WW2 Codebreaking
SYSTEMS, EQUIPMENT AND DECEPTION

This book is dedicated to my wife, Susan, who has put up without complaint with many hours of my researching, reading, and writing on the subject within this book, and the previous two volumes.

WW2 Codebreaking
SYSTEMS, EQUIPMENT AND DECEPTION

A WARTIME GLOSSARY

RONALD KOORM

Pen & Sword
MILITARY
AN IMPRINT OF PEN & SWORD BOOKS LTD.
YORKSHIRE – PHILADELPHIA

First published in Great Britain in 2025 by
PEN AND SWORD MILITARY
An imprint of
Pen & Sword Books Limited
Yorkshire – Philadelphia

ISBN 978 1 39905 354 9

A CIP catalogue record for this book is available from the British Library.

Typeset in Times New Roman 10/12 by
SJmagic DESIGN SERVICES, India.
Printed and bound in the UK by CPI Group (UK) Ltd.

The Publisher's authorised representative in the EU for product safety is Authorised Rep Compliance Ltd., Ground Floor, 71 Lower Baggot Street,
Dublin D02 P593, Ireland.
www.arccompliance.com

For a complete list of Pen & Sword titles please contact
PEN & SWORD BOOKS LIMITED
George House, Units 12 & 13, Beevor Street, Off Pontefract Road,
Barnsley, South Yorkshire, S71 1HN, England
E-mail: enquiries@pen-and-sword.co.uk
Website: www.pen-and-sword.co.uk

or

PEN AND SWORD BOOKS
1950 Lawrence Rd, Havertown, PA 19083, USA
E-mail: uspen-and-sword@casematepublishers.com
Website: www.penandswordbooks.com

FSC
www.fsc.org
MIX
Paper | Supporting responsible forestry
FSC® C013604

Contents

Introduction

This is the third volume of the series of a wartime glossary on codebreaking and it will outline some of the systems and equipment used during and around the Second World War. It will also touch on deception as a tool in war and the post-war period. As there are many publications and websites that deal with the detailed analysis of equipment, this will be more of an overview, and will aim to avoid great detail for the main part. Equipment will not only cover encoding and decoding machines and similar, but delve into areas of radio communication during wartime, transmissions, aerials, specialist tools and methods that may have assisted in collecting and analysing enemy data.

In the Commentary chapter, the author outlines a simplified, brief picture of the challenge that the Allies faced in wartime with ever-changing enemy encoding machines and systems. Reading this part may assist the reader to put codebreaking and intelligence history into perspective.

With war ongoing in Europe at the time of writing in Ukraine and elsewhere, the lessons to be learned in collecting, analysing, and processing enemy data and intelligence is as relevant today as it was during the last world war. Most armed services now have complex, advanced, encrypted radio, and modern telecommunications. Being 'hacked' by the enemy in your communications is a real point of concern, with serious consequences if successful. Cyber-crime and cyber intelligence are demanding large resources to fight back and prevent information falling into the wrong hands. In the Second World War, computers did not really exist as we know them, but to identify enemy encoded messages and read them quickly to gain a military and strategic advantage was part of the objective when you were fighting for survival, as Britain was at the time.

After the war ended, one could purchase much army surplus equipment at knockdown prices, or used equipment during the war. Nowadays, equipment in good, working condition from that era is hard to find, and commands high prices on auction sites. To find a gem that has its original valves, switches and components still working, is quite rare. *Enigma* machines in working order sell for high prices, and are much sought after. Drawings and blueprints are like gold dust, particularly with provenance and a tracked history. The Radio Society of Great Britain (RSGB) has some members with wartime radios and equipment, and the National Museum of Computing (TNMOC) holds a collection of interesting exhibits, many of them restored or rebuilt and working, with the aid of its volunteer members. Private collectors may not always wish to publicise what equipment they have due to fear of theft.

The systems and equipment contained within this volume have been selected as having a specific relevance to codebreaking, intelligence gathering and analysis, mainly during the period 1939–45.However, to improve understanding of developments, I have included several pre-war and post-war items. There are also items that look at the subject from the Nazi and other Axis powers' viewpoint, not just the Allies. The sequence of items may follow events during the war, but in places items are grouped together for simplicity.

As regards the topic of deception, this is discussed using examples of wartime activities involving trickery and concealment of information from the enemy and states that threatened the UK and its allies. Some examples of deception are also contained in the other two volumes of this series, *People and Places* and *Events and Organisations*. There were significant advantages during the war in deceiving the enemy to take a particular action, route, or strategy, buying the Allies valuable time, saving lives, and providing confusion. Not all German generals or officers fell for these tactics, however. One had to be prepared to do enough to convince the majority of influential officers or Adolf Hitler in order to make the scheme work effectively. Not everyone would be convinced by the Operation Mincemeat project that allowed the Nazis to find important strategic documents on a British officer killed when his plane crashed off the coast of Spain. But that ploy did work, although it took some time to be accepted by the enemy as genuine.[1] An initial idea in Britain would be scrutinised in some detail, with some thinking it a waste of time, inconceivable that the enemy would fall for it.

In this book, a 'system' could be defined as any method, process, organisation, or process that assisted the collection of intelligence, the analysis, codebreaking, encryption, or decryption of a message. It could be based on one individual person such as Alan Turing, or be part of a much broader process affecting many thousands of people and different countries. Indeed, a codebreaking machine is just a tool by itself. There needs to be a process, procedure, and activities to enable that machine to do a particular job, and with a degree of some accuracy and repetition.

Systems and processes usually need to be written down and recorded to be repeated, to avoid making errors, or in avoiding making assumptions that may prove to be incorrect. They need to follow a process of logic and reason. The system behind using Bombe codebreaking machines required various specialists to work out instructions and 'Menus' in order for the operators to set up the machines. That process became second nature after a while and was key to the whole process of decoding message settings using machines. Listening stations required a strict protocol and procedures to avoid duplication of work, recording Morse code transmissions in a particular format.

One may ask why deception is included in this volume? It is the case that deception was used both with and without codebreaking activities during wartime. The use of listening stations and methods to crack Enigma and other enemy encoders and ciphers was a form of deception. Misleading your opponent enables them to make errors and mistakes, which can give you a strategic advantage. They may try the same on you, of course. Gathering intelligence using decoding techniques helped to provide evidence of whether an operation was working or not, and how effective it was in practice.

We can look back to those years of wartime conflict and consider ourselves fortunate that most of us never had to be subjected to air raids, bombings, rationing, the uncertainty of war, the threat of invasion of the United Kingdom, or the loss of loved ones who served for their country, in Europe or elsewhere. We can now review the machines, equipment, systems, methods, and processes that may have contributed to the Allies winning the war against tyranny and dictatorship, also acknowledging what equipment and systems the enemy had at the time. Considering this was done at a time when there was no digital technology, and no real computers, it is quite remarkable what was achieved in practice.

Systems

The chapter outlines some of the processes, ideas, protocols, and systems that moved codebreaking and intelligence gathering forward at the time of the Second World War, including periods both pre-war and post-war considered relevant by the author. Some of the items listed may also overlap and be referenced in the 'Equipment' chapter. While some of the systems were initially highly structured and clearly defined, others were almost accidental, and evolved over time into more structured entities and systems, sometimes even using basic trial and error. There are some quotes from historic memos and communications included. By studying these in detail one can get a better overall understanding of how certain individuals were thinking at the time.

Developing Enigma in the early years

The development of the encryption device Enigma was probably triggered by an early Dutch patent in 1919 by Hugo Koch for a rotary-based encryption machine, although two Dutch officers had already developed and invented the first rotary-based encryption machines in 1915. With the concept of providing a security device for banks and finance houses, Arthur Scherbius, inventor of the Enigma encoding machine, had a specific market in mind, but one that was to expand exponentially to the military and other organisations over time. Scherbius was aware the Dutch also were involved in developing rotary-based encoding machines, but had been slow in acquiring patents in this respect. There would be problems and setbacks for Scherbius when his security device was rejected by commercial organisations for being too expensive, too large and heavy for transportation, and too complex to operate. This assessment was a blessing in disguise for Scherbius as it generated a radical review of the design of his machine. He scaled down the cost and size to roughly an eighth of the original, making it more user-friendly and practical. However, in practice it would require two or three people to operate it if the encoded message was to be sent by Morse code. There would be no printing facility, so one had to rely on the accuracy of an individual to write down clearly the encoded illuminated letters on the lamp board, positioned above the keys, after pressing the keys at the front of the machine. But the marketing message had to be that the Enigma was totally secure and the cipher unbreakable if used in accordance with the instructions.

With patents for a rotary-based encoding machine applied for and granted in 1918, it would be shown to the public around 1923 at an exhibition for post office telegraphy equipment. The designer managed to gain some commercial interest, and it was available for any member of public to purchase one. By 1926, the German military services were acquiring Enigma models, and soon after restrictions were placed on its availability to the public for reasons of security. The Poles secretly made copies of the Enigma in a factory before the Second World War.[1] Eventually, Scherbius would acquire Dutch patents for encoding and encryption machines in 1927, several years before his premature death, and be in a strong position commercially to develop codebreaking machines and be ahead of the competition with Enigma. Due to the Versailles treaty, signed in 1919 after the First World War, that restricted Germany in developing or building advanced technical equipment, various patents were established in both the Netherlands and Germany, and Germany was able to use the complex arrangement of German-funded Dutch companies as a cloak to develop advanced machines without international interference in their activities. Effectively, a Dutch company was a cover for the German operation in the inter-war years.

For the reader's benefit, in case they are unfamiliar with the layout of the Enigma machine, it would be developed into several different versions both pre-war, and during the Second World War. Appearing visually broadly similar to a traditional typewriter with keys but no printing facility, it would take considerable vertical force to operate them, with an output of triggering one of twenty-six lamps indicating a letter, which would always be a different one to the key pressed. The top of the machine would have a section for wheel rotors, which would form a crucial part of the encoding process. These wired rotors would be selected from a box based on the code book instructions and inserted in a specific sequence. Some Enigmas would later have an additional wheel rotor, making four, instead of the usual three, making it more secure. The lack of a printing option on Enigma meant that the operator would have to physically write down the encoded letters in any message, by inspecting the lamp board and noting the illuminated letter. Most messages would be sent by Morse code via radio, and message settings were changed by the Nazis every twenty-four hours. The receiving end would need an Enigma and the same code books, rotor wheels, sequence of rotors, and set-up procedure as the sender. Mistakes were sometimes made, often due to pure carelessness by the operator, leaving the Allies a real challenge to decode an intercepted transmission, and sometimes a welcome gift, helping them to penetrate the message settings. For more detail, please refer to the Equipment chapter, where different models of the Enigma machine are listed.

After Scherbius' death in a horse and carriage accident, the company making Enigmas was run by Willy Korn, an engineer. Many aspects of the design would be patented in several countries, including Germany, USA, UK, France, Switzerland, and the Netherlands.

Polish advances in codebreaking

Three young Polish mathematicians, Henryk Zygalski, Marian Rejewski, and Jerzy Rozycki, had broken Enigma manually, many years before the start of the Second World War.[2] They went on to devise and invent a codebreaking machine, the Bomba, built in Warsaw. It would be developed broadly between 1932 and 1937. The Bomba machine would establish the rotor positions of Enigma, taking around two hours to do so. Initially seen as a learning curve for the trio of mathematician designers, it would soon be of little use due to developments of the Enigma system, but their knowledge would be invaluable when it was passed to the French and the British. The Polish mathematicians had analysed Enigma in some detail and discovered certain weaknesses. Their system was to probe some of those weaknesses using an electro-mechanical machine, which saved time. The Germans would make Enigma more robust and secure over time. More advanced codebreaking machines and systems would then become essential.

The Turing concept of the Bombe

Alan Turing had the concept of a machine that could assist with stripping away the incorrect permutations of message settings of Enigma to leave just the correct settings, this being the combination to open the safe and read the decoded messages. This was some years after the Poles had designed and built their machine, but Turing's machine would be completely different to theirs. It would be based upon thirty-six Enigmas with three-wheel rotors per machine, and with a menu of instructions it could be set up to plough through the message settings, eliminating them one by one from the permutations to leave a result or output. This would prove to be Turing's 'system'. He needed assistance to get it working in practice, in particular from colleague codebreaker Gordon Welchman, who would go on to introduce a small circuit to improve the Bombe machine's efficiency and save time. Then it had to be properly designed technically with detailed drawings, manufactured, and built in a factory in secret. It would need to be tested, modified, improved, tested again, and proved to work to the authorities, who were understandably sceptical and impatient. The cost of it alone would take up valuable resources in wartime. The brilliant mind of Turing would be frustrated when things went wrong, and when others doubted his ability. He had foreseen, some years before, that machines could help man carry out work on a large scale, given the right type of machine and the appropriate instructions. One of the issues would be how to meaningfully instruct machines. Electrical switches, electromagnetic relays, brass contacts, and electrical motors would be the order of the day. The Bombe machine would not be a computer. It would be part of a radically new and important system developed in wartime to help break the enemy's codes and ciphers, alongside manual codebreakers.

Production of Bombe codebreaking machines

Initially on a small scale, BTM in Letchworth, Hertfordshire, started fabricating and producing Bombe codebreaking machines in the early stages of the Second World War. They set aside part of their large factory for production and allocated resources. What was unknown at this time was the quantities needed by Bletchley Park over time. The proliferation of encoded enemy messages on a large scale resulted in the need for more skilled staff and more machines, as well as a review of the number and capacity of sites needed for locating and operating them.

BTM would build the units on a modular basis, allocating components to be assembled in other parts of Letchworth, under their control. The Spirella building at the western end of the city was used by BTM for manufacturing components including cables, electrical connectors, and rotor parts.[3] Partly built units would be transported to the main factory at BTM, where they would be assembled on a metal frame. The logistics of organising the huge volume of materials, tooling, processes, power demands, and engineering personnel in wartime while Britain was being bombed and convoys sunk by U-boats was a real challenge. A total of 211 Bombes were manufactured and distributed by BTM, the vast majority going to codebreaking outstations.[4] This was the Cantab secret programme, everyone involved having had to sign the Official Secrets Act. Almost one quarter of the main BTM factory would have to be allocated to construct the Bombes. Many hundreds, if not thousands, of people were involved. The chief engineer responsible was Harold Keen. He would also contribute to improvements to provide High-Speed Keen Bombes (HSK), as recorded in the official Bombe Registers. From time to time, visitors from Bletchley Park would review machine production, quality, and progress, reviewing modifications and improvements across various machines. Each machine would be allocated a number and a name, based on a city, and logged as regards the date of completion, when and to where it was allocated, and any modifications or special features.

A simple table is provided below for production of British Bombes:

Year	Bombes	Comment
Mid-1940	2	Victory and Agnes, first two Bombes at Bletchley Park
December 1940	12	
End of 1941	16	
End March 1942	26	OSS (Stanmore) established Sept. 1942 increased this figure to approx. Forty machines by end of the year[5]
End of 1943	99	OSE (Eastcote) established in autumn 1943
End of 1944	192	
End of war – May 1945	211	Based upon Bombe Registers held at the National Archives

Staffing for Bombes		
RAF	256	Maintenance
WRNS	1,676	Bombe operators
RN	2	
FAA	4	
Civilian War Reserve	4	

Jobs done with Bombes to crack message settings and messages over the course of the war amounted to some 36,002 in number, with an efficiency rate of 97.6 per cent.

Transfer of recorded Morse code from Y-stations

Logged Morse code intercepts from the many and varied Y-stations would be couriered to Bletchley Park by dispatch riders, often WRNS personnel or Wrens, on large motorcycles. GPO dispatch riders were also used. Later, teleprinters would transfer intercepted encoded messages from the outstations to Bletchley. This was also the case for the more advanced non-Morse message intercepts at places like Knockholt, in Kent. That was a specialist listening station that also intercepted the first fax messages. It would grow to house a large complement of technical and support personnel, with large aerials on site.

Teleprinters saved time and were used more as the war developed. The log sheets from the listening and monitoring operators would be passed to Bletchley Park for review and prioritising the messages, to evaluate the message settings using both manual and machine methods. Teleprinters relied upon GPO landline cables between the sites. Just dealing with the large quantity of messages coming into Bletchley huts would put enormous pressure on the specialist teams to allocate the work to the Bletchley Bombe hut or one of the codebreaking outstations that generally had a large number of Bombes available.

Organisation of expansion of Bombe production

The need to expand Bombe codebreaking machine production was dependent upon the quantity of enemy messages intercepted as the war progressed. Bletchley Park, being the British HQ of cryptographic analysis and decryption, was monitoring the messages coming in via the Y-stations, both home and abroad. The volume of Enigma machines in production increased exponentially before the war commenced and during it. They would be used not just by the military but by the Nazi secret service, railways, and their Axis allies such as Italy.

Any message intercepted by the British could hold crucial intelligence that might change the balance of the war. In practical terms, the use of so many machines in active service meant that there would be a lot of trivia and less-important information, which might be filed away to be reviewed later. Managers Alastair Denniston and Commander Edward Travis would give feedback to those security cleared in the Foreign Office about progress made, and the quantity of Bombes needed based upon projections from discussions with their technical staff. There would need to be coordination with the producers of the actual Bombe machines, BTM in Letchworth. Bombes could not just be simply built, the factory had to find the space for their production, the engineers, personnel, production drawings, tooling, materials, and ensure that electrical power was available for production. As production escalated, buildings, companies, and sites such as Spirella, together with other locations in and around Letchworth, would be brought into the manufacturing loop. Progress reports would be issued at BTM via Harold Keen, the chief engineer in charge. The Cantab top-secret project would demand large amounts of resources, but no one knew when the war would end so planning ahead was problematical. The approach was that the more Bombe machines there were available, the more 'attacks' that could be applied to Enigma message settings, giving a better and faster success rate, in theory. This meant that more Enigma messages could be broken, with speed being critical. It was unacceptable to have encrypted messages piling up and not enough resources to deal with them.

Site visits to the BTM factory in Letchworth were sometimes made from Bletchley Park, and this included codebreakers such as Alan Turing and Gordon Welchman. They were visiting to assess progress, help out the engineers discuss technical issues on the Bombes, and report back to the Government Code and Cipher School (GC&CS) HQ at Bletchley. The expansion of the outstation sites was carried out over the course of the war with the penultimate outstation, Stanmore, coming online in autumn 1942, and the final one, Eastcote, in autumn 1943. It would take time to build up Stanmore, aided by transferring a quantity of Bombes from smaller outstations, the same being true of Eastcote, the largest outstation. Some of the smaller country house-based outstations would transfer their Bombe machines to either Stanmore or Eastcote and then close down. Establishing the personnel to run and maintain an outstation, particularly a large base, took project planning, discipline, management, coordination, and leadership. There needed to be effective communication with Bletchley and with the BTM factory at Letchworth in terms of managing the manufacture, transfer, and allocation of Bombe machines, sending them to the codebreaking sites, and returning many of them for technical modification and major repairs. From the author examining the records in the official Bombe Registers, it is apparent that some Bombe machines were effectively put out to pasture as being unreliable or with various faults, and several of those were then used for training purposes.[6] The vast majority of Bombes, however, did appear to be reliable, and worked constantly, night and day, seven days per week, 365 days a year, with routine maintenance carried out by RAF engineers. Major technical issues with a Bombe machine might result in sending it back to the factory for repair and testing, although many repairs were carried out at the codebreaking stations where practically possible.

Commander Edward Travis and H.D. Fletcher, the senior codebreaker and organiser at Bletchley Park, were constantly reviewing the options for providing the space for an increased number of Bombe machines as well as the personnel to operate and support them. Fletcher referred to these as 'Watchkeepers', that is the Wrens and support staff who set up and operated the Bombes at the codebreaking bases. On 4 June 1942 there would be a report outlining that there were twenty Bombes and 210 Wrens to look after them. However, the need was for forty-five machines across Bletchley and the country house outstations, with a projection of 454 Watchkeepers. However, it was a complex situation, as Fletcher explained in correspondence from Hut 6 to Commander Travis:

> The basic number of Wrens required to operate a machine is 8 (four watches of two); to this number has to be added a variable quantity depending on the number of machines in a unit to provide for sickness and leave, controllers, I/C ops., and in the case of Crawley Grange operators of special machines (testplate, click, etc) and about 40 trainees. This is because Wrens are scheduled to arrive at the rate of about 20 a week, and at least a fortnight elapses before they can begin to be left to operate machines on their own.
>
> Present number of Bombes 20. Wrens 210.
>
> Accommodation is therefore settled for a further 25 Bombes and quarters necessary for the operating staff.
>
> British Tabulating Machine Company have been asked to produce a further 70 Bombes, of which it is possible that about half will be high speed (though this depends on the results of various experiments). They will have delivered 25 of them, some standard, some high-speed, by about the middle of September, thus using up the accommodation available. We are faced, therefore, with having to find accommodation for 45 Bombes, arriving between the middle of September and the end of the year, and for 400–450 Wrens necessary to operate them. The actual number of Wrens needed varies with the number of machines, sickness, I/C, ops., etc.[7]

This, then was all about logistics and planning. Planning was for the short, medium, and longer term, although because there would be various unknowns as to how the war would evolve over time, there would be concentration on the medium term, as well as review of existing resources. At the time of the memo in June 1942, neither Travis not Fletcher would have known about the need for advanced codebreaking machines such as Colossus, or the men and women to make that system operate effectively. Everything at the time revolved around the Bombes, the key tool in the Allied codebreakers' arsenal of weapons to attack Enigma. But Travis and Fletcher understood that even if one knew the ratio of Bombe operators to Bombe machines, one had to make allowances for training, sickness, modifications of machines, as well as accommodation for staff. At the time of the memo, neither Outstation Stanmore nor Outstation Eastcote existed as codebreaking outstations. These would be much larger than the country park estates such as Wavendon, Adstock, and Gayhurst, in terms of Bombe capacity. From late 1942, those new sites, starting with Outstation Stanmore, would become a double-edged sword for management. On the one hand, they had very large capacity for machines; on the other, there would have to be various transfers of machines from the smaller sites, and training of much larger quantities of Watchkeeper Wrens and RAF support engineers. The accommodation would be largely on site, an advantage in many respects, but would need careful organisation and allocation of supplies. Plus, the secrecy of the bases had to be maintained.

It must be understood that while Bletchley Park was GC&CS, being effectively HQ in codebreaking and deciphering intelligence, the codebreaking outstations were not. They were onshore naval bases, some on civilian property such as country estates. Their evolution was through the Foreign Office, who effectively requested the personnel on behalf of Bletchley Park. The listening stations were organised through a variety of organisations, so quite a mixed bag when this is taken into account.

In his memo H.D. Fletcher mentions high-speed versions of the Bombes, probably High-Speed Keen, or HSK, as recorded in the official Bombe Registers. However, he also states that output is dependent upon the result of various experiments. There were no British standards or technical books for such machines; the engineers modified them as they went along. They tested them, wrote down and recorded what worked, and what did not.

One can only imagine the level of consternation there would have been among senior WRNS management when they were informed of the number of Watchkeeper Wrens that were needed. The WRNS would initially not be entirely clear as to where its Wrens would be ultimately based, which personnel would need to be billeted, and which of them would be based on an outstation for accommodation. After all, the WRNS was an expanding naval organisation with much demand for its services across the Navy, mainly in the United Kingdom, but also abroad. Training Wrens took time, and training Wrens for Special X codebreaking duties took longer still. On a smaller scale, this resourcing issue was less of a problem with the country house outstations, but was a completely different scenario when the whole project was expanded to what would become five separate, codebreaking outstations, two of them being located nowhere near Bletchley Park but miles away on the edges of north-west London. Communication routes would play a major part between the outstations and Bletchley Park. Dispatch riders would fill in the gaps on motorbikes between the locations, and later teleprinters would make further progress in this respect. Commander Travis would be the director of the project for allocating Bombe machines, liaising with others to help manage the personnel resources and ensuring a relatively smooth and seamless operation. The operation would be like a swan paddling frantically below the surface but appearing to glide about as though it was in complete control. A great deal of cooperation would be required between the various sections and organisations that had become involved in the Bombe or Cantab project started by Turing.

The typed memorandum goes on to consider that larger sites may be worthwhile for management to look into, but that the country house codebreaking sites were falling behind schedule at a crucial time:

> A concentration of machines is easier to administer and operate than a number of small clusters. Protection against bombing is already achieved by present dispersal.

The potential Luftwaffe bombing of codebreaking sites and Bletchley Park was considered at some length by Churchill and his advisers. The Prime Minister was keen to distribute the sites and spread the risk, a sensible proposal also dealt with in the memo:

> As only a little over 3 months remains before additional accommodation is needed, we must begin to make the preliminary moves now. In order to stress the urgency of the situation, it should be mentioned that in the case of Wavendon, although proceedings were started in March, it is only now that building has really got going: My note of May 29th showed the amount of work and effort by Mr Wallace which was needed to achieve this result, and even now its completion in time is a matter of touch and go. In the case of Gayhurst, negotiations were started in February, and the Admiralty say they are going to find it difficult to complete the work by the middle of July, which is the longest we can give them.

The Bombes would be housed in separate hutted buildings within the country estates and not in the main house. Clearly, these were anxious times. Comment was made on the need for a large site to house many machines in one new location:

> The case for making final provision in one fell swoop seems very strong. A place such as Stowe School, which would require very little alteration, would be admirable.

Stowe School would have made a good location for a very large number of machines, and with adequate space for staff accommodation in huts that could be installed on the large estate grounds. It was also not too far from Bletchley Park. However, it was not to be. The reasons for dismissing Stowe as an outstation were unclear. If it had become an outstation, then it would be unlikely that Stanmore and Eastcote would have then been established. The mention of coordination with the Wrens through a first officer was also apparent from the text:

> I understand that First Officer Canale has taken no active steps yet as she is waiting for instructions. She also informs that she has obtained

> authority for an establishment of 228 watchkeepers, and she will therefore require authority for a further 600.

Canale, referred to in the memo, was a senior Wren officer in charge of the allocation of Wrens at Bletchley and at the outstations. She would be billeted at Gayhurst Manor.[8] Depending how one looks at the organisation and support on Bombe operations, the quantities based on 828 Watchkeepers, i.e. 228 plus 600, might imply a projection of around 100 machines, as there were two Wrens to each machine, and four separate watches allocated. (Three watches rotating on duty, plus one in reserve, leave provision, etc). Some allowance for sickness and other factors was necessary, but 100 machines is more than the total of forty-five in the first part of the tabled memo. However, this number makes sense if you study the paragraph on BTM, which says they had been asked to produce a further seventy Bombes. Fletcher continues:

> A slight relief might be obtained if Mr Freeborn vacates Hut 11 before September. This would accommodate the 8 machines which are expected to be delivered between the middle and end of September, and of course quarters would have to be found for the 80 watchkeepers necessary to operate these. We should still require additional quarters by the beginning of October.

Freeborn, mentioned here, was the BTM employee in charge of the Hollerith punched card machines and tabulators at Bletchley, but due to relocate to Drayton Parslow a few miles outside Bletchley to set up the Hollerith operation there and make more space available. However, no new codebreaking machines went to Bletchley Park, they all went to the external codebreaking outstations. Freeborn did relocate his team, though, further down the road, and that expanded over time.

Reviewing the numbers of Watchkeepers, the ratio of them to Bombes appears to be ten to one: forty teams of two Wrens, being allocated two per Bombe machine, and four separate watches. A great number of skilled personnel were deemed necessary to make this work in practice.

From the above, it should be clearer to the reader that these were challenging times for management, and that making the wrong decision could have perhaps changed the course of the war against the Allies. Churchill relied on Bletchley and Commander Travis to do whatever was necessary to gather the enemy intelligence with his team of experts. Bletchley relied upon the efficiency of the Y-stations around the country and abroad, and of the support personnel such as Wrens, at the growing outstations. This was a complex technical operation, with numerous specially selected staff, on a huge scale. A total of 1,676 Wrens became involved in Special X duties. The Bombes could not be set up or operated without them. Furthermore, BTM had a key part to play, as without its engineering, design, and manufacturing skill, Alan Turing's codebreaking Bombe concept would have just been a mere pipe dream.

BTM also assisted in lending/hiring out an IBM 405 tabulator machine for use at Bletchley Park, and further machines were later supplied via the United States' IBM factory. These machines would be used for processing punched cards with data from messages that needed to be analysed. IBM punched card machines would later be used in endeavours such as the Manhattan atomic bomb project at the Los Alamos National Laboratory.[9]

Bombe Menus

Instructions had to be provided by those at Bletchley Park to connect and initialise the British Bombe codebreaking machines before the machine could be started for a run. This was called a Menu, and consisted of various geometric lines joining letters and numbers, seemingly at random to the average person. However, these were not random, but were carefully calculated based on cribs or clues, linking connecting letters for analysis. The Menu would be sent to the Bombe hut or the codebreaking outstations for the Wrens to use as a starting point in order to connect the cables up and set the machines. Most menus were disposed of, but a few have survived. They were formulated by inspecting the log sheets of the messages and carrying out a process to make links between letters. A correct Menu would form part of the overall process of cracking the message settings of Enigma, at least for a limited time. The Germans would change their message settings every twenty-four hours to provide an added degree of security.

The Menu configuration, as written, needed clear instructions to plug cables into connectors of the diagonal board, and identified common 'nodes' by inspection on the diagram, where several lines coincided with a letter. Although highly complex to an outsider, the Wren operators would become used to the Menus and understand instructions on how to use these to plug in long red cables at the rear of the machine, and ensure they were properly aligned for a good fit and electrical contact. The Bombe Enigma rotor wheel terminations would be connected with the wiring/contacts to the diagonal board and common areas. Gordon Welchman designed a diagonal board circuit to improve the efficiency of the Bombes, and these were fitted to the codebreaking machines on a large scale. Without the Bombe Menus there would have been no instructions on how to wire up the Bombes, so they became an essential part of the system. See also Bombe.

Checking machine system

The checking machines at Bletchley and at codebreaking outstations were operated principally by Wrens, and became an important penultimate stage in the analysis of the Bombe machine output, which had been set up to operate from a Menu produced by the codebreakers at Bletchley Park. They consisted principally of three wheels that, unlike the Bombe, could be rotated manually by the operator in either direction, i.e. turned clockwise or anticlockwise. The result gave feedback, which was communicated to Bletchley to await further instructions.

Most checking machines would be in separate rooms, and operators could be seated to use one. However, certain photographs indicate that at Eastcote at least some of the checking machines were actually within the Bombe rooms, the machines being adjacent. Semi-enclosures were provided in an attempt to suppress at least some of the noise of the Bombes, which could be extremely loud and off-putting if one had to concentrate on a task. However, these enclosures were of little benefit other than to provide a seated workstation for the Wren operator. Betty Vowles, based at Eastcote, told the author she was not permitted into the room with checking machines and operators.[10] Some Wrens were permitted to set up Bombe machines and later, on another shift, operate checking machines, but not all. Documents and plans showing the Cobra attachments and Bombes at one of the outstations shows a room for the checking machines nearby, and there is a sketch showing one. A reproduction checking machine is at the National Museum of Computing at Bletchley Park.[11]

Hollerith system

Hollerith was a company and its machines were used as a tool by Bletchley Park and by BTM as part of a system of recording and sorting a large amount of intercepted message information and intelligence.[12] It was an American organisation formed by an inventor of a tabulating machine, Herman Hollerith, an American and German statistician, which became highly successful as a production company both in America and abroad. Hollerith used his machines for census statistics and he went from strength to strength, writing papers on the subject. The company was initially known as the Tabulating Machine Company at the end of the nineteenth century. Later, it became the Computing Tabulating Recording Company, but changed its name again in 1924. In the 1930s, the British Tabulating Machine Company in England (BTM), obtained the rights to market, hire, and sell Hollerith machines across Europe and elsewhere to the British Empire, paying royalties to the inventor. The significance of this was twofold: first, BTM, through its expertise with these machines, went on to win a contract from the British Government to engineer and build Bombe codebreaking machines for Bletchley Park. Also, it would be experts in use of the Hollerith machines to assist Bletchley codebreakers in collecting and filtering data from the enemy that had been decoded through the interception of messages sent via the Nazi Enigma encoding machines. Different versions of Hollerith machines would be provided, some known as pin-box tabulators. These were noisy machines, sorting information on punched cards en masse, in huge quantities, via electro-mechanical operation. BTM had used the machines for census operations for countries as far away as Africa and understood their potential. The Hollerith organisation was the first stage in the creation and development of International

Business Machines, IBM, from 1924, which would eventually dominate the business computing market post-war.

Bletchley Park would incorporate Hollerith machines licensed via BTM and have Hollerith operators in one of their huts, Block C, but eventually the storage of punched cards became a problem due to the large quantities involved.[13] Due to a lack of space, they were all relocated to Drayton Parslow, a few miles away near a local village, and managed by Freddie Freeborn of BTM with a large number of largely female personnel, which ran into the high hundreds. They worked shifts day and night to sort, process and pass data back to Bletchley when requested. Freeborn was assisted by two deputies, being brothers Ronald and Norman Whelan. Those women operators who showed ability and skill were promoted by Freeborn or his deputies, but they saw little financial reward for the additional responsibility. Those staff working on Christmas Day at Drayton Parslow would only be allowed home at 4pm to eat their Christmas dinner as a special concession. Times were therefore hard, and work was ongoing to get the job done. Message information would be processed through a sorter, verifier, collator, and the tabulating Hollerith machine, so this was a complex, and noisy, multi-stage process. There would eventually be dialogue between Freeborn and the senior codebreaker, Tiltman, to prioritise the work, and ensure it was being processed as efficiently as possible. The request for high-priority jobs at short notice would be part of the challenge for Freeborn and his team. The traffic analysis section at Bletchley, later known as SIXTA, would have made use of much of the sorted information to help build a bigger and more refined intelligence picture of the enemy and its objectives. The impact of effective traffic analysis cannot be underestimated as to its significance in wartime.

Establishment of Y-stations

Those who ran listening stations during wartime fell into certain groups, but the purpose was the same – to listen for enemy intelligence that might be of some value to the British and its wartime allies. These were established initially during the First World War. Y-stations were run by the Foreign Office (MI5), the Post Office, the RAF, Army, Royal Navy, and by the Marconi company. The logging of recorded signals manually on log sheets was made consistent, and that made it easier for Bletchley Park to trawl through the intercepts. Listening stations existed before 1939 and the start of the Second World War, however, they were considerably expanded in number both home and abroad, including in Africa, Palestine, India, Ceylon (now Sri Lanka), Malta, North Africa, and elsewhere. A list of the British listening stations can be found in the first volume of this glossary, *People and Places*. When the war in Europe ended, listening stations abroad would remain in service to help fight the war against the Japanese. Many WRNS and other service personnel were transferred after VE day to places such as Ceylon to put on headphones in much warmer and tropical climates compared to Britain.

Y-Station listening and recording process

Listening stations were used extensively throughout the country as well as abroad. Some of these would be on ships at sea and others with mobile army units abroad. Direction finding of message sending locations would often be applied to find enemy positions where practically possible. These were the crucial first links to the codebreaking process; listening for Morse code intelligence from the enemy, much of which would be encoded from the Enigma Nazi machine. ATS, WAAFs, WRNS and other personnel would sit at radio receivers, often in banks, with headsets, and be given specific frequencies and bands to listen to. The data would be recorded on log sheets, providing date, time, frequency, and staff details. Coded letters would generally be written in groups of five. The information would be sent to Bletchley Park initially. Then a large proportion of them would be circulated to codebreaking outstations with Menus of instructions to set up the codebreaking machines. Prior to the Bombes, everything was done by hand at Bletchley. The call sign of the sender of the original message would be of interest as this might help in prioritising the codebreaking work.

Over time, a network map would be established by the British, outlining the structure of the German Army, its divisions and sections, with key communication information identified. This aided the codebreaking work tremendously, but the hard work in the Bletchley huts still had to be done, with many hours spent poring over the messages coming in. The large volume of Enigma machines produced and allocated to the Nazi war machine meant that the volume of encoded and transmitted messages rose exponentially. That meant more work for the busy Y-stations, more work for the dispatch riders, and more work for the codebreakers and their support staff, including of course, the outstations. The listening personnel could detect the Morse 'key' of specific individuals sending messages over time. They could recognise their Morse signature; incredible considering that the Morse was sent simply in a series of dots and dashes.

While there were numerous Y-stations both home and abroad, the main naval listening stations were at Flowerdown and Scarborough. The principal Army station was at Chatham in Kent, and the RAF listening station was in Cheadle, Cheshire. A data collection centre was also based at Arkley View in Barnet, north London, which collected listeners' logged data. There would be more than 600 radio receiving sets used in the war at the Y-stations. Under Lend-Lease arrangements with the USA, some of the receivers would be of American origin. The National HRO receiver was used extensively and was very reliable. Many Voluntary Interceptors used by the Foreign Office were amateur radio enthusiasts who had initially built their own receivers.

Teleprinter system

There was a need for efficient communication between the listening stations and Bletchley Park, and the codebreaking outstations and Bletchley. Telephones were, of course, used extensively, but with the need to transfer large amounts of data and information quickly from place to place, teleprinters would be introduced. Electrically powered, they generated text and numbers at a rate of speed that a good typist would have struggled with. The paper roll would be continuous and renewed frequently as it came to the end. Multiple banks of teleprinter machines would be established at Bletchley, and places such as Knockholt, which was an advanced non-Morse listening station in Kent. Block D at Bletchley would be built with purpose-made teleprinter rooms.[14] The teleprinter areas were often windowless, with poor ventilation. They were stuffy and rather unpleasant to work in for the staff. A permanent teleprinter building was built, managed by Post Office engineers, and relevant blocks would be further enlarged over time. Women operated many of the teleprinters, including WAAFs. The use of motorcycle dispatch riders as couriers between listening stations and Bletchley, as well as from the outstations, would still remain a crucial part of the communications network, but teleprinters were more immediate, and speed was important when analysing enemy signals and intercepts.

Vacuum tube system

A pneumatic system used at Bletchley Park for transfer of information in a tube that was situated at high level on a sort of railway network without rails. Block E would have this system and connect to other blocks such as A, B, and D. Signal traffic and other information would speedily be transported from department to department, saving valuable time. Such systems would also be used elsewhere for speed, such as in selected large Government offices. Similar technology had been used in large departments stores some years before, and was probably developed originally in the USA.

WRNS training

The relevance of the WRNS to codebreaking was that a selection of these military women set up, operated, and monitored most of the codebreaking machines, situated in a variety of different locations across England. Initially these would be the Turing–Welchman Bombes, which started off at Bletchley Park in Buckinghamshire, in relatively small quantities. Most training for Wrens was basic, comprising two or three weeks in north London, in Wimbledon or in Scotland. It was only once this training had been completed that individuals were then selected for their aptitude and intelligence to be considered for Special X codebreaking duties. A Wren would be no wiser when the term Special X duties was mentioned. She would have had an interview to be told she was being allocated to these duties, but she would not have been told the details until she arrived at either Bletchley Park or one of the outstations. There she would sign the Official Secrets Act.

The National Service Act, passed in 1941, would commence formal conscription of certain categories of women for wartime work. That included single women and those without children aged between 19 and 30 initially. Later, the upper age limit was increased to 43. The choices for conscripted women were either the WRNS or the equivalent Army female force. Fletcher, the senior codebreaker and organiser, had written to Commander Travis at Bletchley Park in 1942 concerned that there must be sufficient Bombe codebreaking machines to carry out the job in hand in breaking Enigma ciphers, but also highlighting the need for enough trained Wrens to operate them. In the typed memorandum, Fletcher would refer to the Bombe Wrens as *Watchkeepers*. In one way, they were exactly that; overseeing, setting up, and operating the machines, looking after them as if they were their children. The communication would project both the numbers of machines needed, as well as the quantity of Watchkeepers. They all had to have accommodation too, either on site or in a billeted location in the local community. Many Wrens on *Special X* duties at outstations would be accommodated on site.

There would be training at the outstations about the setting up of the Bombe machines, installing the wheel rotors, the plugging and connecting of cables, the use of the Menus, the checking machines, as well as rules and regulations on the shift work, working in pairs, security, meal allocations, expenses, uniform and clothing allowances, reporting off sick, and miscellaneous information. Enigma would not be mentioned, at least not unless it was essential to the task. They would be told their work was highly important and could help to defeat the enemy, but that attention to detail was absolutely critical. Checking of each other's work on the codebreaking machines and working together in pairs on lengthy shift work would become the norm. It would not be too long before new recruits were aware there was more than one outstation, but only if a colleague had worked elsewhere was this information available. Of course, some may not wish to talk about their experiences at another site, but many would due to the intense boredom of the work. Several hundred Wrens proficient in radio communication and Morse code would also work at various Y-stations, listening to enemy radio and Morse transmissions, and they would have to be specially trained, a process that could take up to six months to obtain a proficient technical standard that was considered acceptable by the military. It would be 1942 when the WRNS choices were expanded for women, and their duties could then include radar direction finding, gunner dome operation, and bomb range marking.[15]

After the war ended, around 3,000 Wrens would be retained to support the naval service at home and abroad. Around 2.25 per cent of Wrens worked in codebreaking during the war, a relatively small number of the 74,000 total. In contrast, Bletchley Park had approximately 8,000 females working there during the war, across a wide range of duties.[16] Many of these would be WRNS or ATS females, plus civilians. Wren First Officer Canale, who worked at Bletchley Park from December 1941, helped coordinate WRNS resources to reflect the numbers of trained Bombe operators across HQ and the outstations. This would become an extremely challenging task.

Naval administrative system for codebreakers

The Royal Navy had specific views about its naval personnel on codebreaking support duties. Initially known as *Special X* duties, this was changed to Pembroke

V or HMS Pembroke V for administrative purposes. This name applied to each of the five codebreaking outstations, plus the hut that contained the Bombes at Bletchley Park operated by Wrens. Wrens being trained at one of the training bases in England or Scotland would not be aware what Special X duties were, as they would receive initially only basic training. It would be senior officers who would look at their performance record and aptitude for codebreaking work, and allocate a relatively small quantity of them to perform such duties at Bletchley or one of the five codebreaking outstations.[17]

Traffic analysis

This is an important stage in the processing of enemy messages and intercepts. The traffic analysis section moved to Bletchley Park on 5 May 1942. New huts were constructed for this purpose. This would be specifically radio traffic, incorporating everything about the intercepted messages, including frequencies, call signs, identification of transmitting units, time of transmissions, and supplementary information. It was a separate process to the cryptographic process of decoding messages. It would occur before the decoding, or in the early stages of the decoding. On 5 February 1944 the section became officially known as SIXTA. The abbreviation or name may have been based on the sections that came together to form the unit, with TA standing for 'traffic analysis'. Hut 6 was also relevant for intelligence reports and could have been the trigger for the new name. This combined service was arranged several months before D-Day.

An early example of traffic analysis was seen in the tracking of the *Bismarck*, where direction finding and other means were useful in locating the German battleship. Bletchley Park combined the processes of SIXTA and cryptographic work. Caxton Street in London was also an important location for intelligence gathering and analysis. Call signs of the enemy were particularly of interest, and discovering networks and 'keys' of the enemy communications. Log readers compared messages with message data. A few log readers in the early years would initially be trusted with knowing about the Enigma encoding machine being broken. Gordon Welchman, codebreaker at Bletchley, was keen on keeping people informed about the work they were doing.[18] This would improve morale and probably the output too. Card indexes and Hollerith machines were used as basis for a database of detailed processed and sorted information from the messages intercepted. Connecting network diagrams with lines, arrows, text, and markers would be produced on a large scale to mark the communications links of the enemy, based upon the traffic analysis carried out. This was a visual prompt for the Allies to follow, and to learn about how the enemy was communicating and operating. It was equivalent to establishing a map of the enemy's military structure and the different parts involved, and indeed diagrams of this nature were produced from intercepts and adding together message information that had previously been thought to have no practical use.

Traffic analysis was formulated as a key system for intelligence gathering and evaluation, evolving over time, and was essential to the decryption process at Bletchley Park. Even in modern times, traffic analysis forms part of military strategic operational work, to probe the enemy organisation network. It can help prioritise which part of the network to concentrate on for future intercepts and analysis.

Voluntary Interceptor recruitment

The need for voluntary radio reception listeners in wartime was recognised, and licensed amateur radio enthusiasts were recruited by the Foreign Office to listen around specific frequencies for radio transmissions. The purpose was to identify enemy agents transmitting, or transmissions of interest from Europe, which might include U-boats or similar. A contact would be made with the ham radio amateur and he or she would be invited to become involved. Instructions were issued after the Official Secrets Act was signed. Although mainly men were recruited for this work, some women also became Voluntary Interceptors (VI).

The Voluntary Interceptors were unusual inasmuch as they were distributed among the British Isles. This may have assisted in ensuring as many signals were intercepted as possible due to atmospheric conditions, which would vary across Great Britain. The benefit to the Government was that the VIs were often using their own equipment and their own homes and electricity to power the receivers. This made it a very economic enterprise for the state. Some improved-quality receivers and equipment would later be provided to the VI radio amateurs. As these radio amateurs were licensed before the recruitment drive, they had certified skills in listening for, transmitting, and recording Morse code. Another relevant aspect of their operational work was that the amateurs had experience of listening to less than perfect signals being transmitted under a variety of conditions. Therefore, weak and fading signals would be less of a challenge, perhaps, than others who had less experience. Standardised abbreviations and letters for signals and shipping would be commonly known to the VIs. In other words, the radio amateurs who made up the VIs for the Government were highly skilled, certified, and tested operators, with useful experience that could be applied in wartime. The interception of encoded Morse code would be something that most had not come across, but providing they logged the incoming signals carefully, others could deal with the decryption.

It can be stated that the combination of official Y-stations in conjunction with Voluntary Interceptors during the war gave Britain and its allies a great advantage in collecting intelligence, both military and civilian-based. The number of VI personnel was considered to be somewhere between 1,000 to 1,700 men and women, although male VIs would be in the majority. The VIs were the idea of Lord Sandhurst, who recruited them with the support of the Foreign Office. Background checks would, of course, be carried out to ensure there was no security risk to the state. The Official Secrets Act would have to be signed by each amateur operator and nothing about their work could be revealed to their friends or family over the course of the war and beyond. Indeed, it would be the late 1970s before the VIs could speak openly about their wartime work. Some may have decided to never speak about what they achieved in wartime. See also VI processes.

Voluntary Interceptor processes

When a VI listened in to radio traffic for the Foreign Office, they were given frequency ranges to concentrate on. When feedback indicated something of interest, they were further instructed to focus on specific frequencies to obtain further intelligence. The date, time, frequency, and other key information was logged and sent to a PO Box address in Barnet, north London. Atmospheric conditions affected the recording of information, so that one day the signal may have been relatively clear and on another almost unintelligible. Many VIs were dotted across the country, and there were a good number near the English coast. Listening both for possible agents and Nazi transmissions from abroad was an incentive to switch the radio equipment on, and listen for several hours at a time. There would be little success in recording enemy agents, but many opportunities for collecting frequencies and signals of interest.[19]

Over time, equipment would often be acquired, modified, or built by the VIs themselves, and some American receivers were issued, which proved relatively reliable. The only giveaway for a VI would possibly be the large aerial mast array required in the garden or on the roof or terrace. Some might have got away with wires internally in the room connected to the receivers, but this would severely limit the range of possible intercepts and signals. But as licensed amateurs they would be entitled to have such aerials, subject to any local planning rules, and nothing would normally indicate they were carrying out specialist listening work for the British Government. Several VIs would later be called up for military service and end up in the Radio Security Service, using their skills and working on a range of equipment.[20] Some would intercept Nazi *Abwehr* signals in their work. Where these were encrypted Morse code, the AIs would not be aware of the significance of the work they had done in wartime. It was the equivalent of the Wrens spending several years in Bombe codebreaking machine huts, setting up and operating the machines to identify message settings, yet never being aware of what those messages stated, or their significance to the Allies. Operationally, VIs were sometimes involved in direction-finding work to pinpoint the origin of transmissions.[21]

Y-station organisation

We outline briefly some of the organisation of the Y-stations that acted as the ears for Bletchley Park and the country during the war. It is little known that until the Y-station service was fully established, a private company, Cable and Wireless, would help to provide the cabling network and infrastructure for signals communication.

The signals traffic would be carried on C&W cabling and components. While the 'Y' in Y-station was thought by many to be an abbreviation for 'wireless', other schools of thought indicate that it could have been a procedure or protocol, Naval Procedure Y, which was in place as far back as 1925 as a system of military rules in naval communication. This was an important stage in fleet wireless telegraphy that helped form the standards by which the Y-stations would be established.

The system developed over time, with Signals Intelligence based at Caxton Street in London before moving to Devonshire Place in 1939. Teleprinters would be used more for communication and had to have telecommunication cables routed, tested and in place to expand the service and make it less reliant on dispatch riders on motorcycles. Provision had to be made for approaching 1,000 lines via the telephone exchange. This was now a large operation to reflect its importance as war commenced. Bletchley Park would have a communications terminal manned by RAF personnel, which would be used constantly. Training was expanded and developed further in late 1940 via MF8, which also covered intelligence, policy, and liaison, the latter important with coordination via foreign allies such as the US later on as they entered the war following the attack on Pearl Harbor.

October 1941 would bring both expansion and new ideas for the improvement of efficiency of the service. A Deputy Director would be appointed later in April 1943. The direction-finding (D/F) part of the Y-service was becoming critical for traffic analysis, and some reports indicated around 2,000 signals bearings per day had to be intercepted and communicated to those at senior level, including Bletchley Park. Bases were expanded, extended, and fitted out with more modern equipment, receivers, larger aerials, teleprinters, etc. Beaumanor became a key site, as did Forest Moor near Harrogate in Yorkshire.

The use of female ATS personnel became the norm with support by RAF listeners. Training initiatives for being considered for Y-station work revolved around strict tests based upon accuracy and speed. Much work occurred in training in 1940, in the early stages of the war. Although training to be a Y-station listener with radio and Morse skills took around six months, in reality it could take a further six months to a year for someone to be proficient. This was down to the experience they needed to gain on the job, listening in a different range of atmospheric conditions, with fading signals, working on direction finding, recognising an enemy Morse key, and so on. Some GPO worker staff with limited radio communication skills were tested, but only a few could meet the high standards required on the tests, so the remainder had to be rejected. The ATS women appeared to have a higher pass rate, meeting the standard. RAF listeners were also in a supervisory role checking their staff for accuracy and providing technical assistance where needed. Keddleston Hall was one base used for training Y-station listeners.

As regards liaison with allies abroad, the US Army Signals Service designated a captain to review the Y-service in the United Kingdom. This went further still, examining arrangements for signals communication in North America. The Canadians' army and navy had six listening stations, but its air force had none.

It was eventually decided to provide an integrated Y-station signals listening service combined with the United States. The Canadian Y-service processed several thousand intercepted messages per month, and was able to erect substantial arrays of aerials and wires for long-distance reception, covering thousands of miles. Y-stations would be established in places such as Hong Kong, Kenya, Malta and North Africa. Information from abroad was highly valued at Bletchley Park and the location of such stations sometimes resulted in stronger signals from the enemy transmitters, although weather dependency for quality of signals would be a challenge during dust storms, torrential rain, high winds, etc. Aerials could collapse in high winds, requiring prompt recovery operations to get the station back into service quickly. Y-stations would be used to communicate with allied agents in the occupied countries from time to time. The RAF would establish 26 Signals Group back in the UK, with more than 3,500 staff across four departments or sections, with a mixture of officers and subordinates. ATS women would represent three quarters of the War Office Y-station group working on intercepts.

Advanced Y-stations organisation

By 'advanced', we are referring to those Y-stations that intercepted non-Morse messages from the enemy. The initial detection was from the Metropolitan Police building with a listening station, in Denmark Hill, Camberwell. It was useful as a Y-station for non-Morse work from mid-1941 into 1942, although it was originally established in 1939. This was the location that originally raised alarm bells and asked for the opinion of GC&CS HQ personnel from Bletchley Park about very strange and unusual transmissions being received at high speed and unlike normal Morse code. St Albans Post Office site was established and used for non-Morse intercepts from mid-1941 into 1942. Knockholt, at Ivy Farm in Kent, was established from mid-1942, taking over a farmer's site using wartime formal acquisition powers and developing it over time into a huge base, with large, rhombic aerial arrays, and under the direction of FORDE. It would be acquired together with 30 acres of land, but eventually be further expanded to some 160 acres by July 1942. The original farmhouse would house technical equipment, but many other buildings would be constructed on the site. Then, Wincombe Hill, near Shaftesbury in Dorset was used from late summer 1943. This was followed by Hawklaw near Cupar, Fife, in Scotland, from May to June 1944, and nearby Kingask near Cupar from June 1944. Keddleston Hall in Derbyshire, an army site, was of considerable importance, also used for training in non-Morse reception, and was used from late 1944 on non-Morse interception. Genval, near Brussels, was established from January 1945.

Therefore, in total, around eight separate advanced outstations were in operation listening out for non-Morse messages, although the most sophisticated of these was probably Knockholt, which also intercepted the first facsimile transmission. Its relatively high geographical elevation and location were specially selected for effective radio reception. The rhomboid aerials were substantial in size and scale.

Staffing at Knockholt would grow substantially over time, as demonstrated in this table showing staffing during the war:

Month and Year	Staffing personnel	Remarks
June 1942	6	Established around May 1942
June 1943	120	
June 1944	600	
May 1945	685+ 84 ATS+ 46 FORDE	815 personnel total

NB. Knockholt Y-station was also known as Knockholt Pound.

Billeting of staff was assisted by newly constructed special hostels taking in staff in Halstead and at Sevenoaks, Kent. A canteen and a galley kitchen were eventually built by the Ministry of Works in February 1944 to feed the large quantities of personnel on the base. Knockholt would have at least two radio receivers searching continuously for non-Morse transmissions. Other receivers would be engaged and assigned to a direct search pattern. Staff involved in advanced Y-stations on non-Morse work could receive specialist training abroad in North Africa, Sicily and Italy as the war progressed. RCA 88 radio receivers were generally used by operators, with around a quarter of them being female.

The antennae of the aerial arrays would be 105ft high, with masts formed from pairs of 50ft-high masts fastened together at the bases and stood on end, and then guyed with strong steel cables from the mast joints to be secured to large concrete blocks in the ground. There would be a total of twelve rhombic antennae, horizontally 900ft across the main diagonal, and 600ft across the minor dimension. The incoming signals from paired rhombics to paired receivers were amplified, detected, flat topped, added together and the combined signal received by Marconi undulators and recorded using paper tape. The large aerials could easily be seen from the air, but although that was a potential risk to attack initially, it reduced over time as the RAF became more in control of the skies above England.

Doris (Jenny) Stockdale (née Gummerson), a worker at Knockholt recalled her experience of working there:

> The station consisted of a cottage with one Nissen hut in which the Wireless Operators worked and leading off it, at the rear, a very much larger Nissen hut, and somewhere in the grounds at the back of that a canteen. Although I believe it is called 'Ivy Farm', I do not remember there being a farmhouse as well as the cottage. I do remember being told that the cottage was for the farmer's daughter who died just before she got married, so we all used to feel rather sad about the cottage.
>
> I attended an interview at Knockholt Pound, which was given by two females whom, I presume, were Civil Servants. I was accepted

> as a typist and then, after signing the Official Secrets Act, I started work in the larger Nissen hut, having first to learn how to read ticker tape and punched paper tape. No ATS girls were there until around the last year and then very few, maybe six. The Wireless Operators were men, plus one woman, and they were either ex-Forces or men not fit enough to go into the Forces. The rest of the staff were Civil Servants or, like myself, drafted in as temporary Civil Servants. The only other non-civilians on site was a Sergeant on the gate and occasionally an Army officer, but they had no authority over the civilians.
>
> I hated being in the large Nissen hut as it was rather like a typing pool, which I was not used to. I was fortunate in managing to get a position in the Wireless Operators' hut. I think there were six radio operators per shift, two typists, and also sometimes a Scotsman in charge, usually in the daytime. The operators spent their time searching for signals, and as soon as they tuned into one the ticker tape would start operating. I know I had to decode the ticker tape, type it out and, whilst I was typing, the punched paper tape machine, attached to the typewriter, started working. Whatever came through was in code and that had to go to Bletchley to be decoded into a proper language. I do realise that what we were doing must have been useful to Bletchley but on the whole it was pretty boring.
>
> Seeing the word 'FISH' in your posting (referring to a posting on the Kent History Forum website) reminded me that each operator's station was called after a different fish. How I wish there were photos of the inside, as there are of Bletchley, because I would remember so much more!
>
> We had three shifts: 0700 to 1400, 1400 to 2200, and 2200 to 0700. The staff were taken to and fro by a double decker bus from Orpington Station and Knockholt Station to the Pound. I lived at my parents' home in Lee for the first few months and travelled by train from Lee via Hither Green to Knockholt Station. On the late shift I would get to Hither Green well after 2300 hours and then have to walk to Lee in pitch black and sometimes air raids.
>
> Dispatch motor cyclists used to come from Bletchley to collect special consignments. In the large Nissen there was a teleprinter sending work straight to Bletchley.[22]

This brief description shows that much of the work was boring, but that it was an essential component of the race to crack enemy codes and ciphers, continuing to the end of the war. Cycling was an essential and inexpensive form of transport at times when there was petrol rationing and limited fuel supplies. The billeting of staff needed the assistance of the local communities. Officers of the law could sometimes assist in finding new billets for staff, using a little gentle persuasion.

Local towns and villages around Knockholt, such as Orpington, would be part of the area and radius considered appropriate for locating billets. The reliance on 'modern' teleprinter technology for communication back to Bletchley Park is apparent from the account.

There is no recollection by the listener-operator of the main farmhouse at Knockholt, which contained certain advanced technical equipment with access restricted to those with the appropriate clearance. Training was given on the job, but those who had to listen for transmitted messages and similar would be expected to pass a rigorous technical test in advance of taking up their positions at the listening station. Those in a support role such as filing data would be less challenged technically. Doris Stockdale explained the training she had to go through to read punched tape. This would have been based on the Vernam-Baudot system. It would eventually be processed, at least in part, via codebreaking machines back at Bletchley Park, such as the Robinson, and later Colossus, reading the tape through an optical sensor or magic eye. Thousands of valves would act as digital switches, in what was an early digital computer. Then it would be passed over to the Testery, some yards away from the Newmanry, to let the codebreakers manually determine the remainder of the cipher to be able to then put it through a Tunny machine for the final output.

In time, the operators and staff became more familiar with the layout of the site and the local surroundings. Security was high on the agenda, and pep talks to staff would remind them of the need for confidentiality and discretion in their work, with them not being permitted to inform their families or friends. It is appropriate to state that Knockholt was organised under FORDE, i.e. the Foreign Office, and was not a military base. It had mainly civilians as operators and technicians. The engineers employed on aerial erection and maintenance were probably from the RAF and similar. The Germans, had they known of the lengths the British had gone to read the enemy ciphers and codes, would have been surprised at the system that had been developed from scratch, its complexity, and the resources of vast quantities of skilled personnel in many different locations needed to make it work in practice.

Shift work at Bombe outstations

Work at codebreaking outstations would be round the clock on every day of the year including Christmas day. Shifts for personnel would be eight hours, and three shifts with different staff per day. The allocation of shifts would be based on the watch you were allocated to, such as 'A' Watch. Breaks were generally limited to half an hour for a meal, but many staff at Eastcote Outstation did not bother going across to the galley dining huts at break as it took time to get across there and back. At night this was even less inviting, particularly as one Wren had been assaulted by an unknown person along the public footpath that separated the two blocks of the site. Fortunately, this was an isolated incident, not to recur. Finishing a shift at an outstation, one could be called to Parade, or 'Divisions', irrespective of the time, day, or night, or of the weather conditions. During the shift, Wrens would generally work in pairs checking each other's work. A few lucky Wrens could operate the checking machines and sit down for the shift, not so if you were working on setting up the Bombes. Tea breaks would introduce the 'tea boat', as it was referred to in naval terminology. Shift work was long, arduous, and mostly quite boring for the main part. There was little natural daylight in the rooms, and it was extremely noisy with the click clatter of rotor wheels turning, like the sound of hundreds of knitting needles. The sound would be quite reverberant, as there were hard acoustic surfaces and no acoustic dampening provided. Some women complained later that they had lost the high frequencies of their hearing due to the intense noise at work. It was at a time when Health and Safety was not a priority for workers.

RAF engineers would come in to maintain the Bombes and carry out much of their work at night, during quieter times. Wrens needed small metal tweezers to align and correct the sharp needle wires that were within the Bombe rotor drums, and making electrical contact with the brass contacts on the main frame. Short circuits caused by wires touching another sector were common and had to be addressed to avoid equipment malfunction.

Food at meal breaks was basic and not wonderful. A sick Wren, fatigued from exhaustion over many weeks of operational work on the machines, was recovering in a separate room on the base. She had not eaten anything for several days until her Jewish mother was allowed to deliver her half a cooked chicken, which the Wren devoured with thanks. The brief access for her mother to what was a secret codebreaking base was unorthodox. The Wren was back at work within a week or two, refreshed after a short period of leave. Exhaustion and nervous breakdowns of the Bombe operators and support staff would occur from time to time due to the pressure of work, meeting targets and output. Periods of leave for staff were highly valued but relatively infrequent.

When the Americans arrived at Eastcote, there was more opportunity for sharing better food and attending their dances and social events at other bases, where food and entertainment would be plentiful and a welcome relief from the drudgery of outstation work. Eileen Hughes, a Wren who worked at Eastcote and Stanmore, recalls hearing the sweet sound of a nightingale early one morning at Eastcote, after a long arduous night shift on the Bombe machines.[23] That seemed to bring her back to some reality in the world, at least until the next Bombe shift in the evening. Wrens would get callouses on their fingers from adjusting the sharp contact wires within each rotor wheel on the Bombe machines with tweezers, and sometimes just bending the wires with their fingers. Some would receive slight electrical shocks from the machine, as confirmed by Eileen, but thankfully, no one was electrocuted, at least not officially.

The cabins the Wrens slept in were named after Navy battleships and aircraft carriers, and they had to follow naval discipline, including saluting on the quarterdeck. They would check their uniform was spotless at all times, and that of their colleagues who were about to start a codebreaking shift. Leave was but a luxury, but had to be planned in advance for outings into a local town or central London, to see a show, or go up town for dancing. Fortunately, both Stanmore and Eastcote Outstations had relatively good travel connections into London. Many staff had a bicycle, which was economical. A friendly RAF engineer might even repair your puncture for you. Transfers to other bases, including to Bletchley Park, would occur from time to time. This was an opportunity to meet new people, check out the food and conditions, and possibly meet up with colleagues who were also at the Mill Hill Training Base. But was this an antidote to the boredom of working on the noisy, oily, and smelly Bombe codebreaking machines? Probably not.

When American 6812th US Signals engineers came to Outstation Eastcote to work on a selected number of codebreaking Bombes, they would be based in Ruislip Woods, initially, in tents. The shift work would entail marching to the outstation and back again. It could not have been good for morale to know the Wrens were in dry and heated permanent huts with bunk berths for sleeping in, as compared to their draughty tents. Any night shifts for the Americans would mean getting back to their tents in the dark through the woods. As the war progressed, more comfortable accommodation may have been found for them in the locality, billeted in houses. The experiences gained by the US Signals personnel at Eastcote were highly valued and as the war progressed technical reports were produced outlining the process of the Bombe codebreaking methodology. They clearly had a very good understanding of how the machine was set up and worked.

Resourcing of support staff for codebreaking

Codebreaking during the war expanded considerably in terms of knowledge, machines, equipment and personnel. However, there were initial concerns at Bletchley and elsewhere as to how the service would be staffed, particularly as many men were either called up, in training, or carrying out essential work in factories, the utilities, and industry such as the manufacture of steel and aircraft production. Part of the answer was the use of female personnel on quite a large scale. Some would be billeted at Woburn and commuted into Bletchley. Others were tasked with supporting the outstations, such as Stanmore, Eastcote, or Wavendon, and these would be the Wrens. RAF engineers would also act as support staff to maintain Bombe machines.

Initial use of women on codebreaking machines was thought to be not such a good idea, with a certain amount of prejudice against females and their capabilities by some senior managers. However, tests carried out with Wrens operating Bombe machines and other tasks proved not to be a problem for most. Memos were circulated at high level to raise the issue of how the increased number of codebreaking machines could be produced, and how they were to be staffed when operational. Estimates of personnel needed were listed and these had to be revised upwards as Bletchley required more and more machines to crack Enigma ciphers and codes.

Similar in some ways to a projected cash flow forecast, the projections senior management had calculated future productivity based on staffing and the number of machines. There would also be an additional allowance for staff leave and sickness into the calculations. Liaison with the BTM factory in Letchworth and PORES in Dollis Hill was essential, as they produced the codebreaking equipment. Those concerned with staffing resources asked the question: 'Can enough numbers of Wrens be trained in time to operate and maintain the Bombe codebreaking machines which are being produced at the BTM factory?' The conscription of Wrens helped to a degree. This occurred later in the war, and concerned women of a certain specific age group. Not all Wrens would be suitable for this work and apart from basic training at places like Mill Hill, they would have to be selected for Special Duties X work, by senior staff, and specially trained to operate the Bombes and ancillary equipment.[24] The situation was highly complex as machines and personnel were sometimes transferred from one base to another. For example, one could have been trained at Mill Hill or in Scotland, then sent to Outstation Stanmore, and later be transferred to Outstation Eastcote. Others would be sent to Bletchley Park, and billeted at Woburn, some distance away. Shift work was introduced at all the outstations and at Bletchley on Bombe machine work. Some of the smaller outstations were a bit more flexible for the staff than the larger sites, which was noticeable if you started at say Outstation Wavendon, and were later transferred to Stanmore, a much larger Bombe outstation and base. The larger sites were much stricter in discipline, adhering to military protocols and in procedural aspects.

The resourcing of support staff also extended to those who were tasked with operating Hollerith machines, Typex machines, or to provide administrative duties such as typing, filing, and record keeping. The shortage of men in wartime meant that a substantial amount of this personnel would be female, and be a mixture of both civilians and military staff. Drayton Parslow, in Buckinghamshire, would be run by men but relied totally on women operators of the Hollerith equipment. Those who demonstrated aptitude at work would be promoted to a more senior role. Their pay rate, even when promoted, hardly changed if you were female. Women were used in large quantities during wartime, but were relatively poorly paid and valued. Equality in employment was still a long way off. Three quarters of the staff at Bletchley Park during wartime were women.

Codebreakers at Bletchley Park who worked on analysing the messages and looking for cribs or clues were often mathematicians but could also be linguists, classicists or be studying at university. It was Cambridge that supplied many of the specialist codebreakers, including Max Newman and Alan Turing. Not all recruits adapted easily to the work, but support from fellow codebreakers on learning the ropes would prove beneficial. Many would become specialists in their own way, and develop systems, methods, or procedures to make the processing more efficient over time.

Dilwyn Knox was one such codebreaker, who set up his own team of mainly women at Bletchley and these became 'Dilly's Girls'. He appeared to have an approach that encouraged experimentation and even a tolerance of minor mistakes by young recruits, providing they learned from those mistakes. Team players such as Mavis Lever would go on to achieve great things in their work, making an important difference in cracking enemy codes and ciphers. She was a mathematician but also knew German, which was an asset for the work. Providing there were more successes than failures, and a consistent approach to the work, 'Dilly' was allowed a degree of flexibility with his team of codebreakers. Morale was relatively high in the cottages at Bletchley that housed his female team, and this proved to be most beneficial in respect of output. Unfortunately, Knox fell seriously ill while working at Bletchley and his girls would have to go on without him when he sadly passed away on 23 February 1943.

The backroom personnel would have a range of duties to perform at Bletchley, outstations, and at Y-stations. Women would dominate many of the roles, that included typing, translation of German and Italian into English, cataloguing, and filing records. These records could include everything from messages intercepted from Europe and the Mediterranean, the Y-station intercept log sheets, to recording statistics on operational staff at bases. There would also be confidential files on important enemy generals, admirals, commandants and other officers, organisation charts of the enemy groups and divisions to be kept up to date, plus calculations of the quantity of supplies needed to keep bases operational and active. As no one knew how long the war could last, it was difficult to predict how many replacement valves one might need for Y-station radios, or how many radio receivers. How many Bombes should be ordered from BTM? Was there a need for another codebreaking base, or could they manage with the newer established bases at Stanmore and Eastcote?

Staff would either be billeted in nearby villages and houses or sometimes on site, such as at codebreaking outstations. All the billets had to be checked out by the official authorities and registered. These questions and more would need careful consideration. Management meetings would table questions on a range of detailed agenda and send in comprehensive reports as well as requisitions for materials, personnel, equipment, and supplies. Training of personnel would be an ongoing operation, with tests and examinations held for the more challenging roles, records kept of progress and the level of skills acquired. Morse code speed and accuracy tests would be one of the criteria for selecting skilled personnel for Y-stations. Not all would pass the rigorous tests, based upon GPO radio licence standards. See also Organisation of Expansion of Bombe Production.

Lend-Lease

The Lend-Lease Act, enacted on 11 March 1941, was a key tool in providing funding and resources to allied powers by the USA during the war. It was subtitled 'An Act to promote the defense of the United States'. Churchill had even suggested the concept of lend-lease to Franklin D. Roosevelt at the end of 1940. After Pearl Harbor it would be easier to pass the Bill through Congress. Extraordinary large sums of money and equipment was provided to Britain, Russia, and many other countries to help with the war effort. This included a considerable amount of radio equipment for transmission and for radio receivers. Much was used in various Y-stations or wireless listening stations in the UK and abroad, being robust and with ample spares for maintenance. The agreement stipulated that items not used at the end of the war should be returned back to the US or were to be paid for. The Lend-Lease facility was a saviour for the UK, inasmuch it enabled a bankrupt nation to rearm and prepare for further conflict with the enemy, and as part of a much greater Allied force together with the United States. Britain was one of the first countries to benefit from the Lend-Lease Act, and other countries would soon follow.

The process involved the Office of Lend-Lease administration allocating resources to Britain and others in huge quantities. The US would receive around $10 billion of so called 'reverse lend-lease' as compensation, and a number of financial settlements post-war, although a fraction of what the US had supplied. The money would generally not have to be paid back, although other loans made to Britain did have to be reimbursed. In October 1941 the US Senate passed a $5.98 billion Supplemental Lend-Lease Bill bringing the total commitment to around $13 billion at the time. This would later increase substantially as more and more countries were added to the list of recipients of wartime aid. By early 1945 the US had spent around 15 per cent of its entire war budget on Lend-Lease to other countries.

The investment into the Y-stations as regards equipment would ensure Bletchley Park and the outstations would be kept operational in decoding the enemy intelligence to the benefit of the Allies. A complication under the Lend-Lease agreement involved the convertibility into Sterling, which had to be later adjusted and then dispensed with as it disadvantaged the UK post-war in terms of trade with the US, affecting British monetary reserves. The US Treasury received their final payment in December 2006 for a post-war supplementary loan to GB. The amount borrowed under Lend-Lease was some $50.1 billion across some thirty-eight countries. This was the equivalent value of $690 billion at 2020 rates for comparison. Considerable levels of funding and military equipment would also be provided to Russia by America when it was an ally fighting Nazi Germany together with the West. It was a logistical challenge during wartime, and there were concerns by President Roosevelt that urgently needed machine tools for US factories were being sent abroad to other countries. A balance had to be struck as regards the priorities in food, fuel, armaments, materials, and other resources that left the shores of America.

Arctic and Baltic Allied convoys would take great risks transferring American goods and supplies to Russia via Lend-Lease agreements, trying to avoid the U-boats patrolling the area. British merchant ships and military support ships played their part here. Convoys could start from England, Iceland, or North America for the long sea journey and the Arctic route. Navies participating included the Royal Navy, Canadian Navy, and US Navy. Around 1,400 merchant vessels would take part with Allied naval escorts. Extreme weather in winter would ice up the ships and risk capsizing them in rough seas. Intelligence reports of the latest enemy positions and weather were critical for survival. Reports indicate that around 6 per cent of merchant vessels were lost at sea, mainly due to enemy action, some due to adverse weather conditions. The area was extremely complex geographically and politically, as for a time Finnish forces would attack Russian vessels in the area. It was hard enough for the Allies trying to evade the Germans and arrive back home safely without losses. Without these much-needed supplies, Russia would have quickly run out of ammunition, vehicles, tanks, materials, and equipment, as well as food. Just under eighty convoys made this dangerous journey over the course of the war, with some gaps that saw no convoys occurring in some years. Without Lend-Lease agreements and the Anglo-Soviet agreement hardly any such convoys could have been funded or organised. They would make a significant difference to assist repelling the Nazi invaders and driving them back over time.

Academic recruitment for Bletchley Park

The search for potential codebreakers to fill Bletchley Park huts would start with trawling academic institutions, the universities such as Oxford and Cambridge, to recruit bright young men and women. Mathematicians were particularly of interest, but also linguists and even classicists, where language structure and even the recognition of obscure patterns in language could be relevant. Alan Turing, Gordon Welchman, Donald Michie, and others would be attracted to work at Bletchley, in cold and draughty wooden huts, to help decode the German Enigma and advanced encoding machines. Turing joined Bletchley in September 1939; not a moment too soon as war was commencing in Europe. Over time, this would become a huge undertaking involving many staff with different skills and abilities, trying out old but tested methods, introducing many new ideas, and developing innovative and groundbreaking codebreaking machines. While initially Bletchley was looking for highly qualified academics and 'men of the professor type', over time there was a degree more flexibility in selecting personnel, considering the range of duties and tasks across the GC&CS organisation. Indeed, 7,500 women worked at Bletchley during the war, around three quarters of the total staff. Some had university degrees in mathematics or physics, and several had knowledge of German or Italian, which was valuable to codebreakers. The class system was alive and well at GC&CS, with daughters of titled ladies and debutantes selected for clerical and administrative work. Those who were particularly good at crosswords, and who had other languages as a skill, may have come to the notice of some of the management for further interviews and consideration to be engaged in a more technical role. WAAFs, ATS, and WRNS personnel would help to support the GC&CS machine at Bletchley and elsewhere.

Setting Enigma daily key

The setting of the Enigma machine depended initially upon reference to Nazi code books to find settings for the rotors based on the date. However, there would also be a daily key, and the sender would first send through the rotor positions unencoded, followed by an encoded rotor setting, This would make up the key for sending and receiving the encoded Enigma messages. The British would unravel this system eventually at Bletchley Park, but cribs or clues would be needed to help decode the message settings.

Banburismus

A technical and cryptanalytic system devised by mathematician and codebreaker Alan Turing to attack the Enigma ciphers. It worked to identify and analyse the most likely wheel positions in the right-hand rotor, and the middle rotor of the machine's rotor wheels. When correctly applied, this would reduce the amount of work the Bombe codebreaking machines would need to do. It was a combination of manual work and using the Hollerith punched card readers for sorting and data processing. The Banburismus process was used in Hut 8 at Bletchley Park. It is dependent upon a non-random letter distribution and sequential probability of the positioning of letters. This process was used for a period of two years until 1943. The increase in production of Bombe machines later in the war became significant, giving more time for message setting analysis.

Cillies

These were 'silly' clues identified at Bletchley because of sloppy procedures and laziness by the Enigma operator. Effectively, it would be information inadvertently given by the enemy operator that gave those at Bletchley Park an indication to the message keys for the Enigma encoding machine. These would be exploited to save time in cracking the ciphers. Some reports indicate that the term had been arrived at because of a German operator who sent messages referring to his girlfriend as Cillie.

Zygalski Sheets

A series of overlaid perforated large paper sheets stacked on top of one another. The process was one of elimination to reduce the apertures to one single remaining aperture, which could give information as to the message key used on Enigma. The name comes from the Polish codebreaker Henryk Zygalski, who developed the system. Careful alignment of the stacked sheets would be essential, and the depth of them meant that it was still difficult to see through the apertures.

Jeffreys' sheets

Similar to the principles of Zygalski sheets, Jeffreys' sheets were based upon the layering of paper with aligning apertures to assist with codebreaking. John R. Jeffreys was both a mathematician and codebreaker recruited to Bletchley Park in 1939 from Cambridge University. He worked as a researcher alongside Dilly Knox and specialised in using the Polish-designed Zygalski sheets. He was in charge of managing the manufacture of two sets of Zygalski sheets at Bletchley. However, he had developed his own version of paper perforated sheets to aid cracking the Enigma cipher, and these were known as Jeffreys' sheets. They aided the cipher attack on Enigma by looking at the combined effect of any two Enigma rotors and the reflector within the Enigma machine. Polish cryptologists working in France in January 1940, most probably at the secret codebreaking base, Château des Fuzes, used Jeffreys' sheets to help decipher one of the first wartime Enigma messages. In Hut 6 at Bletchley, he would work with Gordon Welchman, sharing duties. He would be in charge of sheet stacking and improved the quality control of the system. Jeffreys fell ill in 1942 and died in January 1944. His fiancée at Bletchley had also worked on hole punching and organisation of the sheets. Jeffreys' sheets can sometimes appear to have similarities to modern QR codes in respect of the patterns produced, but these work on different principles.

Rodding

A method to aid codebreaking developed largely by Dilwyn Knox. It was used to break messages that did not have a plugboard or 'steckerboard', and was invented in 1937. The Italians used some Enigma machines without a plugboard, and Knox's rodding method managed to crack some of the messages in 1941. Rodding would also be used to crack the Nazi Railway Enigma models too. This process worked on the complexity of the Enigma machine in that when one pressed a letter, say K, and an 'A' lit up, in the same position pressing an 'A' would result in a 'K' being illuminated. One could also never generate the illumination of the same keyed letter, so that 'A' keyed by an operator would never produce an 'A' lit up on the machine. This would turn out to be an inherent weakness in the Enigma. Knox made a series of lettered strips of cardboard, which he referred to as 'rods'. There would be one of these for each rotor wheel. The exact description of the entire process of rodding from a technical viewpoint can be found elsewhere, but suffice to state it involved making up tables on a grid system, and with the possible rotor positions analysed in detail. Knox had trained his female team of codebreakers on the rodding system, and it was used to good effect by Mavis Lever against the Italians, which had an impact at the Battle of Matapan in the Mediterranean by giving the Royal Navy the element of surprise.

Turingery

A manual system of codebreaking the Lorenz teleprinter attachments, devised by Alan Turing in July 1942. It relied on a degree of trial and error but a process was applied to help identify part of the wheel settings of the Lorenz machine. The method was also jokingly referred to as Turinismus by some of his codebreaking colleagues at Bletchley Park.

Direction-finding processes

Direction-finding or D/F relies upon the concept of triangulation and intersection of two or more points to establish a location. This was used by both the Allies and the enemy in wartime. The direction-finding process was used by utilising more than one listening station to target a transmission from, say, Europe. It was critical that the angle between the stations should be relatively large for accuracy. More than two listening stations could assist in a more accurate location of a transmission. Mobile units on trucks or lorries could also carry out direction-finding work. The Nazis used D/F extensively in the occupied countries to identify illegal radio transmissions from the underground resistance fighters, and agents planted in the countries by the Allies, perhaps working alongside SOE. They would listen in at one location, then drive a few miles away and tune into the same frequency to get a plot and a bearing. The next stage would be to make radio contact with the armed forces to arrest the culprits. This process was also used by the Allies to locate enemy agents. The shorter the transmissions, the less chance of finding the position of the sender. Agents making long radio transmissions took a huge risk of being captured, tortured, and executed.

Managing and handling agents and double agents

Throughout wartime, and even in peacetime, various states would plant agents and spies in other countries to gather intelligence to aid their position of strength against potential enemies, and against neutral states such as Switzerland. The Nazis had spies around the world even before the Second World War commenced. Japanese spies were in Pearl Harbor before the attack on the American fleet, to pass information as to the vessels in port and other activities. A number of operations were assisted greatly by using agents and double agents on both sides. Communication devices would range from use of invisible inks or secret ink writing to the use of microfilm, photographs of military sites and factories, clandestine radio transmissions using portable transmitters, penetrating official organisations such as the Abwehr, and use of safe houses to operate from. Transmissions by radio could be in plain language, Morse code, or in encrypted Morse.

Recruiting agents and double agents was a tricky and risky task for the Allies. One had to be entirely sure of the loyalty and commitment of the people who would gather intelligence and communicate with the enemy, often in occupied countries such as France or Belgium. A handler would often be appointed to control the agent from Britain, and to give instructions and monitor messages passed to the enemy if a double agent was involved. One mistake could give the game away and expose the spying initiative.

Agent Garbo, or Juan Pujol Garcia, was taken on after much reluctance by the British, but they eventually realised he had good enemy agent contacts in Portugal and Spain and could be of some value. Originally, he was code-named Bovril, after the famous drink, but that was changed some time later to Garbo, and he was known as Arabel to the enemy. He came to Britain in April 1942 and his handler kept him in a private house in Hendon, north-west London, writing and sending messages to the enemy, giving false information together with some facts.[25] Garbo had a fictitious network of many supporting agents in Britain, and it appears that his contact was convinced this was a reality. That is not to say that there was not some tension between his handler and himself in the double agent operation. There would always be some doubt as to whether Garbo was just too good to be true, and was possibly a triple agent on the side of the Nazis, duping the British. MI5 wanted frequent reports of the progress made, identifying the threats and the opportunities available. If Garbo fell suddenly ill or died, they would be left in a difficult situation as to exactly how to proceed. The Nazis may then have expected one of the other senior networked agents under Garbo to fill the gap, but they did not exist. It could all collapse so easily, like a house of cards.

Tomás Harris was Garbo's handler for the security services, monitoring him day and night. It was Harris's role to ensure that Garbo kept to the script the Allies gave him, to feed the enemy just enough intelligence to make them interested and wanting to know more. The messages were sent to a post office box in Lisbon, Portugal. Garbo had a habit of including sometimes unauthorised information, as he may have been considering himself somewhat of an actor playing a part in an important play, but a play that could go so badly wrong. He was fortunately mostly kept in check by Harris, so as not to go too far astray in his information and messages. The ultimate prize would be that the Nazis would fall hook, line, and sinker for the Allied Fortitude South operation, and the concept of FUSAG, an American army awaiting to invade the Pas-de-Calais instead of Normandy. This was feeding intelligence to the enemy at the highest level, and even Adolf Hitler would see some of the messages from Garbo.

The MI5 officers had various levels of experience handling their agents, and many were fluent in more than one language. This helped considerably, as if an agent was communicating in German, one needed to understand exactly what was being sent to the enemy. Most of the German agents, both in England and in the US, had been discovered, exposed, and turned into double agents working for the Allies. The Y-stations helped here considerably, listening into hundreds of thousands of radio messages and Morse code, passing that intelligence to Bletchley Park for analysis and decryption. A system by MI5 and the equivalent in America, SIS, had been developed over time, and was much more sophisticated than that in the previous war, partly due to the explosion of radio communication and advanced cryptographic processes.

Use of rare languages and dialects in ciphers

One way of confusing the enemy is to use a rare language that is spoken only by a handful of people, and dialects of that language, to create a cipher for military or diplomatic communication. This technique was used by the Americans during the war, using indigenous Indian tribes that spoke a language that was known only by a few. The language had to be supplemented with a few more modern words to be able to communicate items such as 'tanks', 'grenades', and others. Such dialects were used against the Japanese, and were extremely successful. Navajo Code-talker Marines are an example of military use of a rare language used as a cipher. Their cipher communication was used between 1942 and 1945 across the Pacific islands. It was never broken by the enemy. Such systems are quite unusual, but one problem was that if someone using the system was killed or injured, there needed to be another code speaker who spoke the same language and had been specially trained in the operation. There would be a constant pressure for military commanders and communications officers to ensure there were sufficient Navajo code talkers available to fill in for men who may have been killed, injured, or who had gone missing. Some reports have indicated that without this system in use, the Pacific Island of Iwo Jima would never have been taken by the Allies.

The system was considered after someone realised that Navajo soldiers would often communicate to fellow Navajo colleagues in their mother tongue. An entire training regime was established from 1942. Something similar may have occurred in Australia, where indigenous people had their own language and a degree of rarity in the dialect. The Japanese were never able to decipher the Navajo dialect communication, so its use was considered to be a complete success.

Photo reconnaissance

The use of photo reconnaissance in identifying potential targets, places of interest, troop and supply movements, and of key geographical features, should not be underestimated. This intelligence, added together with codebreaking intercepts, could assist the armed forces and their commanders considerably. This is also where piecing together trivia and miscellaneous intercepts using the Hollerith punched card system could prove fruitful at times. There would be Hollerith machines and operators at Bletchley Park and later at Drayton Parslow, not far away. This would act as a storage of data facility and be set up for retrieval of searched data, which was catalogued and cross-referenced in a specific way.

The photos obtained of occupied Europe and elsewhere provided intelligence that would be matched up with encoded intercepts where possible to build more of a picture and help prioritise enemy targets. Resistance fighters and the SOE would also play their part to add more bits to the jigsaw puzzle. The original section involved would be the Photographic Development Unit. Managing the information collected would be a challenge, particularly as it could rapidly become out of date. Specialist reconnaissance personnel would spend many hours reviewing aerial photographs using technical and optical equipment on large tables. Stereoscopic viewers could be used to help identify heights of buildings and structures, such as V1 and V2 rocket launch sites. As the 2D pictures were overlapped when photographing sites by around 60 per cent, this made it possible to view them in the stereoscopic viewer with a binocular to gauge height, as well as distance. Shadows on sunny days were extremely useful when assessing images, as they could give an accurate indication of height, such as at the Peenemünde missile development site. The detail required to evaluate some of these sites was such that a special WILD photogrammetric survey machine was required to be of use. These machines were obtained via Switzerland and Germany under a clandestine operation, and brought to RAF Medmenham for use by personnel. (The machines were used principally in peacetime for land survey work.)

The Allied Central Interpretation Unit, which superseded the Photographic Development Unit, and the Photographic Interpretation Unit, would coordinate the work. This was mainly compiled at RAF Medmenham. Danesfield House was the focal point for the photo reconnaissance activities there, with many skilled photo-interpreters scanning images for long periods. This site was approximately 60 miles west of London, and top secret.

Photo reconnaissance was a tool to aid the war effort and would assist in the Allies confirming enemy movements, which could be verified at times via Enigma intercepts, through the wireless listening stations. The aircraft for photo work varied in type, although some Supermarine Spitfires and de Havilland Mosquitos were adapted and proved very successful. To gain sufficient altitude and range, some were stripped of their machine guns and ammunition, reducing weight but leaving them vulnerable to air attack. Cameras in the planes had to be specially heated to avoid malfunction and freezing up completely at altitude.

Beatrice Schilling, an engineer, would play her part in making technical improvements to the Spitfire's carburettor to ensure it could operate without power loss when in negative G. Her unique engineering solution was a specially formed tiny brass fluted component with a curved orifice to control flow of fuel in the carburettor, but one that made a huge difference to performance. Schilling had a building named after her at University of London, Royal Holloway, Surrey Campus. A glass cabinet contains a replica of the fluted component, which was made specially by British Aerospace for the university as a commemorative item. A selection of Schilling's personal papers and documents were also bequeathed to the university by her family. Some US planes were also used for photo reconnaissance. Some 36 million photographic prints were made during the Second World War, and their storage and filing was a vast undertaking by itself.

Billeting of codebreaking military personnel

While some codebreaking support staff could live at their bases, such as at some of the codebreaking outstations, most could not. Billeting would be arranged by a billeting officer, identifying accommodation for staff in surrounding areas, towns, and villages. Woburn was such a place and numerous Wrens were billeted there, some staying in the actual Woburn main mansion house within selected rooms. While houses and flats were mainly used for accommodation elsewhere, some alternatives were also used such as a golf club, and even empty stables on farms or estates. With some of the codebreaking Bombes also in concealed stables at some of the country house outstations, the conditions were not always pleasant, with smells, odours and standing water in places making it often damp. However, the majority of billeted premises were adequate for the purpose of providing a bed and a meal for hard-working staff. The advantage of being at Woburn was being surrounded by many acres of beautiful landscaping, with natural wildlife nearby. In spring and summer this would be appreciated by the women, although various parts would be out of bounds. Eton College and other sites near Windsor were used to accommodate Wrens. Many of the military personnel, or civilians working in a support role at Bletchley Park, the outstations, or bases, both male or female, would walk or cycle to work, or use the local bus. Cycling was very popular during wartime, and avoided the problems of buying petrol, which was rationed, and also kept the person relatively fit when cycling a few miles every day. Wrens who worked at the Western Approaches bunker near Liverpool and Merseyside were generally billeted in nearby houses, but some stayed for several nights within the bunker, particularly if there was a critical planning phase, event, or activity. Events such as the approach to D-Day were so important in terms of security that personnel were restricted in their movements and may not have returned home for several days. Sleeping in bunks and beds on site became the norm, at least for a time.

Security

Security in wartime and even post-war was essential to guard secrets and systems, but was applied in different ways. Signing of the Official Secrets Act by those who had access to confidential information applied to codebreakers, those at Bletchley, and the outstations. Armed guards, who were sometimes from the Royal Marines, guarded installations and outstations. Information was provided on a need-to-know basis to personnel. Staff were issued security passes, and their backgrounds checked and vetted. However, all this did not prevent serious breaches of security by agents and spies, such as one at Bletchley Park in the codebreaking huts. Post-war, MI5 would become complacent and allow traitors such as George Blake, Guy Burgess, and Anthony Blunt to pass British secrets across to the Soviets. Blake would be imprisoned eventually, but would then escape, resulting in a national manhunt that proved to be a failure as he went over to the East, hidden in a friend's camper van.

There is no such thing as perfect security, only varying levels, with the state constantly trying to close gaps and loopholes. Wartime breaches of security were very serious, as if the enemy found out about Bletchley Park, the codebreakers, the Bombes, and the outstations, things would be have been very different and the war might not have ended as it did in summer 1945. Fortunately, although there were some close calls, the Nazis never caught on. Part of this was down to the character of Hitler, who dismissed warnings by his generals and advisers about Enigma and other related issues. Indeed, it was the failure of the Nazi Enigma operators to follow the security protocol for setting up and operating the encoding machines that gave clues, cribs, and openings for the Allied codebreakers to penetrate the enemy systems. Their laziness and incompetence was useful to the Allies.

Security was also particularly relevant at codebreaking outstations, such as at Outstation Eastcote, where an old public footpath effectively split the site into two, dividing Block A and Block B, the latter containing the Bombe codebreaking machines.[26] This was a less than ideal scenario, with the public wandering up and down the path day and night, close to top-secret machines and operational Navy and RAF personnel. Royal Marines guarded the perimeter of the site and entrances off the footpath.

The scale of the Second World War and its complexity meant that it was virtually impossible to have total security, with possible breaches of security likely, either through accident, incompetence, or via active enemy agents. The latter were less of an issue as most of the German agents had been identified and many turned to act in favour of the Allies. Before the war, enemy agents had acquired detailed maps of England and taken numerous photographs for record purposes of the London Docks, military installations, airfields, harbours, industrial sites, etc. Japan had done something similar in the Hawaiian islands before the Pearl Harbor attack, planting agents to report the movement of Allied ships. They blended into the community in what was a busy harbour and support infrastructure. What may also have been a factor in their success is that few believed Japan would launch an attack on the US, and probably not in the islands. When radar equipment was erected in the north part of Oahu, it was manned by a handful of bored military personnel with just basic training. The discovery of a radar image detected early on the Sunday morning of the attack was telephoned through to a superior officer for instructions, but was dismissed as probably local aircraft. Complacency by senior military officers would have a severe impact on the US Navy due to the losses on 7 December 1941. Lessons would have to be learned from mistakes made and the rule book rewritten.

A memorial was developed for the Pearl Harbor attack after the war, and an architecturally designed platform bridge has been erected over the sunken USS *Arizona*, at right angles to it and only a few feet above the water. One can still see the outline of the ship through the relatively clear harbour water, and traces of oil glistening in the water. It is a spine-chilling experience to stand on the platform looking down on to what is effectively a war grave.

United States codebreaking and security

OP-20-G was the US Naval intelligence division and would be the enabler of the American four-wheel codebreaking Bombe, built in the latter stages of the war. The Office of Chief Naval Operations explains the 'OP' part of the somewhat awkward abbreviation. This division would be principally for signals intelligence and cryptanalysis for the Navy during the war. OP-20-G was established on a relatively small scale in the early 1920s. The division expanded and became a key focus after the catastrophic events of Pearl Harbor. Their monitoring of the Japanese diplomatic messages prior to the attack had only been partly successful, and this had dire consequences. This was partly due to the rivalry with the Signals Intelligence Service (SIS). In 1942, the division was based at Mount Vernon College for Women, which was acquired by the Navy.

The impact of the attack by the Japanese on Pearl Harbor would awaken a sleeping giant, and that meant intelligence gathering and processing became critical. As the US's enemies were not just the Japanese, but now the Italians and Germans, the network of intelligence gathering had to be on a broad scale, also utilising allies at Bletchley Park in England, and coordinating operations in Malta, North Africa, Australia, and New Zealand. The establishment of a network of listening stations would evolve over the course of the war in the US, the Mediterranean, and the Pacific. Some of those listening stations back home could pick up messages from many thousands of miles away. Indeed, they collected useful data for the UK.

The apportionment of blame arising from the Pearl Harbor attack by the Japanese was considered after the war ended at the highest level via an official inquiry. Some senior military officers including Admiral H. Kimmel, commander of the US fleet in Hawaii in December 1941, were considered to have been made scapegoats for the communication and intelligence failures, and even in 2024 the grandson of Admiral Kimmel, Tom Kimmel, is fighting to clear the name of his grandfather. His family claims to have certain documents that prove Washington had key intelligence information that was not passed on at the appropriate time and could have otherwise avoided the complete lack of preparation for the Japanese attack. Although Kimmel was stripped of his command and accused of dereliction of duty, the charges were later dropped by the Navy, although his career was cut short. In 1944, both a friend of Kimmel and a naval cryptanalyst involved in deciphering codes told of Japanese intercepts in early December 1941 that an attack by the Japanese was imminent on the United States. Kimmel claims never to have been made aware of this. He retired a rear admiral and was not allowed to use his four-star admiral status. An official Senate hearing allowing the family to be heard was held in April 1995, with senior representatives of the US Defense Department attending. Lieutenant General W. Short, who was the Army equivalent senior ranking officer of Admiral Kimmel, was also discussed at the hearing. In 2000, Congress passed a bill, sponsored by Senator Joe Biden, to reinstate the rank of Admiral Kimmel. Several books have been written by military historians stating that Kimmel and Short were both scapegoats, based on evidence examined in detail, and not responsible for communication failures before the enemy attack on Pearl Harbor. This is an ongoing topic being investigated and researched by military historians, fitting together the different parts of the puzzle based on historic documents and accounts.

The year 1942 would be a pivotal one in the exchange of information and technology between Britain and the United States, with reciprocal visits to the US by codebreaker John Tiltman, and to Bletchley Park by US Navy cryptanalysts. In that same year, in March, a contract was organised between the US Navy and the NCR company in Dayton, Ohio, to establish the Naval Computing Machine Laboratory (NCML). When OP-20-G decided to develop an American version of the British codebreaking Bombe, funding had to be applied for before work could commence. The machines built were principally used for decoding U-boat Enigma messages, with some 55 per cent of activity the deciphering of German naval keys and the remaining 45 per cent against non-naval ciphered messages, including use of the British Bombes in England against Enigmas used in occupied Europe. By spring of 1944, some ninety-six four-wheeled Enigma-based Bombes were breaking U-boat messages in Washington. Sharing intelligence information with their British allies, the system worked effectively and reduced shipping losses in the North Atlantic.

Sharing intelligence with allies and policy

The degree of sharing of British military intelligence during wartime depended upon the relationship with the particular ally. For example, America was treated rather differently than Russia. There were concerns that security leaks via Russia could compromise British operatives by identifying the source of the intelligence. Russia had also previously been an ally of Nazi Germany, so some suspicion remained. Even sharing information at times with Britain's US allies was a sensitive issue. The Americans would eventually take the design elements of the Bombe codebreaking machine and develop an improved four-wheel model, to be used in Washington against U-boat messages. There would, however, be exchanges of personnel during wartime between nations such as the UK and the USA, and a contingent of American specialists and signals engineers visited Britain to learn about its codebreaking systems and apply their knowledge practically. This occurred at Bletchley Park and at outstations such as Eastcote in Middlesex. When a Swedish mathematician cracked the *Geheimschreiber* Nazi secret writer advanced encoding machine based on landline tapping, the British, Russians, and later the Germans found out about it. This might have made things difficult for the Allies, as the Russians would then be aware there were methods being utilised in intercepting and cracking the enemy's cipher machines, which the Allies could take advantage of. As William Tutte and others pursued the advanced teleprinter-based machines, Bletchley Park and the Western Allies would have to keep their sources secret, or at least disguise them, when providing intelligence to the Russians.

The cryptanalysts in the US would later agree with those at Bletchley to split the workload between the countries, with America concentrating on the Pacific war and Bletchley on the European/Atlantic war. However, that did not quite work out, and the Americans were forced to concentrate a large amount of their resources fighting the U-boat threat in the North Atlantic, as well as gathering considerable intelligence from the Italians and elsewhere.

An important visit to Bletchley Park by representatives of both the US Navy and Army occurred during early February 1941 to share information and exchange ideas. Four men, including Weeks, Currier, Rosen, and Sinkov, were met at Sheerness in England en route to London, and then on to Bletchley Park, after a long and arduous journey across the Atlantic and then down from Scapa Flow. They would be met initially when docked by Captain Sandwith, head of Naval Signals Division 9. This would possibly be considered as the equivalent of OP-20-G. John Tiltman may have been present from Bletchley, but this is not confirmed. At Bletchley, among the various discussions, the Americans had brought a 'Purple' analogue machine to demonstrate to the British codebreakers. The bulk of verbal interchange was around non-Enigma enciphering systems such as the Luftwaffe lower-grade field ciphers and systems used by the SS, SD, and *Abwehr*. Italian and Japanese crypto systems were discussed at length. Hollerith machines at Bletchley were inspected in the huts, and as these were American design and sourced, the visitors were already broadly familiar with them.

Management at Bletchley had mixed feelings about sharing the Enigma codebreaking work with the visitors, which seems rather peculiar given the nature and purpose of the visit to GC&CS. Eventually, Stuart Menzies agreed subject to certain conditions being fulfilled, such as controlling those who had access to this secret information. Churchill, as Prime Minister, had to be consulted, and he gave his formal approval on 27 February. Confidentiality agreements were drawn up in early March, and offered to the four visitors to sign, which they did even though initially they were reluctant as they were relatively junior officers. Bombe machines were then disclosed to them and demonstrated, with a full explanation given of how they were set up and operated, including Menus and how they worked in practice. Without this access to Enigma-based codebreaking, the visit may have been deemed a failure, or at the very least not particularly productive. No captured Enigmas were handed over to the Americans in exchange for the analogue Purple machine they had brought for the British, mainly because Bletchley did not have any spare to give. Trips away from Bletchley included a visit to the Marconi Wireless factory, and there the Americans were able to review British direction-finding equipment. This technology would have been relevant to U-boat detection. Other jaunts included visiting various listening 'Y' stations and discussing HF-DF systems at Scarborough.

The conclusion is that there was some tension between the hosts and the visitors over several weeks of exchanging information, ideas, and proposals. It was relatively early on in the war, and Bletchley had relatively few Bombes, and very few Enigmas to share, if any. The Americans later commented that they should have been better briefed by senior staff before their visit. Things would later improve over time, but at least this was a first step on the ladder of joint cooperation between allies.

Organisation of WAVES in US Bombe production

It would not be until early September 1942 that funding for the US Navy four-wheel Bombe codebreaking machines was applied for and granted. The four-wheel Bombe became a priority as the U-boats were causing havoc in the North Atlantic, sinking massive amounts of shipping, and communicating using the newer four-wheel Enigma machines. Bletchley had some challenges to decode these, and the US Navy was becoming impatient. The costs would be considerable and the resources too, in terms of personnel, materials, equipment, machinery, and secure space to build them. Admiral Redman of the US Navy approved the funding based upon the formal application by Commander Wenger, deputy chief of OP-20-G. To help build the machines designed largely by Joseph Desch at NCR, in Dayton, Ohio, a number of WAVES personnel would be trained up to fabricate components and construct them, along with sailors, engineers and NCR civilians.

All was top secret, and personnel were only allowed into certain rooms or areas if they could prove to the armed guards that they needed access to do their jobs. Senior engineers would even create colour-coded wiring templates in such a way that it was difficult for the assemblers to understand how many different permutations of the wiring there would be. Instead of just producing twenty-six wiring circuits, one for each letter of the alphabet, twenty-eight loops were created. The need for security was almost of paranoid proportions at the time of development of the machines. Initially there were as few as seventy women on the project, but this built up to more than 600 over time. Shift work was round the clock, and revolved around the sequence 8am–4pm, 4pm–12 midnight, and 12–8am. It was a major task to learn how to wire the components, drums, and frame, based upon intense training. A relatively small proportion of the WAVES were allocated this work compared to the thousands who worked for this organisation in the war.

When the machines were ready for operational use, they went to Washington, where personnel were allocated to set up and run them. Photographs exist in the database photographic gallery of the National Cryptologic Museum of female operators setting up the naval Bombes. The reader should bear in mind that while Wrens operated British Bombe machines, they did not become involved in their manufacture, although civilian female factory workers did assemble components for the Bombes in Letchworth, Hertfordshire.

Operational aspects of the US Navy Bombes

The prototypes of the US Navy Bombes were termed Adam and Eve, and were largely finished by early May 1943. However, new buildings being constructed to house the machines in Washington were unfinished and some would later end up with tarpaulins over them until the roofing was completed. Of course, initial testing of the early machines over several weeks was carried out prior to dispatch to Washington. The quality control of the work had to be meticulous, as mistakes could not be tolerated in the assembly, which would otherwise have compromised their output and impact. By the end of May, the testing of prototypes was under way but there were technical problems back at NCR in Dayton. However, the two machine prototypes operated similarly to one another, which was encouraging as to the output. The initial results of the test, speedily sent over to Washington, were analysed and surprisingly a German U-boat message setting code was found to have been cracked, which brought much relief to both NCR and the end users in Washington.[27] A special secure communications line had been established between NCR and Washington naval comms. The results in the summer of 1943 would bring dividends with the sinking of several U-boat tankers that supplied the U-boats, and all due to the use of the new N-530 machine. Things were now looking up for the Allies.

In Building 4, Nebraska Avenue, Bombes started to be installed in rows, with WAVES and naval personnel trained in their operation. During initial induction talks senior staff had threatened the recruits that if they breathed a word to anyone about what they were doing, 'We will shoot you!' If that did not put the fear of God into the naval operators, nothing else would. The initial induction, partly based upon security and need to maintain it, and the remaining part technical and procedural, would form the elements of training that were so essential to success, and elimination of errors and mistakes in operation. This, then, was part of the 'system' to formalise the operational procedures, and maintain efficient working, as the output was crucial in saving thousands of lives of men and women, by helping to neutralise the U-boat threat over time.

Bombe bays would each hold four machines, served by four operators, together with a supervisor to check the work. Compare this to the British Bombes, which were often eight machines to a finger-block at the outstations, where staff worked in pairs, checking each other's work. Menus were a key part of the process and operators had to be trained in converting the strange diagrams into instructions so as to load the wheel rotors and set up the machines. Eight columns of four rotors were provided with each Bombe. The fastest wheel rotor would spin at 1,725 rpm, giving a twenty-minute operation cycle, all other things being equal. The equivalent of the British three-wheel checker machine was an M9 checker, which largely carried out the same process. Supervisors would arrange the checked output complete with the analysed plugboard connections of the Enigma, to be forwarded to the codebreakers following logging of the output. Of some interest is the fact that some of the WAVES personnel decrypted German messages themselves with the help of M9 or M8 machines, which were effectively Enigma emulators. There would be an electro-mechanical printout of the output message, which finally needed translation from German into English. This is a simplified description of the complex process, but it worked and was reliable and robust. Even those at Bletchley Park had to admit that as time went on the Americans should concentrate on breaking four-wheel Enigma codes and leave the British to work on three-wheeled Enigma messages.

Around 80 per cent of the four-wheel Bombes were working constantly in Washington by the end of 1943. As more Bombes came through in 1944, improvements resulted in a newer, more efficient model termed the N-1530.[28] We do also have to acknowledge that the British specialist engineering teams later achieved success with providing four-wheel-based Enigma/Bombe decoding machines. These amounted to approximately twelve Post Office Research Engineering machines, including Cobra attachments, and around fifty-nine BTM-built machines.

Monitoring enemy listening stations

Both sides in wartime would monitor each other's radio and Morse transmissions. Specific bases in France and the Netherlands were established by the Nazis near the English Channel and North Sea to obtain good reception from Britain. They also used direction-finding techniques where possible. Britain's network of listening stations, or Y-stations, both home and abroad was considerable. Some would specialise in naval transmissions, as at Scarborough. As the war progressed, the British had to build specialist Y-stations such as at Knockholt in Kent to monitor and intercept the Nazi Lorenz and secret writer transmissions, which relied on 'non-Morse' messages. Thousands of military personnel would be engaged on a 24/7 operation in shifts, listening to specific channels and frequencies, during both day and night, and identifying enemy call signs to build a bigger intelligence picture for the Allies. Traffic analysis would then follow from scrutinising the information at Bletchley Park, using specialist teams. The vast amount of radio and Morse transmissions received meant that a substantial quantity of trivia was collected, which may have been considered of little use. But pieced together with other relevant information, a small portion of that trivia may become more useful, and reveal enemy plans, tactical movements, and even strategic targets. Resourcing this process was a challenge, but had to be done. As the Channel Islands were occupied by the Nazis, enemy listening stations were then relatively close to England, but in the event this had no apparent adverse effect on the D-Day landings in June 1944.

The source of the transmissions received at Y-stations varied from teleprinters, *Hellschreiber* equipment, and of course encoded general Morse code over the radio. The specialist Y-stations would be kept busy as the war progressed.

UGHQ, Hampshire

UGHQ (i.e. Underground HQ) housed Combined Headquarters (COHQ) at Fort Southwick, near Portsmouth, in Hampshire. The COHQ was set up principally to coordinate the British and Canadian beach landings for D-Day, and the operations of the Second British Army and Naval Commander Task Force. It contained a mass of underground tunnels housing some 700 personnel across the Army, Navy, RAF, and the Allied nations, both men and women. Wrens and WAAFs were in large numbers here carrying out a wide range of duties including direction finding and passing information received to those in senior command.

The tunnels had been designed to be bombproof, being some hundred feet under the surface. Staff coordinated radar information with shipping data to inform the commanders of the situation as D-Day evolved in June 1944. There were Crypto Rooms in the tunnelled areas. The tunnels were built in 1942 by the 172 Tunnelling Company, Royal Engineers, and took almost a year to complete. The tunnels were largely formed on a rectangular grid pattern, and rooms included areas for meteorological experts, and many radio operators working long shifts. By December 1942 they were ready for fitting out, and received both sophisticated air conditioning and a gas filtration system. There was no lift but three steep staircases formed the access.

Supreme Commander General Eisenhower, as the head of SHAEF, would be based about a mile away in Southwick House in the build-up to D-Day, but he later moved to command the forces from a military tent in an encampment nearby. More than 1,000 personnel would be above ground helping to coordinate supplies and organisation in a support role. COHQ staff would be a key part of the communication and coordination system on the build up to D-Day, collecting intelligence, mapping it, and passing it to those in a position to make decisions. Information passed back from shipping crossing the Channel was of particular interest.

The tunnels and HQ were top secret, and there would be a back-up site at Newhaven to take over in the eventuality of the base being put out of action. An underground radio station was also built at Paulsgrove Chalk pit, near to the site. The underground tunnels were also used in the Cold War era.[29]

SIGINT and the Jewish people

It would be as early as 1938 that GC&CS in England broke into German police Morse code radio ciphers on matters regarding the extermination of Jews in Germany. The initial intercepts were based on a combination of Police 'ORPO' units and later SS and Gestapo. By 7 August 1941, a summary report had shown that 30,000 civilians, mostly Jews, had been shot by the German police in the central sector. Winston Churchill would receive a summary from SIGINT via Sir Stewart Menzies, head of SIGINT. Churchill has horrified and commented that atrocities were happening in Germany for which there was no name to reflect the level of crime. The early intercepts gave an indication of the start of the Holocaust, which would accelerate as the war went on, and the exposure of concentration camps in Germany and the occupied states. The set-up of the police and other organisations was as follows in respect of transmissions in the early years:

ORPO	Simple hand ciphers
	Medium Grade hand ciphers
	Roulette Enigma (Machines)
Gestapo and Kripo	TGD ENIGMA
SS Military Units	Orange II Enigma
SS Concentration Camps	Orange I Enigma

Apparently, it was only TGD Enigma that would remain impenetrable by the allies.

The police had a combination of battalions and cavalry brigades, the latter with some mounted police, but were still effectively ORPO or *Ordnungpolizei*, and carried out mass murder on behalf of the Third Reich. Intercepted reports from SIGINT in July and August 1941 indicated that more than 4,700 Jews were shot at Slonin and in the Minsk area alone. A further report added well over 10,000 shootings and executions of Jews and 'those incapable of labour' by the police.

As the invasion following D-Day accelerated and 1945 approached, there were considerations as to whether concentration camps should be bombed to stop the ongoing mass slaughter of civilians, but there were other priorities and limited resources of aircraft that could do the job. No one at SHAEF high command would take that decision, as it would be a mixed blessing with the potential deaths of Jewish people caused by Allied forces and be open to criticism in the future years. The prime target was to rapidly overcome the Third Reich, despite fierce resistance from the Nazis. Enigma would be used by the Nazis to organise the efficient movement and transfer of Jews and others to the concentration camps, as though it was some sort of game. Ironically, although his process was all about speed, the head of ORPO decided to stop using the fast Morse code radio transmissions for communicating the statistics of shootings and mass executions, and instead reported them to Berlin by the slower use of couriers in the early years of the war. French decrypts in late August 1941 had intercepted intelligence that indicated 5,130 Jews had been shot that day by a combination of the SS and the German police. Cooperation of mass executions between Nazi organisations and different departments appeared to be working, a thought that sends shivers down one's spine. Even though the Allies had known of some of the atrocities carried out by the Nazis, partly due to intercepts and partly due to accounts from escaped prisoners, they had no idea of the scale of the problem until they had ended the war and discovered numerous sites of mass execution.

Magic and SIS

'Magic' was the name used by the Americans for decoding the Japanese intelligence intercepts in wartime. It became a project using the Army's Signals Intelligence Service (SIS), and the SCU, the US Navy's intelligence unit, to decode as much intelligence from codebreaking machines termed 'Purple' and others as possible. This was a cryptanalysis project involving considerable resources and personnel. Early Japanese ciphers before the war included 'Red' and 'Blue'. Purple, in comparison, was developed during the war, and was the principal objective for the Allies. Bletchley Park also contributed to analysing Japanese intelligence. Purple was based on modified Enigma machines that were originally supplied to the Japanese by the Germans. Purple was far more complex to crack than either 'Red' or 'Blue' ciphers, and was used for diplomatic transmissions. The Americans realised that if they could break this cipher then they would be privy to Japanese intentions in the Pacific, and military planning, which could be of a major and significant strategic advantage. Naval movements were of particular interest as the Japanese moved carriers and battleships around the ocean, and the Pacific islands that they occupied, or planned to invade, such as *Midway*. The process of cipher-message interception, decoding, translation, and technical evaluation would be organised such that it would revolve around coordination between the SIS and the SCU.

There would be intense arguments after the war and a heated public enquiry via Congress to try to establish if the attack by the Japanese on Pearl Harbor could have been avoided, as a series of structured Japanese diplomatic messages had been read by intelligence staff as they were transmitted. There was a delay in communicating the last part of the message to the Commander in Chief at Pearl Harbor, and some confusion as the Japanese burnt and destroyed their paperwork in preparation for the attack. The Japanese were able to achieve complete surprise when attacking the American fleet. The Americans knew something was up, and building as the diplomatic messages were transmitted and intercepted, but they did not know the date or exact location where the Japanese attack was planned. The failure of the intelligence system to identify this event in time would haunt the American people for decades.

Pearl Harbor is currently one of the most popular tourist attractions for Japanese tourists and visitors in Hawaii. Despite ultimate defeat of the Japanese in 1945, it is seen by many as an event that was a great victory and success. The incident brought America into the Second World War, to Churchill's delight, as Britain needed US resources to help win it.

Australian input

In 1941, on the other side of the world, Australia was gearing up to provide Allied intelligence support, with Melbourne concentrating on Japanese diplomatic codes. A Central Bureau would be established and have links to wireless units, the Fleet Radio Unit, the Australian Special Wireless Group, the US Army, and the US Navy to share information. Some of the codebreakers would be trained at Bletchley Park. The Central Bureau would be interested in monitoring the Indian Ocean and Pacific areas, principally to attack Japanese intelligence. The 4 Special Wireless section was active in Crete, Greece, and Palestine, and would acquire critical encoded German radio messages. Eric Nave and Jack Newman were cryptographers within the signals and communication network.

The development and evolution of the *Australian Naval Special Intelligence Bureau* pulled together listening stations, cryptographers, and those who concentrated on traffic analysis. A Women's Emergency Signalling Corps, or WESC, was also founded at the start of the war. The training they gave in signals intelligence included both men and women, and ran into thousands of personnel. The organisation would be established by Violet McKenzie, who would appreciate some of the work of the WRNS done in Britain and apply her own version to the Royal Australian Navy. This then resulted in the signals training team being absorbed within the new Women's Royal Australian Naval Service, initially with just under 600 personnel.

The year 1942 would prove to be an important one for development and organisation. Thus, there would be an evolution of organisations, sub-organisations, and systems, just as there were in Great Britain and the US. Procedures would be set out, officer training improved and adapted, examinations, and high standards set for those allowed to train others. While mainly military personnel attended the training classes, several merchant ships would also benefit from signalling and Morse code instruction.

Enigma on U-Boats

U-boats were the German *Kriegsmarine*'s ace card in the fight against Britain and the Allies. The intention was to cut off supplies initially to Britain, and later to Russia and the United States. Communication was via Enigma encoded transmissions and code books were used, including the Short Signals and Short Weather ones. Messages would be received in code and then the operator would look in the code books to identify the rotors to be used in the machine, the sequence of rotors, and so on. Transmissions could only be received when surfaced, so a pre-check with periscope was carried out to ensure there were no enemy ships close by. The Enigma used would be the four-wheel type, principally the M4, which had greater security and with many more permutations of letters than the three-rotor versions. The decoded message using the correct Enigma settings would give instructions as to location to meet up with other U-boats for a 'Wolfpack' attack. Messages could also be sent back to command in an encoded form if convoys had been spotted.

The success of the U-boat strategy for the Nazis was as much to do with communication and enciphered Enigma messages as with the crews and boats themselves. The Enigma M4 would provide an effective barrier to infiltration from the Allies for lengthy periods, allowing much shipping to be decimated by the U-boats under Admiral Dönitz, head of the Kriegsmarine. The machines were often situated within the radio room, and the code books kept safe. Without these books, the Enigma would be just a pile of metal and wiring. Sometimes the machine would be in the captain's quarters, while some U-boats carried two Enigmas. This was to ensure a smooth changeover between different message Enigma keys around midnight, when keys would change to further confuse the enemy. When a U-boat was threatened with capture or forced to surface by the enemy, the instructions were to throw the Enigma rotors overboard, and the code books too, as the machines were useless without either. There were times when this went wrong, and rotors and code books were captured by the Allies.

Bletchley Park would struggle to decode the four-wheeled Enigmas for some time before they eventually had some success. The Turing–Welchman codebreaking Bombes were configured around three-wheel Enigmas, so had a disadvantage. However, thousands of tons of shipping in both convoys and isolated vessels crossing the Atlantic were sunk by U-boats, and were Churchill's greatest concern. America later hit back by designing and constructing a four-rotor-based codebreaking machine specifically targeted against the U-boat intelligence and intercepts. More than 120 of those specialist machines were eventually built.

Research and development in wartime

Technology brought great strides towards ending the war as systems and equipment were developed. Organisations such as the Telecommunications Research Establishment (TRE) in Malvern, the Post Office Research Engineering Station (PORES), at Dollis Hill, and work at Bletchley Park and in Letchworth, Hertfordshire, all made a difference. Yet all this occurred without modern computers. Radar technology was relatively new and not well understood by those who used it in aircraft or shipping. Britain was ahead in radar development, with Professor R.V. Jones one of the pioneers. He was able, with some assistance, to develop systems that could distort or bend enemy tracking radio beams. Chaff or Window, long foil strips dropped from aircraft, were developed by a female engineer, and are still used today as a defence mechanism in military aircraft against incoming missiles, confusing their homing radar. PORES developed the first semi-programmable digital computer, and many other pieces of equipment. This was only possible as Tommy Flowers, a senior research engineer, had investigated the possibility of using valves as digital switches before the war. Few other people around the world had looked at this option at the time.

Research was also ongoing in Nazi Germany during the war, and a huge push was made to develop the V1 and V2 weapons, which could become devastating and neutralising them was virtually impossible once they had been fired. Heavy water or deuterium production in Norway became important to support a potential nuclear bomb. Fortunately, SOE managed to stop the production with a daring raid on the factory and the wagons transporting the heavy water on a ferry across a deep lake.

The main issue of wartime research was that firstly it was a race against time, with the Allies trying to be one step ahead of the enemy. Secondly, it took up large amounts of resources, men, materials, energy, and power, as well as organisation. Some scientists and engineers were forced to work under the Nazis in occupied Europe.

The process of research and development of codebreaking machines reflected the advancements in the Enigma models and improved security. The introduction of advanced, teleprinter machines would also trigger the need for new codebreaking systems. It seemed that there was nothing the Allies could not deal with, given time. The National Cash Register Company (NCR) in Dayton, Ohio, USA, would develop the four-wheel Bombe machine, and that was originally based on the British Bombe, but with several improvements in the design.[30] It is worth noting that many of the Allied organisations involved in wartime research and development went on after the war ended to develop other equipment, processes, and systems, as diverse as hearing aids, computers, and lottery randomising machines such as

National Savings' ERNIE. This was truly random due to its highly technical design, which was an essential specification component for a national gaming machine of chance.[31]

PORES moved into military and SIGINT support as the war progressed, with constant requests by the Admiralty, RAF, GC&CS and others to design equipment for various purposes. As a comparison, in July 1938, only 9% of its work supported the armed forces with hardly anything for SIGINT or security services. By 1945 half of PORES' work would be support to the armed services and the remainder for the security services, SIGINT, and HUMINT.[32] PORES would be involved in projects along with TRE and BTM, and there would be their share of disagreements along the way, but progress would be made.

TRE had experts such as Dr Charles Wynn-Williams, who contributed significantly to many projects involving the codebreaking machines and improvements to them, among others. TRE was an amazing collection of skilled individuals, often working in specialist teams on top-secret projects, such as radar and the bending with radio waves, to counter the Nazi *Knickebein* bomber alignment beams from German aircraft. There are those who consider the war against the U-boats and war in the air were both won on the playing fields in Malvern. Malvern was a boys' school in a town of that name, where TRE had relocated to from Dorset during the earlier part of the war.

The site became a vast village itself, of civilian scientists, academics, and many support personnel. Organising the meals alone for staff and support people became a mammoth operation. TRE had teams constructing a model at Malvern to measure the radar signature of V1 flying bombs. This would be incorporated into Radar Anti-Aircraft Mk1 code-named 'Rugger Scrum', and linked to Bofors guns to shoot down and destroy the V1s. Oboe was a high-precision bombing unit radar developed for the Allies. H2S was another and was very successful. Window, strips of aluminium foil, would be developed here too, and they would be used in vast quantities dropped from the air in large bundles, spreading out over thousands of yards to confuse the enemy on their radar screens. The development of centimetric radar at the site may have helped change the course of the war in the Allies' favour against the U-boat threat. Now, the smallest projections of conning towers above the waves could be detected by aircraft tuned into the appropriate radar frequencies. When the King and Queen visited TRE in wartime, the location and purpose of the secret site was kept quiet from the public and the press. It was the largest engineering factory in Europe at the time, and all those working on projects there had to sign the Official Secrets Act. It was considered by some that the main purpose of TRE was to buy the Allies time in war. This they achieved, but they also developed systems and equipment to transform the RAF and other armed services to use new technology to fight the foe.

Jodrell Bank radio telescope would later be established by astronomer Sir Bernard Lovell, who worked on radar projects at TRE in wartime. An 'atom-smasher' piece of equipment was developed at TRE, being the forerunner of the Hadron Collider used for research on plasma and atomic particles.

Newmanry and Testery

The Newmanry and Testery were highly specialist departments established at Bletchley Park during wartime to help crack the advanced Nazi encoding machines, such as the SZ40 and SZ42. The cracking of the enemy ciphers on advanced machines was problematical for those at Bletchley, inasmuch they had never seen the Lorenz encoding machine.

The process of cracking the ciphers would be in two discrete parts. Firstly, the testing of machines and setting up of them, to analyse the non-Morse message settings based upon work done in the Newmanry. The second stage was a more manual approach with codebreakers in the Testery, using the analysis output from the advanced codebreaking machines. These were separate departments and initially communication was not good between them. Management then instructed for there to be a fluid dialogue between the sections, to improve efficiency and results. Real progress was made and improved substantially when the Post Office engineers at Dollis Hill designed and built the Colossus machines and delivered them to Bletchley Park. The machines would carry out work to reduce the setting permutations of non-Morse messages, a process known as to *de-Chi* it. The results were then passed to the Testery team, whose experienced codebreakers would find the final settings after eliminating the other permutations. A true team effort. Max Newman had established the Newmanry and Ralph Tester, the Testery. The Mark 2 Colossus machine in June 1945 worked much more efficiently and five times faster than the Mark 1 version. These improvements filtered through to the codebreaking sections.

Training of codebreakers at Bletchley

Codebreaking was not a profession before war came. It had to be learned over time, from experienced cryptographic experts, using special techniques, methods, and processes. It required the recognition of patterns, the understanding of languages, and identifying the frequency of letters used in text. Trainees had to learn how to obtain various cribs and clues to make attacks on the enemy codes and ciphers easier and more reliable. Staff were encouraged to develop new methods and systems such as Banburismus, the identification of 'Cillies' and other tricks that would save them time. The promotion of certain codebreakers and key staff gave opportunities for other less-experienced personnel to come in and receive training by those more expert than them. Mathematicians and others had to learn to recognise patterns and apply logic to crack the various ciphers, learning from others.

Roy Jenkins, who later went on to become a Labour Home Secretary, was engaged at Bletchley on codebreaking activities from April 1944. He was an Army officer and quickly became competent working on challenging problems in the huts. Jenkins would work in the Bletchley 'Testery' on advanced codebreaking. It was here that some of the most proficient codebreakers and cryptographers worked. They included Donald Michie and Jerry Roberts. Michie had similar ideas to Turing in the field of machines and particularly in artificial intelligence, which he exploited further after the war ended. By comparison, Turing had limited time after the war ended to pursue his goals in this field. The Testery would have around 118 staff, including a handful of specialist cryptographers/codebreakers and twenty-four ATS staff in a support role. It would be almost like a post-graduate university, with a particular specialism, and using work from the Newmanry to assist them crack the Nazi and Axis powers' message settings.

William Tutte was nearly overlooked as a candidate for a new intake of codebreakers at Bletchley, yet he went on to dismantle the cipher of the German Lorenz advanced teleprinter attachment without ever having seen it. Mavis Lever and others were trained by Dilwyn Knox, who appeared to be patient with his largely female team of codebreakers and encouraged experimentation using previously tested methods. Lever went on to crack an Italian message that was of extreme importance and significance in the Mediterranean, giving an advantage to the admiral of the fleet in that sector. The female codebreakers were effectively nurtured and developed into efficient codebreakers by Knox, and respected as team players in what was otherwise largely a man's world full of prejudice against women. It was sad that Knox fell extremely ill and was unable to live long enough to appreciate the outcome of the war and his contribution to ending it. Lever would go on to marry Keith Batey, another colleague at Bletchley.

Data transfer communications via dispatch rider

When Y-stations recorded and logged the encoded Morse code messages or non-Morse information, the information had to be communicated promptly to Bletchley Park. This was initially done via dispatch riders on motorcycles, and later via teleprinter on GPO landlines. The couriers would ride to and from Bletchley Park in all seasons and all weathers, through day and night. Many of the dispatch riders would be Wrens. On receipt of the information it would be logged immediately and then processed. It would be the responsibility of those at Bletchley Park to identify as much relevant information as practically possible about the messages, and after traffic analysis and looking for cribs or clues, develop Menus of instructions for others to set up the Bombe machines and other equipment. This was a stage termed 'traffic analysis', a stage prior to the creation of the Bombe menus. The motorcycles used for the courier service were large, robust, and reliable. However, teleprinters were preferred due to the specific advantage of speed in communication.

Log sheets

Log sheets would be allocated to Y-station radio and Morse code listeners at the wireless stations, at both home and abroad. They would record the date, time, and where possible the call sign of the transmission, and the radio frequency intercepted. Some transmissions would be in Morse, many of them in German.

Encoded messages such as via Enigma machines would be logged as five-letter blocks on the sheet, for later decryption at Bletchley Park, and sometimes using codebreaking outstations to find the message settings for that particular day. The operator would have to cope with fluctuating weather conditions affecting the transmission. Some stations would be used for direction finding (D/F), and the location of the transmission source would be of great interest to the Allies. Sometimes, other listening stations would pick up the same transmission simultaneously, and adding the two intercepts one could pinpoint the source more accurately. This was even better if there were three stations listening in to the same source transmission, so careful triangulation on a map could be applied to find the intersection point of the source. With practice, the Y-station listeners could detect a sender's Morse key, by the characteristics of the transmission, so they may be able to recognise that a specific person was on the air again. Messages from agents in occupied countries were also transmitted back to Y-stations, sometimes in code. Use of code words, such as 'Broadsword' or 'Market Garden' could provide a degree of security provided that the Allies had the code book listing the word or phrase, and the implication of sending it. A W/T Red form can be seen at Bletchley Park museum that was used for Enigma-encoded transmission logging. Four vertical columns allowed entries of the code letters in groups of five at a time, and if the message was long, then several log sheets had to be used to take the message down, and the sheets numbered. The left-hand margin was for Bletchley Park experts to enter text and was possibly used by the SIXTA section for traffic analysis referencing.

Wheatstone's Playfair cipher

A cipher was invented by Charles Wheatstone in 1854 to advance the use of secret telegraphy messages. This was used in the Second World War by the Germans, including the Army, SS and *Kriegsmarine*. It was unusual in that it enciphered pairs of letters rather than single ones. It would take a great deal of time to decipher by the enemy. Originally it was shown to the British Foreign Office, which considered it far too complex for its staff. It was used in the Boer War and in the First World War. The system was known as a bigram substitution cipher, and was much harder to crack than a cipher with the simpler substitution of a single letter. There would be around 600 potential bigrams as compared to twenty-six single letters to decode. Apparently, the system was used also by the Government of New Zealand during the war, but is no longer used today due to the advancement of automated computing methods. The 'Playfair' name is due to the person who demonstrated the cipher in 1854, Lyon Playfair, First Baron Playfair of St Andrews. The existence of the system demonstrates that applications were being sought to advance telegraphy in the nineteenth century, and eventually typewriters would be used and modified, including the use of electrical relays. This was before rotary-based encoding machines were developed in the early part of the twentieth century, principally by the Dutch and the Germans.

Identifying new codebreakers and cryptographic personnel

While initial recruitment of codebreakers was via the academic institutions and universities, as time progressed there was a programme to recruit via advertisement and tests in London. A crossword puzzle was placed in a newspaper along with an invitation to those who had completed it within a specific time to apply for an interesting opportunity. Those applications were then filtered and selected persons invited to carry out tests in a large room with others, a type of written examination. A select few were then invited to join Bletchley Park, and the majority of candidates who were unsuccessful were merely thanked for their time. Bletchley was looking for people who had an aptitude with logic, words, patterns, and numbers. No one taking those tests would have known their purpose. Dilwyn Knox, a skilled codebreaker at Bletchley, would encourage women to develop their skills within his codebreaking team, and they were known as 'Dilly's Girls'.

Experimentation with codebreaking machines

Few codebreaking machines were left unmodified, and without improvements being made to varying degrees. One example was Gordon Welchman's Diagonal Board improvement to provide greater efficiency and eliminate unnecessary processing for the Bombe. BTM in Letchworth, which built the Bombes for Bletchley Park and the outstations, constructed a large version comprising four Bombes connected together, the 'Giant'. It was proved to be rather unreliable, so was eventually split up back into the four individual Bombes and these distributed for operational use. Giant was not the only experimental machine using Bombes, but it may have been the largest. So heavy and large was Giant, it could not be lifted as one unit.

The Enigma encoding machine was constantly developed and improved over time, and became portable before the war started, making it a valuable and practical tool to be used in all types of locations and situations. When the Americans developed the four-wheel Bombe during the war, they only did this after they had studied the British Bombe in some detail. They decided to improve the efficiency compared to the original version, and used it against U-boat messages in the Atlantic. Of course, the British had their own successes, and developed the RAF Type X machine, which was an improved copy of the Enigma, and it was used to test message settings to display decoded messages. The Type X was used at Bletchley Park in large quantities as well as abroad. It was used after the main decoding operation had been carried out, either manually by human codebreakers or by Bombe machines.

Enemy agents and systems

While the majority of Nazi agents in the UK and the USA had been promptly exposed and 'turned' by the Allies to work for them, there remained an effective agent network in occupied Europe run by the Germans. Intelligence was obtained before the Nazi invasion of Russia, although initially it had limited success and dismissed much of the valid information passed to it via the German military attaché in Moscow. Indeed, the eastern intelligence network was far more effective than the Nazis' attempts in the west of Europe, via the *Abwehr*, the German secret service. After 1944, the intelligence network units would be renamed intelligence units and sub-units, or FAKs. The front lines of the enemy were infiltrated by agents via FAK Is, with FAK IIIs being heavily involved in counter-espionage, and further complemented by use of signals intelligence. Also relevant was the identification of Allied spies behind the German and Italian front lines that fed back intelligence to their HQ. Although it is estimated that only 20 per cent of messages intercepted by German agents in Russia were of interest, and of any use, these would be significant in helping the Nazis identify pockets of resistance, the build-up of Russian forces, assembled military positions, and other useful intelligence.

In the West, the situation was different, and not as helpful as in the East. Until D-Day, there was effectively no front line to penetrate by FAK I agents. With the *Abwehr* being reorganised in early June 1944, the timing was less than satisfactory as there would be confusion, mistakes, and many lost opportunities for the Nazis. The Allies had the advantage of cracking both the Enigma and Lorenz encoding systems, and were fairly well organised in this respect, decrypting enemy messages on a large scale. They knew from the Colossus decodes during and after D-Day that large Panzer divisions would be kept intact in northern France near Calais, awaiting the fictitious FUSAG assault over the English Channel. All the Allies needed now was more data and intelligence on the tactical operations and build-up of reserves, equipment, armament, fuel, food and supplies, which armies relied upon. Break the chain of supply to the enemy and he would rapidly run out of resources, allowing troops to break through the lines. That was the theory, at least. Hard fighting by the Germans, and many captured Russians and other foreign nationals who were 'encouraged' to fight the advancing Americans, Canadians and British, together with great resistance, would slow down the Allies after D-Day around Caen and the Bocage country, where hiding places for the enemy were like a gift. White Russians, Cossacks, and many Ukrainians were seen as pro-German in the East and easier to recruit to become spies and agents against Communist Russia. There would be considerable *Abwehr* successes in Italy, where the evolution of the *Abwehr* and new changes made appeared to be far more effective than in the West. The lack of a continuous front line in the East of Europe made it far easier to send enemy agents in through the notional front lines, and carry out effective damage, collecting key intelligence. Where the agent had local knowledge of that part of the country and population, it made a huge difference in the results obtained. However, among German commanders and higher senior officers, there was a reluctance to feed back important information to intelligence officers in the field, and the role of the intelligence officer became one of self-doubt, with morale declining significantly at times. These were again lost opportunities to work closely together, have respect for each other's military role, and to make the best of exchanging ideas between relevant personnel. Duplication of work would sometimes hamper progress in some sectors.

The Allies may not have been perfect in the field of gathering, sorting, filtering, and analysing enemy intelligence, but their overall organisation was far better than the Germans. Of course, this is a generalisation, and there would be highly efficient exceptions in the German Nazi war machine, but probably not enough in terms of quantity and consistency.

Enemy listening stations

The enemy, principally the Germans, but with some Italian input, set up listening stations in Europe, the Mediterranean area, North Africa, and particularly near the coast of France, Netherlands, and Norway, to listen to Allied radio and Morse code transmissions. A number would also be mobile units in trucks, useful for detecting resistance operators and spies locally. The fixed units included Hardelot, Étretat, Saint-Malo, Paramé, Neum, and Husum, Norway. Their stations were termed Hochstelle, and four principal SIGINT, *Abwehr*-controlled listening points monitored British and Allied movements from the French coast. Units in Norway took in Oslo and Trondheim, but concentrated on monitoring internal parts of the country. Denmark would use listening bases in Copenhagen. Further south in the Mediterranean, Rocca di Papa in Italy and Montpellier on the French coast would monitor Allied shipping, with Rome, Sicily, and Sardinia also being active with monitoring stations. An estimated 12,000 German army personnel would be engaged at the stations by the end of the war.

When the Russians occupied the Baltic states, their shortwave radio transmissions could easily be picked up by the Germans and acted upon to their advantage.

Mapping the enemy organisation

Using a technique called traffic analysis, a diagram of the organisation of the German armed forces was established in great detail, with different divisions, units, and command centres. This took a good while to fill in all the missing gaps, a bit like completing a vast jigsaw puzzle, but the individual pieces had to be added based upon the intelligence via Y-stations and use of agents. The final diagram was extremely detailed, and gave the Allies a head start in understanding how the Nazi war machine worked, and how communication was structured between units and different areas. Call signs were particularly of interest, and were recorded by the Y-station listeners when they had identified them. Direction finding had its place too in this project. Knowing how the enemy structure was arranged meant that communication weaknesses could be more easily identified, and routes of enemy communication could be mapped, with varying degrees of priority. Log-reader personnel at Bletchley would analyse the Y-station listener logs provided to them, and draw diagrams with lines and direction of travel of the messages intercepted. A bigger picture could then be understood when the various lines and information was collected together, and arranged more formally as a sort of block diagram. The advanced network of non-Morse messages using the Lorenz teleprinter attachment was sent through a network of specific cities and given Fish identification names. Only by understanding the complex arrangement and how it was used by the Germans could the Allies start to intercept it on a large scale and decode enemy messages. Later, Bletchley Park would be decoding and reading messages that had yet to be read by the senior officer the message was intended for. Some were dictated by Adolf Hitler himself. SIXTA was the largest of the sections at Bletchley during the war, covering traffic analysis of the German Army and Air Force Enigma intercepts. The volume of Enigma messages was far greater than that of Lorenz. This was because many more Enigmas had been made and distributed, tens of thousands of the machines, in several different versions. While most SIXTA personnel were of Army origin, there would be some Foreign Office personnel too. ATS staff would support the work further by logging data from Y-station intercepts. While scattered around various huts, SIXTA would be moved to Block G at Bletchley in autumn 1943. SIXTA originally stood for 'Hut SIX Traffic Analysis'.

Transporting and organising the codebreaking machines

Security issues were raised early on as to which might be the most appropriate and secure method to transport and transfer codebreaking machines from the factory at Letchworth to Bletchley Park and the codebreaking outstations. Options included a convoy of vehicles, armed guards, or transporting items in the early hours of the morning in darkness. In the end, the management decided it was going to be a low-key security operation, using a large truck with a tarpaulin cover to conceal the Bombe codebreaking machines. One single driver would be alone in his cab, only 'protected' by a letter from Winston Churchill pointing out this driver had important business and that no one should obstruct him in his duties or else they would have to deal with the Prime Minister himself! Whether such threats would work against a rogue or villain in the twenty-first century is of some doubt. The Bombes would need to be strapped down securely to the truck as they were basically a vertical, rectangular, tall, and extremely heavy metal box containing delicate components and wiring. Excess vibration along the route would not do the soldered wiring connections much good, and when the unit arrived at Bletchley Park or the outstation it would have to be carefully craned off the truck and wheeled into place on some sort of trolley. It would then need to be plugged in and tested before it could be considered satisfactory for operational use. The log would indicate whether it was a modified machine, and the date of initial operational use. It would receive both a name and number, appropriate to the bay or section it was installed within. For example, the Greek Bombe bay may have 'Athens' or 'Corinth' or 'Larissa' as the name. Names could change if the Bombes were relocated elsewhere, so tracking them was essential to avoid confusion.

Many Bombes were moved around different locations at different times and this had to be carried out as part of a specific protocol and procedure. This would be to ensure that first there was a clear tracking record of where the Bombe originated from and where it would be deployed to at another site, and second, to ensure that it would be decommissioned temporarily in a sequence that avoided damage or malfunction. Some would go back to the factory for modifications, while others could have minor modifications on site via RAF engineers.

Packing of the valves in more advanced machines would require several assistants taking care to wrap them and label the boxes and crates. Valves were an extremely expensive wartime resource, and even some at Bletchley criticised Flowers for his 'wasteful' use of them in Colossus.[33] This was later proved to be a working advanced machine and the valves were essential to the effective and efficient operation.

The whole process of moving and transporting machines became a major operation in itself, but was largely well organised, with checklists to ensure that all parts were accounted for and none were missing. BTM, the factory in Letchworth, had the pressure of ensuring the output of Bombe machines was maintained to meet Bletchley Park's targets, and that the quality was also maintained. Once the machines were loaded on the truck, BTM could concentrate on production. While there were several minor mishaps in the transportation, unloading, and commissioning of equipment and machines, overall, the system appeared to work well.

Planning the codebreaking outstations

The codebreaking outstations were not considered back in 1939 when war started. It would be the fear of the risk of mass bombing of Bletchley Park, it being the codebreaking headquarters, which might destroy both machines and skilled Bombe machine operators, that led to consideration of using outstations. Churchill was in agreement that the risk to the machines and operational staff had to be spread. More locations for the Bombe machines were required, it was just a matter of identifying where. Country estates near to Bletchley Park were selected, and eventually there would be a total of three of these for Bombe operations, run by the WRNS. Adstock, Wavendon, and Gayhurst comprised the three initial outstations, the first of a total of five. They were remote enough to be away from potential bombing targets, but near enough to quickly courier the Bombe output to Bletchley by dispatch riders.

As the volume of messages increased in the war years, space came at a premium and a much larger site was needed for processing intercepts and decrypts. Stowe School was considered and promptly rejected, for reasons that are unclear.[34]

Outstation Stanmore, or OSE, would come online in autumn 1942. This would be a substantial site near to Stanmore railway station, and not far from Edgware and Elstree. Hundreds of Wrens would operate the machines here on a shift basis. A cover story for security purposes would be that the site was for WRNS administration, a proposal approved by Commander Travis at Bletchley Park. Machines would be sent to Stanmore directly from the BTM factory at Letchworth, and several Bombes were also transferred to Stanmore from the country house outstations. The quantity of Bombes needed to keep up with the enemy messages still increased as the war progressed, and there was a concerted effort to try to identify another outstation of substantial size. This would become Outstation Eastcote in Middlesex, not far from Ruislip in west London, and not a million miles away from Outstation Stanmore. OSE would become the final outstation to support Bletchley Park, but also the largest, housing some 103 Bombes at the end of the Second World War.[35] OSE was available from autumn 1943, and its previous planned use as a military hospital for D-Day did not proceed for a variety of reasons. Codebreaking operations had the priority at Eastcote. It too would be managed and run by Wrens, working on a shift basis, 365 days a year.

Taking Bletchley Park into account with its Bombe machines, six locations would operate Bombes, although some special versions were also operated at the BTM factory in Letchworth for a relatively brief period. Including those specialist machines, such as Giant, the number of locations then amounted to seven. This excludes the American four-wheel Bombes built in the USA, and operated in Washington. The progress of identifying outstations to support the HQ at Bletchley was an evolving process, which started quite small and grew to a substantial operation using hundreds if not thousands of mostly Wrens, with some RAF engineering support and Royal Marines to guard the bases. The costs of setting up, supplying, managing, and running the sites must have been considerable, but a great deal was at stake here, and the need to crack enemy intelligence decrypts was of the highest priority. Churchill was quite forward thinking as a politician to realise how important Bletchley Park and the support structure was to the nation during wartime. It was probably something to do with his military background and his natural tenacity and determination.

Constructing the outstations required the requisition of large quantities of building materials, and installing drainage, water, gas, electrics, telephone lines and other communications. External lighting for paths and roads as well as security were required. Teleprinters would later serve some of the outstations and speeded communication. How much coordination there was with the relevant local authorities is not clear as the bases were intended to be top secret. While most people could see many of the huts and buildings from the road or a footpath, they would not have a clue as to what activities were taking place inside them, nor the skills and training of the personnel on site. Planning permission for development may have been waived for reasons of wartime. Local authority building inspectors were probably not allowed on site if the bases were military. However, the outstations were a combination of country estates and semi-military bases organised via the Foreign Office and the Ministry of Works in a supporting role. Some of the builders may have been military personnel from the Army, engineers, etc. There would be key deadlines to work to, programmes to achieve.

The Battle of Britain Bunker at Uxbridge (not far away from the site of the proposed Outstation Eastcote in Middlesex) was built just in time for the start of the war in 1939 by a well-known private contractor, Sir Robert McAlpine. It was an amazing feat of engineering built in record time, mostly underground. It is 60ft below ground and accessed by seventy-six steep steps. It contained all the necessary services to control and direct the RAF's 11 Group during wartime via the operations room, complete with a master control panel on the wall with illuminated coloured lights.[36] Pre-dating the computer by many years, this is an amazing piece of equipment intended for effective communication to chief officers and support staff to direct RAF forces against the enemy.

Some outstations had hatches built into the Bombe rooms to pass instructions across from an adjacent administrative office and results of the output from Bombes back to a senior member of staff. Years later, a few Wrens managed to draw sketches of the layout of the machine room and the peripheral activities to support it. The checking room would be off the Bombe room at one end, with several Wrens at desks waiting to put the output results from the Bombes into the checking machines. In the early days of the codebreaking machines there was little to use as a template for construction of a Bombe layout and support, other than perhaps those few machines installed at Bletchley Park. At the end of the machines were rotor wheels that could be studied and their output recorded.

The trained personnel knew what their specialist roles were, when to request assistance, and how to work alongside their colleagues in setting up and running the machines. A senior Wren would contact Bletchley with the results of a Bombe run and then receive further instructions. Bletchley Park even had a mechanical communication cylinder system that ran overhead to send and receive information quickly between certain offices. Similar systems were utilised in large department stores and some factories. All this equipment needed to be planned, drawn up, designed, and installed by engineers and construction workers. By the time the final outstation at Eastcote was established, the system and protocols to manage and operate the codebreaking machines had been fine-tuned, and generally operated efficiently. Even the US Signals engineers, who had ten Bombes at Outstation Eastcote to themselves, were impressed. With one exception – the food at Eastcote left a great deal to be desired!

Evolution of Bletchley Park during wartime

Bletchley Park evolved over time after being established in 1939 as GC&CS. The quantities of both codebreaking and support personnel increased exponentially as the war progressed, to several thousand staff. This was not so much a system as an evolution. The buildings on the site also went through considerable change, with some huts merged together, others newly built, some even demolished to make way for new structures. The use of women in wartime was accepted as progress, and while there was some initial prejudice using women to perform certain tasks, in time this would be largely overcome, with Wrens operating the Bombe codebreaking machines and later the advanced machines, too.

The relocation of the Hollerith punched card operation to a different location was a significant change, and to a degree Bletchley lost some of the direct control it had previously over the message data, then relying on a BTM manager from Letchworth to decide priorities and actions. It was effectively outsourcing some of the systems to make more space for traffic analysis and support teams. Outsourcing departments will always be a double-edged sword, with positives and some negatives in the transfer of resources elsewhere. Communication was not quite as effective as if that department was still on site in one of the huts. However, space was required rapidly as the enemy messages increased in quantity, and as the commanders of the armed forces required more and timely feedback as to what the enemy was planning and doing. Hollerith processing was really about holding and managing a very large manual database, with punched card machines to help with sorting, filtering data, and feeding it back to Bletchley when requested.

Bletchley Park, as HQ, would transition from manual codebreaking to an organisation relying heavily on codebreaking machines, and then to another stage where it had the challenge of attacking and reading the non-Morse messages transmitted via another group of enemy advanced teleprinter attachments. Yet, very few personnel on the site would be privy to the detail of these new challenges, with information communicated largely on a 'need-to know' basis for security purposes. People would need technical training in operating a whole range of new equipment, from Bombes, to checking machines, Typex machines, Tunny machines, Robinson, Colossus Mark I, Colossus Mk II, etc. The Post Office and PORES would assist where they could with input to equipment manuals and instructions, but all the training needed to be managed effectively, with personnel evaluated for their suitability to be trained, and staff monitored frequently on their performance. At the same time, the Wrens operating say, the Robinson or Colossus machines, did not need a detailed technical knowledge of the design or workings of the equipment. It was only necessary to give them sufficient instruction as to what the stages of setting up the machines were, the sequence to be followed, checks to be made, and how to deal with minor glitches and malfunctions. Perhaps also, in the case of the Colossus machine, there was a need to monitor the high temperatures due to the massive quantity of valves used in the equipment. Just as not all car drivers understand the workings of the internal combustion engine, or of the design of the motors and batteries of an electric car, they are still able to drive it with appropriate manuals and instruction. They can also recognise certain failures and malfunctions that might require specialist technical expertise to resolve. All credit to the management of Bletchley Park, who generally permitted the Wrens to set up and to operate the advanced codebreaking machines at a time when female roles with advanced technical equipment were not always seen as appropriate by their male counterparts. ATS women were also allowed to operate Tunny machines. Progress then, even in relatively small doses, but still a long way from true equality.

As D-Day approached, those at Bletchley and the outstations would be placed on high alert, processing large amounts of data, and they were under intense stress, whether a codebreaker or operating a Typex machine. The stress was not contained just at Bletchley, as it would also be equally felt at BTM, where the Bombes were made and at the Spirella factory, making components for the Bombes, in Letchworth. The PORES engineers working on Colossus, Y-station operators, and many others would be losing sleep, keeping up with their targets and timeframes to produce specialist equipment, systems, output, and results to bring Britain and its allies closer to winning the war.

The system for decryption of Enigma keys in stages

We set out below the key stages in decryption of an Enigma message by the Allies:

Y-station intercept of encoded message

↓

Coded message logged and transferred to Bletchley Park via courier or teleprinter

↓

Booking in information

↓

Traffic analysis

↓

Intercept control

↓

Crib hunt

↓

Menu

SYSTEMS

↓

Allocation to either Bletchley Bombe hut or outstation

↓

Setting up Bombe codebreaking machine with rotors and cabling

↓

Bombe run

↓

Checking machine

↓

Feedback to Bletchley Park of settings

↓

Typex machine at Bletchley

↓

Deciphered German text

↓

To intelligence huts

↓

Additional Traffic Analysis

↓

Distribution of message

The above is a simplified flow chart of activities. While it may appear relatively straightforward, in practice there would be some mistakes and errors made, malfunctions, and machine breakdowns, air raids affecting progress, resourcing issues of skilled personnel, sickness, etc. Mistakes made in taking down the

Morse code at the listening station or gaps in the code would make the life of the codebreakers more difficult. The fluctuating radio or Morse signals under different atmospheric conditions would challenge the station listeners attempting to tune their receivers to capture the transmissions. That would be the first stage in the system and process. As the codebreakers became more experienced in attacking the Enigma cipher, they would try out a variety of clues or cribs to identify individual letters in the code. Indeed, it would be the application of cribs that would help formulate a Menu of instructions for the Bombe machine operators. The Menu would be a starting point to set up the machine and test it. Strange graphics with lines and letters would become familiar to trained Special X authorised and security-vetted Wrens setting up the Bombes at Bletchley or the outstations.

The working conditions would be rather unpleasant and extremely noisy in the Bombe rooms. At least most of the checking machines would be in separate isolated rooms where Wrens checked the Bombe output after a 'stop'. Some checking machines were within the Bombe areas, however, but they were often partly enclosed with a metal or wooden screen for the checking machine operator, where she sat awaiting patiently to check the results. A telephone call to Bletchley would then be made. Bletchley would have the final say in whether the output communicated back to them was a good stop, or whether the Bombe run needed to be repeated. The Bombe runs could take as little as twenty minutes but others much longer. The Wrens would be kept busy aligning and realigning the sharp metal brushes, effectively long metallic steel needles within the Bombe drums, to make electrical contact with the brass contacts on the machine frame behind the wheel rotors.

The Typex operators back at Bletchley in the huts would be kept occupied typing in the messages using the decoded message settings, with a machine that had effectively copied and improved on the Nazi Enigma. The display of German text in front of them after typing in the message would indicate success, even if the operator did not read or speak German. Some of these messages were read by the Allies and codebreakers before the Nazi enemy officers had even read the message. It was the constant changes to the message settings by the Germans that would keep the codebreakers on their toes, together with slight 'tweaks' and improvements to the Enigma machines as different versions were coming off the production line in the factories licensed to build them. There could be no room for complacency on the part of the Allies in attacking the Enigma ciphers.

Vernam cipher system

Gilbert Vernam, an American, devised and invented a polyalphabetic stream cipher and patented his system in July 1919. To apply the cipher, each bit of the binary character code for each letter of the plain text undergoes an 'XOR' operation with the corresponding bit of each letter of the binary character code for the corresponding character from the key stream. This creates the cipher text. In simple terms it is a method of combining text and characters with a random stream of data of similar length. For it to be effective in terms of security the keystream of random data must be of equal or the same length, and be used once only. It therefore can be considered a highly secure 'one-time pad' and the basis of a secure encryption method. A modern example of a one-time pad is the number generated by a bank on a handheld security device for the user to then enter on a computer screen. The number cannot be used the next time around if it is truly random, and therefore it would be of no practical use to others. However, usually that number is not revealed for additional security and is destroyed or deleted on a screen, having been used once. By comparison, a list of predetermined numbers in a code book may be more vulnerable to being identified. The computational security of a cipher system is assessed by the probability it can be deciphered in a set amount of time and with sufficient cipher text. Used correctly as intended, the Vernam cipher is the only one that is considered to be perfectly secure, due to the one-time pad system. It has been mathematically proved to be unbreakable irrespective of the time spent attacking it. The only exception would be a lucky guess, and that is unlikely given the complexity of the system.

The plaintext of the message to be encrypted is converted to binary, which is the language that modern computers understand. The random key must also be converted to binary code. The two are added together in binary form with the plaintext converted to ASCII values, which is the standard system used nowadays for text conversion. The combined addition of plaintext and the cipher key is the ciphertext in binary form, a series of zeros, and ones. Applying the Vernam cipher system algorithm, one can encrypt and decrypt the message relatively easily. It is known as a symmetric encryption method as it works both ways for encryption and decryption. Because the ciphertext addition is random, the combined ciphertext with the plaintext of the message also becomes random, and therefore secure. It is, however, extremely difficult to generate truly random numbers in practice, and if the message is long, say many pages of text and numbers, the random ciphertext key must be at least as long as those characters, and preferably longer still.

Both sender and receiver of the message will need access to the cipher key for the system to work. How that key is communicated to another party could expose a weakness, and leave the system insecure if the method of communication is poor. Imagine Person 'X' having the launch codes for a nuclear missile, and that must be communicated promptly to an operator, person 'Y', on a military site with a nuclear bunker, several miles away, and the secure key is sent by post in a letter to the operator. How secure would that be? Not at all, it could easily be intercepted by a third party. If it were transmitted in an email on the internet it still would not be secure as someone could intercept it. If it was an encrypted message and sent using the Vernam one-time pad over the internet by email, then it should be very secure, but one needs to be sure the cipher key was truly random, and not just pseudo-random such as someone just calling out a range of numbers, apparently at random. Patterns may exist from using a stream of pseudo-random numbers, which can be analysed by other parties with cryptographic knowledge. There is a view among cryptographic experts that computational security is good enough, and that perfect security may not be wholly practical in real-life situations.

The one-time-pad key was apparently outlined in 1882, but taken more seriously in later years in 1917. It is of interest that the one-time pad is used by internet organisations, finance houses, banks, and others in conjunction with modern battery-powered electronic devices to generate random numbers and to feed back those numbers or cipher 'keys' to the organisation in order for the customer to access secure data and information. The three-digit security number on the rear of your credit card or debit card is *not* a one-time pad as is used for multiple transactions. It is used purely for convenience, providing a very basic level of security.

D-Day decisions

The build-up to D-Day in June 1944 meant many months of planning the event, agreeing strategy, order of battle, and synchronising many operations and events that would make D-Day and the drive forward into France effective against the enemy. Intelligence gathering was crucial, identifying changes to the Atlantic Wall in France, the positions of artillery and the Panzer divisions and forces that could be mobilised quickly. It needed to be ascertained whether the enemy could be deceived by convincing them the main attack would come across the shortest Channel route, or whether they had other ideas. The key decision-making for the final invasion plan would be established in the lecture theatre at St Paul's School in Hammersmith, London, attended by King George VI, General Eisenhower, senior Allied commanders, and Winston Churchill on 15 May 1944.[37] The actual date of invasion would be delayed from the end of May to 5 June, then finally 6 June 1944. By this time, Bletchley Park, the codebreaking outstations, and the Y-listening stations had helped to paint a more accurate picture for the commanders and for Eisenhower as to how the enemy were planning a possible response to an invasion. It would be the state of the weather that tipped the balance to 'go' on 6 June. No single individual person could have more responsibility on his shoulders than Eisenhower, as Supreme Allied Commander.

Identifying the specific beaches for each of the attacking forces and routes inland, together with the timings of each assault, would be crucial. There would have been calculations for anticipated number of losses, dead and wounded in the invasion, bringing home the harsh realities of war. Then, advice from the military logistics experts as to the resources needed to sustain the assault and create the bridgehead to drive further into France and capture towns and villages en route. Intelligence from photo reconnaissance would be pored over to review the enemy strength, different Panzer divisions, condition and situation of bridges, railways, roads, physical features, and pinch-points that would affect the rate of progress. Could the quantities of fuel be sustained to support the tanks, trucks, and landing craft from the Pluto fuel line via the Isle of Wight? Where would the German generals be on the morning of D-Day and how quickly would they react to the invasion? Would the Mulberry harbours do their job as intended or would they sink en route in the Channel, leaving no berthing place for the ships to reinforce the troops? Would the use of *Window* and the deception around it make an important difference, and was the plan to jam of enemy radar going to buy the Allies sufficient time? What was morale like in France with the enemy, and what was the morale of the attacking troops, most of whom had not set foot in France before. Was their training enough to counter the hardened German troops, many of them experienced in battle from the Eastern Front or elsewhere? How could so many ships and troops be coordinated effectively against the enemy without failure? Would the enemy U-boats and mines destroy half the attacking force before they arrived at the Normandy beaches? So many ifs, buts, and uncertainties, but one man ultimately had to take the final decision with the odds against him, and the lives of many thousands of brave men in his hands. The common goal would be to bring down Hitler and end the war in Europe. For many of the American soldiers, they had in the back of their minds that even if they survived this battle, and the war in Europe was won, many of them would later have to be redeployed in the Pacific against the Japanese. The chances of survival across both theatres of war were relatively low and the picture bleak.

Eisenhower would rely on his experts for advice, and the final decision to proceed would be made on the condition of the weather in the Channel, which in the turbulent summer of 1944 was more like winter, with high winds and rough seas. The one positive thing was that, given the weather conditions, Rommel and others German commanders thought it would be madness for the Allies to invade at this time, and allocated time to go to Berlin to purchase shoes for his wife's birthday. Rommel would be in for a shock once the invasion started, and there would be a difference of opinion with Field Marshal Gerd von Rundstedt as to deployment and mobilisation of the Panzers. Disagreements and confusion would help the Allies' drive into France, but it would be tough and Caen would be a tough nut to crack militarily, slowing progress for a time. The enemy was not going to roll over without major resistance and counter-attacks, and they tried to drive the Allies back into the sea before they could establish a bridgehead. Allied losses were significantly lower at Normandy than first anticipated. That was down to effective planning and determination.

The Colossus Mk II machine built for Bletchley by Tommy Flowers and his Post Office Engineering team would be engaged operationally just a few days prior to D-Day.[38] Final tweaks, improvements and adjustments to the machine by Jack Good and Donald Michie would ensure it could help crack the latest encoded 'non-Morse' enemy messages efficiently. After all, it ran five times faster than the original Colossus, and had 2,400 valves glowing, set up and managed by competent WRNS personnel. They would not realise they were operating the second version of the world's first semi-programmable computer.

Equipment

Note: The quantity and type of machines and equipment under this subject is vast, and we can only provide a selection of some of them. It is not possible to list or describe all. There are technical websites that can provide additional information. We have also included some auxiliary equipment such as antennae, aerials, and certain specialist components. While machines such as the codebreaking Bombe, Colossus, Robinson, are listed, as well as Enigma, models of Enigma, and other encoding machines, the reader will be able to see from the listings below that some of those machines relied heavily on other items of importance, such as valves, relays, etc.

Adcock antenna D/F

The Adcock Antenna system was developed in 1916 by an engineer, Frank Adcock, initially as a concept. The system was designed to aid direction finding of transmitted radio signals from long distances, and a hut with reception equipment was surrounded by four tall aerial masts, often 10ft high. These were positioned at the points of the compass. Under good atmospheric conditions, the reception for locating a bearing of a signal for frequencies more than 5MHz could be up to 160km. Technically, when properly set up the arrangement eliminates errors due to horizontal polarisation. Several such stations were established during the war for direction-finding duties. It is sometimes referred to as the U-Adcock system, although an H-Adcock version has a slightly different arrangement. For vertically polarised radio waves it operates similarly to a loop antenna. The disadvantage of an Adcock arrangement is that the antennae must be physically very large, whereas a looped antenna can effectively be folded and much smaller in size.

Autostritcher, Superstritcher

These were additional codebreaking machines designed and built by the Americans during the latter stages of the war. They were used to break into traffic using the pluggable Reflector D. The Autostritcher was electro-mechanical with relays. The Superstritcher used around 3,500 valves.

Bomba

Three codebreakers and mathematicians, Zygalski, Rejewski, and Rozycki, developed and built the Bomba codebreaking machine in Poland to crack the Enigma ciphers. This would be nothing like the later Bombe machine built with input from Alan Turing and Gordon Welchman in England some years later. It would, however, become the first proper codebreaking machine in relatively modern times, and it proved that the Enigma could be analysed with the aid of a machine designed by mathematicians. The Bomba had a limited useful life as the security of the Enigma machine improved over time. For example, additional rotor wheels were added by the Nazis in December 1938, increasing the permutations of message settings. The German setting up procedures would also change. With the Bomba using six sets of rotors, it could work out and replicate every position the Enigma wheel rotors could be in to produce a result or solution, although this process could take up to two hours. With Enigma, a three-letter message key was sent by the German operators before the main message. This was repeated exactly, and was intentionally duplicated as part of the procedure. Sometimes the plaintext letter yielded the same ciphertext at three positions in front. It is this that was of interest to the codebreakers. Initially the Bombas may have been hand-cranked but later were electrically powered. There would be a casing with many switches on the front but with rotor wheels and geared wheels on top, quite complex from a visual perspective. The Bomba, when set up correctly, could establish the rotor order, the rotor positions, and the ring settings, leaving only the plugboard cabling to be determined.

The Bombas were all destroyed by the Poles in 1939 just before the Germans invaded their country. A replica was made of one in 2019, but the use of computer software simplified the engineering to a degree. This was constructed at the National Museum of Computing in Buckinghamshire, led by Jeremy McCarthy, who had an IT background. The project was assisted by the Pilsudski Institute in West London (Instytut Jozefa Pilsudski). While the original drawings were destroyed, one of the co-designers produced papers in 1967 and 1979 with sketches of the machine.[1] The replica used a combination of both hardware and computer software in design and construction. It may have not looked like the original Bomba but emulated its workings to produce a valid output.

Bombe

The Bombe codebreaking machine was the concept of Alan Turing at Bletchley Park, aided by fellow mathematician Gordon Welchman. It would be a large electro-mechanical mechanism with multiple rotor wheels emulating an Enigma three-wheeled machine, designed to eliminate the wrong settings to arrive at the correct remaining setting for decrypting enemy messages. Constructed on a large steel frame, the Bombe would be built in large numbers in Letchworth, Hertfordshire, by the British Tabulating Machine Company. Project Cantab was the coded name for the Bombes, and part of the main factory would be set aside for their manufacture and assembly. Components were made in other locations in Letchworth and brought together in the main factory building for final assembly.

The Bombes were operated by the WRNS at both Bletchley Park, plus five codebreaking outstations. The process of using the Bombes to break message settings involved obtaining a Menu of instructions from Bletchley Park, loading the rotor wheels on to the Bombe, plugging in numerous cables at the back of the machine and setting up the machine to start a Bombe 'run'. Eight Bombes would be located in a bay, which may be a finger block on an outstation.

A checking machine operator would carry out a detailed review of the output if the machine stopped, by rotating wheel rotors manually to specific positions. Checkers were usually in separate rooms or areas, although some would be in the Bombe machine rooms too. The penultimate stage would be for Bletchley Park staff to enter the results in a Typex machine, to hopefully read the message in German. The final stage would be translation into English by translators at Bletchley Park.

A total of 211 British Bombes were manufactured and used during the war. The Bombe was not a computer as such, but contained some of the processes with human interaction and setting up and crude programming physically, with plugged in wired connections, that might later be applied in a modified form to use in future computers. There would be 104 electrical contacts to each rotor wheel, arranged in four concentric circles, with twenty-six contacts each. Drums would be fast, middle, or slow. Millions of sharp contact needle wires would be inserted into the rotor drums to make electrical contact with the rear plate, which had brass electrical contacts, and were in turn connected to the electrical cables and wiring looms. The Wren operators would be tasked with aligning the stiff needle wires, using tweezers, otherwise the machine may not make electrical contact correctly or may short out, giving incorrect output. The Bombes were generally maintained by RAF engineers, based on site, but minor maintenance was down to the Wrens.[2] A person at Bletchley Park helped to track and coordinate the allocation of the Bombe machines, and track the movement of them. One needs to understand and appreciate that while some machines were delivered from the factory in Letchworth to the codebreaking station and stayed put, many did not, and were modified, relocated to a different site or for a different purpose such as training operators. This is why several of the Bombes had more than one name during their lifetime even though they generally had one number for identification.[3] A simple table is set out below with specific information relating to the Bombes:

Bombe Type	**Quantity Built**
Early three-wheel 36-rotor Enigma	73
Four-wheel 36 Enigma (BTM High-Speed Keen)	57
Four-wheel 36 Enigma (PORE/BTM) Cobra	12
Later three-wheel 36-rotor Enigma (high-speed Siemens-type relays)	69
Total	**211**

Bombe Type	Quantity Built
United States Navy four-wheel based machines (see description next to equipment entry)	121
Grand Total British and American Bombes	**332**

Although we are unsure of the exact quantity of Enigma machines produced during wartime, on the basis of, say, a total of 100,000 Enigma machines, then applying the British Bombes to this quantity gives a ratio of 1 Bombe for every 474 Enigmas. Add in the American four-wheeled Bombes and the ratio reduces to 1 Bombe for every 301 Enigmas. Of course, the Bombes were kept busy processing message settings from many of the same Enigmas just on different days and different times when the settings were changed every twenty-four hours. But the ratios give an idea of the challenge the Allies had at the time. Manual codebreaking was also used in parallel to the Bombe machines, but there would be a limited number of skilled men and women to carry that out successfully and consistently.

A Bombe was 2.1m high × 1.98m wide × 0.61m deep (Approx. 7ft × 6ft 6in × 2ft). Each Bombe would have 108 positions to locate rotating wheel rotor drums, in groups of three, to reflect the three-rotor Enigma models. There would be a full rotation with twenty-six positions for electrical contact on a drum. When the top row of drums rotated a full revolution, they triggered the next row of drums below to rotate 1/26th of a rotation, and a full rotation of those drums would rotate the bottom drums 1/26th of a rotation. Each wheel rotor contained 104 spring brushes comprising nineteen separate wires per brush unit, in sets of four. This calculates to some 1,976 wires in each individual Bombe rotor drum. Applying thirty-six rotor wheels to a Bombe, that makes 71,136 wires inside each one loaded up for a Bombe run. If even one of those wires short-circuited, the Bombe would malfunction and need attention. The Wrens would have to identify where the problem was and use fine tweezers to straighten the wires. The Bombe brushes were made by women workers in the Spirella factory under the direction of BTM management. Spirella had been a ladies' foundationwear and corset factory in Letchworth, which also made parachutes, until BTM requested its use for making Bombe components.

At the end of the Bombe metal cabinet were Menu sensing switches, and an indicator panel for the operator to read and take readings from. Control switches were at the bottom of the panel. More involved technical repair and maintenance was carried out by RAF engineers.

Ten Bombes were operated at OSE in Eastcote, Middlesex, by the 6812th US Signals Security Detachment APO 413, US Army Engineers. A photograph of two of the engineers are shown in the photographic plates in this book, one operating a checking machine and checking output from a Bombe named Rochester.[4] This was the last of the ten Bombes allocated to the engineers and became operational in

September 1944. The following table lists the names of Bombes that were allocated to the American engineers at Eastcote within Block 'B':

Bombe Name	Operational From	Remarks
Ming	March 1944	Bombe reference No. 4. Started at B/Pk before transfer to OSE
Houston	May 1944	Bombe reference No. 286. Started at OSA ref. No. 11 before transfer to 'Works' [BTM factory] and then to OSE
New York	May 1944	Bombe reference No. 16. Started at OSW before transfer OSE
Chicago	June 1944	Bombe reference No. 19. Started at OSW before transfer OSE
Atlanta	July 1944	Bombe reference No. 297
Minneapolis	July 1944	Bombe reference No. 299
Philadelphia	5 September 1944	Bombe reference No. 307. Delivered to OSE on 30 August 1944
Omaha	5 September 1944	Bombe reference No. 309. Delivered to OSE on 30 August 1944
San Francisco	5 September 1944	Bombe reference No. 303. Delivered to OSE on 30 August 1944
Rochester	6 September 1944	Bombe reference No. 313. Final allocated Bombe machine to US Signals engineers[5]

Sources: *Backing Bletchley – The Codebreaking Outstations from Eastcote to GCHQ*, Ronald Koorm, also the official Bombe Registers at the National Archives.

Note there is some evidence that the Bombe machines under the responsibility of the Americans were operated from 1 February 1944, but these might have been for training purposes initially, with WRNS personnel assisting. Additionally, please note there were only 211 British Bombes built at BTM. The numbering reference system in the official Bombe Registers is strange in places and finishes at number 318. Some Bombes had more than one number, probably based upon machine modifications, and transfer to other outstation sites. It would usually take a few days from delivery of a Bombe machine to test it and to have it fully operational, loaded with rotor drums and breaking message settings, e.g. Bombe 309, Omaha, delivered 30 August 1944, operational 5 September 1944.

Bombe naval USA (four-wheel) N-530 and N-1530

The need for a reliable four-wheel Bombe codebreaking machine was identified early on in the war, but it would be the Americans who would decide to design and build one, independently of the British, and use it to tackle the U-boat losses in the North Atlantic. The department responsible would come under OP-20-G, the machines being built by the NCR company and moved to operate in Washington DC. Initially, prototype machines were made and called 'Adam' and 'Eve'. These were plagued with oil leaks and short circuits but were a stage in the development of more reliable versions. 'Cain' and 'Abel' would follow, being much more reliable. The Bombes had sixteen sets of four groups of rotor wheels, to emulate the four-wheeled Enigma machines. The use of WAVES, or *Women Accepted for Voluntary Emergency Service*, for constructing and assembling the US Bombes would help speed up the production considerably. Seventy women would initially attend the factory in Dayton, Ohio, to start construction. The machine was loosely based on the British Bombe, complete with rotor wheels that emulated the Enigma, but would be more advanced and more efficient. The relevant message data was shared with Bletchley Park once in operation, after the Bombes were transferred to Washington.

More than 200 WAVES were eventually at Dayton to help with assembly. They received detailed training at a facility named the 'Sugar Camp' after some maple trees along the avenue. Around 100 male officers, engineers, and enlisted men also assisted in building the Bombes. Originally, Sugar Camp was a training school for salesmen, but was handed to the Navy in 1943. Some staff came from the Naval Communications Annex (OP-20-G). It was a very large site extending to 31 acres with numerous buildings and excellent modern facilities for both training and study. WAVES would become competent in making certain repairs of the Bombes.

The development of these Bombe machines was not always straightforward. False readings were being given, and there was even a doubt as to whether the design would work practically and reliably in Washington. The management considered that solutions had to be found as enormous amounts of money, time and resources had been put into the project. Joseph Desch, the lead engineer on the project, discovered that the Bakelite wheel rotor drums were running at such high speed that they were distorting and affecting the electrical contacts. Slowing the wheel rotors from 3,600rpm to 1,725rpm made a significant difference. The machines were transported to Washington for operational use before the full-scale testing programme had been completed. Thankfully, they proved to be reasonably reliable.

Consideration had been previously given by Desch to use valve tubes for the processing instead of wheels turning around and revolving at high speed. However, both he and others knew that to abandon the rotor wheels and develop a machine with many hundreds if not thousands of valves would take much additional time, and this they did not have. The reliability of valves was not that certain, and repeated failures in valve tubes could not be tolerated. In hindsight, they were wise to use a more trusted but basic technology, and proceed on that basis. True, it was about risk taking, but the risks had to be carefully calculated in wartime, where human lives were at stake.

After a four-wheeled Bombe completed a run in Washington, a WAVES supervisor would check the printed results on a checking machine, designated the M9. She would continue to check each result, looking for the correct wheel order or sequence. Then she could use the M9 to fill in any missing plugboard positions. When the WAVES supervisor found the correct wheel order, rotor positions, and steckers (plugboard cable connections), she would send the results back to the library. There, the cryptanalysts and WAVES personnel would use an analogue machine to decrypt the message using the settings they had finally established. That final stage and machine would be the equivalent of the British Type X machine. Very short messages could even be decrypted in the M9, but longer messages needed more input with an analogue machine.

The N-530 model was the initial version of the four-wheel Bombe, but the improved N-1530 would later be produced, and the total quantity of machines was 121. They were successful in attacking the Nazi Enigma four-wheeled encoding machines, which then reduced the impact of U-boats to a degree in the North Atlantic. The use of centimetric radar by the allies would also make a difference to the U-boat threat, so that it would not be true that the codebreaking machines solely eliminated the Atlantic U-boats later in the war. It would be a combination of developments and systems, and with much teamwork to provide effective results. The original plan by the Americans was to build 336 naval four-wheel Bombes, one for each wheel order, but this was not done.

Alan Turing was aware of the Bombe production in Dayton as he had visited the NCR factory and laboratory there in 1942, but he was quite scathing about the project. However, the Americans went ahead with design and production, and were quite successful with both the Bombe output and the operational side. Reports indicate that around 3,000 personnel were organised to operate the American Bombes in Washington on a shift rota. Around 500–600 WAVES would operate the Bombes in the building on Nebraska Avenue, Washington. Reports indicate the machines operated up to six times faster than three-wheeled Bombes, although this may have been an exaggeration.

The challenge to the Allies was that four-wheeled Enigma machines had increased the use of the rotors to a choice of eight wired rotor wheels, the fourth rotor often remaining in position, and the preceding three rotors selected from a code book. This increased the permutations of message settings considerably compared to three-wheeled Enigmas.

The US Model N-530 cost $45,000 to build, weighed 5,000lb and was 8ft × 7ft × 2ft. It incorporated 1,500 vacuum tube valves, which were a transition and change from the relays used in the British Bombes.

Bulldozer

A US Navy four-wheel Bombe, a statistical machine where there may be no clue or crib found. It analysed the frequency of plain text and stopped when a settable threshold was reached. Thirty-two of these machines were constructed.

BTM fourth wheel attachment

An unpowered, free-standing unit on castors. It was set up by hand and allowed a further set of thirty-six very fast drum rotors to be connected into the Menu, while in another version cross-connected cables were plugged in. This was not exactly the same as the Cobra attachment, which was electrically powered with a motor.

Checking machine

The three-wheel checking machine used at Bletchley and the outstations was necessary to carry out a check prior to contacting Bletchley in respect of communicating the Bombe stop positions.[6] The principal three rotor wheels could be rotated by the operator in either direction, clockwise or anticlockwise for speed. These would represent the Enigma encoding machine rotor wheels at the top of the machine, under the lid. The checking machines were usually operated by Wrens in a separate small room, but there is some evidence to show that some checkers would be in the main Bombe rooms, which would be a noisy environment to work in. Metal 'hoods' were constructed at some of the outstations to limit the noise, but were probably unsuccessful. Some photographs exist courtesy of GCHQ showing checking machines at an outstation. Some checking machines may have had only three rotor wheels, such as at the Cobra installations at Outstation Eastcote. This was indicated in sketches of the installations using Cobra attachments, where a picture of a checking machine was shown with three rotors.

The Americans also used checking machines when they developed their own versions of the British Bombe. Those were designated the M9 and used by the WAVES personnel prior to the final stages in exposing the decrypted messages.

Cobra

Cobra was a specialist motor-driven attachment for a Bombe machine to help it support or emulate a four-rotor Bombe. Commander Travis at GC&CS, Bletchley Park, had asked for assistance with the design from the Post Office engineers. Parts for Cobra were built at TRE in Malvern, Worcestershire, under Dr Wynn-Williams, and also at PORES, in Dollis Hill, north London, by Post Office technical engineers, and classed as a special project. Another engineer involved would be Harold (Doc) Keen of BTM, the factory that built the Bombes. It was a team effort, at least in theory, but there were some disagreements in the design on technical issues between Charles Wynn-Williams and engineer Thomas Flowers at PORES. While Wynn-Williams recognised Flowers' technical ability and knowledge, he considered him slow to grasp certain concepts, probably because he was not a physicist, whereas Wynn-Williams was. There would be an electronic sensing unit and a commutator as part of the design.

The machine was originally built in Dursley by Mawdsley. This, connected to the three-wheel Bombe, became known as Cobra, driven by a large electrical motor and fed by a substantial power supply.[7] The Cobra was connected to the Bombe by a very large and thick cable. It had a push-button starter made by Allen and West. In early 1943 the prototype was taken to Outstation Stanmore and connected to a specially constructed Hollerith three-rotor Bombe, and later with a four-wheel machine. Technical problems included one of 'brush bounce', which was difficult to resolve, but operating at slower speeds rectified the problem.

The four-wheel Mawdsley machine version was used for extensive testing at Stanmore. Construction included commutators, brush rings, all positioned on a long single shaft driven by a motor. It appears that from reading detailed technical reports on Cobra, Outstation Stanmore was used for Cobra testing and problem solving, and production versions were later installed at Outstation Eastcote from mid-1943. The whole prototype when moved, went to Eastcote to be called 'Warsaw' in the Polish Bombe bay. Wrens operated it, and were rather brave to do so as it was highly complex, noisy, and extremely dusty. RAF engineers were allocated to maintain the Hollerith Bombe machines used with Cobra. In the summer months, the heat generated by the operational machinery was almost of tropical proportions, and very unpleasant. Diagrams of the Eastcote layout for Cobra and the Bombes reveals long racks between the Bombes and the Cobra attachments purposed for drums and plugging-up cables. At one end of the section there was a frequency changer, a power/rectifier room, checking area with checking machines, and a technician's workshop.

Cobra was not particularly successful, and other systems would eventually supersede it. However, it served a purpose, and technical advancement was made that was applied to other equipment. Twelve of these attachments were built to connect to the Bombes.

American engineers had a different approach to dealing with the four-wheel Enigmas and designed and constructed their own machines.[8] Some reports indicated these machines could do the work of six British Bombes, and they were substantially larger and more complex.

Post Office Engineer David Whitehead, who was at Eastcote in 1945, wrote a detailed account of Cobra and how it was operated. According to drawn diagrams and plans, in Block B at Eastcote, twelve Cobra attachments machines were located by specific Bombe bays or sections, near the 'Poland' and 'China' Bombe sections. These were close to the American-allocated Bombes.

The Post Office engineers engaged on the project were given the grade of 'Acting Skilled Workman Class I', but were not transferred to the RAF. It would be this service that generally maintained the Bombes at the outstations and Bletchley Park. The Cobras were also used to run conventional Bombes at high speed, particularly from 1945 when the U-boat threat was much diminished.[9] Cobra was considered as being unreliable in use. See also Bombe.

Colossus Mk1

This codebreaking machine superseded the Robinson and was the development of a joint enterprise including Max Newman of Bletchley Park and Thomas Flowers of the Post Office Research Engineering Station at Dollis Hill, north London. Newman realised he needed a machine that was more sophisticated and faster than the Robinson that was in use, and Flowers had proposed a solution using many valves as digital switches. Flowers had researched this potentially specialist use of valves many years before the start of the war, so was aware of the challenges. Using valves would be controversial, and some thought the project was a waste of valuable resources. Welchman, in particular, would be critical of the project but was ultimately proved to be wrong.

Flowers assembled a team of engineers from the Post Office Engineering resource and spent months working on what was to be the world's first semi-programmable computer, Colossus. This machine would be used to attack the non-Morse message settings from the Nazis' advanced Lorenz and similar teleprinter attachments for sending encrypted messages. The data was put on to punched paper tape, and read by an optical sensor at great speed, the tape on large reels with pulleys and tensioners. Around 1,500 tube valves were used in Colossus, the valves being kept switched on permanently to avoid premature failure.

Professor Max Newman established a specialist section at Bletchley called the Newmanry, and this would have personnel working on the first stages of the decryption process using machines such as Robinson and Colossus. A second, manual stage would be needed after the output was recorded from the machines, and that would be the responsibility of a separate section, the Testery. Ironically, apart from Newman, Bletchley Park did not generally support the Post Office team, and it used the existing less-reliable Robinson codebreaking machine with all its problems and foibles, even though it did work. Flowers resorted to putting in £1,000 of his own savings to finish the project, as money was extremely tight. He was supported by his boss, W. Gordon Radley, which was fortuitous and gave the project momentum.

When sent to Bletchley Park, Colossus had to be dismantled at Dollis Hill, transported to the Park, reassembled with Flowers in charge of the work, and then tested. It was delivered to Bletchley on 18 January 1944. The tests proved that it worked as intended, and reliably too. A team of Wrens were then instructed to operate it, and it was in use to start the initial stages in cracking the enemy non-Morse messages. It would read the paper tape at up to 5,000 characters per second, which was a phenomenal speed compared to other systems. The non-Morse system was based upon the Vernam encoding system, which was originally devised in the USA by Gilbert Vernam around 1919. A telegraph code devised by Emile Baudot was also relevant to the overall process using the paper tape and encryption.

By 5 February 1944, Colossus had broken its first enemy decrypted message. While the Turing–Welchman Bombe codebreaking machine could only carry out one specific task, Colossus could, in theory, be plugged in and switched to do other tasks such as calculations. However, its prime role was to attack the Nazi encrypted messages from the 'Tunny' machines, and this was a high priority. Colossus was a much bigger machine and took up considerably more space than a Robinson. The challenge that Colossus and the codebreakers had was to strip away large chunks of possible permutations and combinations of settings, a process sometimes referred to de-Chi settings. Lorenz had twelve-wheel rotors, so many more possible message settings permutations than on Enigma. However, Colossus was not intended to carry out all the work, with the work of the codebreakers in the Testery at Bletchley being a last stage to obtain the final output and message settings solution. The quantity of 'Tunny' or 'Fish' non-Morse messages were far less than from Enigma machines as the teleprinter attachments were intended for use by the German high command, whereas Enigmas were used extensively due to the large volume of machines. More machines meant more messages sent.

One advantage of using Colossus was that it only required one single reel of tape and not two as on Robinson, which had to be synchronised carefully and accurately by the Wren operators. This reduction in tapes and reels saved time, and was far more reliable in practice. The Wrens would still have to use a heated glue gun to join long paper tapes together, as they did on the Robinson machine. Paper tape had a habit of breaking from time to time. They experimented with tape speeds on the pulleys and found they could achieve almost 60mph before the tape broke. A safety margin was then built in, and reliable operation was generally obtained in practical use. The Wrens also had to frequently clean the photoelectric eye sensor that read the tape holes and apertures. They would become expert at these tasks over time. There were reports that a printer attached to Colossus for printed paper output vibrated so much that it virtually moved across the room by itself when operating. The Wrens had to resort to using rope and naval knots to tie it in place. So, one could say there was even a use for using naval knots at shore-based stations. One wonders what effect the vibration would have had on the many hundreds of tube valves in the machine, as those were rather delicate. In the event, the valves appeared to be relatively unaffected, and did their job acting as digital switches. See also Robinson, Colossus Mk2.

Colossus Mk2

An advanced version of the Colossus Mk1, it was five times faster than the previous version, and had 2,400 valve tubes. It was delivered to Bletchley Park a few days before D-Day, in June 1944, and was promptly put to good use. Codebreakers

Jack Good and Donald Michie made some slight modifications to improve the efficiency even further. Non- Morse messages were processed at a critical time with some speed, although specialist codebreakers had to complete the decryption in the Testery section once the output from Colossus had been recorded.

Colossus Performance
Mark I character speed: 5,000 characters per second.
Mark I input tapes: Two tapes to be synchronised together
Mark II character speed: 25,000 characters per second
Mark II Input tape: One single tape
Sensor: Photoelectric sensor reading tape cipher text.
Colossus characters deciphered from the enemy in the Second World War across all models: Circa 63 million.

The Mark II Colossus, due to its high-speed of operation, could process a complex message in around four days, as compared to weeks of operation required before it. Flowers had used parallel processing in the Mark II design, a concept used in modern silicon chip processors and advanced for its time.

Colossus, mostly the Mk I at this stage but with some use of the new Mk II, had two major advantages relevant to D-Day. It assisted in providing information and intelligence about the enemy in the order of battle, resources, supplies, and troop movements. Additionally, it also provided some evidence of credibility and the confirmation that the FUSAG deception aided by a key double agent in Britain was working, and that large Panzer divisions were being held back for the invasion across the Pas-de-Calais, which of course never materialised. The clever part of Colossus, apart from using the valves as digital switches, was in applying statistical analysis to identify machine settings that produced output that exceeded random counts. This would result in application of a 'processing tree' to help target the most likely settings and Colossus could use relatively high-speed processing to test the results. It was far better than simple trial and error, and much more productive. To be fair, the statistical analysis was applied with the codebreakers' input, and Jack Good at Bletchley made constructive progress with this application. Bear in mind also that the rules for efficient operation of Colossus were being established as the codebreakers experimented, learning from their past experience with the Robinson, and other machines. Lorenz and the advanced secret writers were still relative newcomers to be attacked effectively and efficiently by the Allies, but results were encouraging, particularly as the D-Day landings developed and France and the occupied countries were penetrated further by the Allied armies.

While two Colossus machines ended up at GCHQ Eastcote after the war and then moved later to Cheltenham, all the machines had essentially been dismantled and destroyed by the mid-1960s. One of the machines was dismantled in 1959 following fourteen years of post-war service. There was a fear by some in Government that the Russians would use the Colossus technology and put the West at risk. Whether this was an over-reaction at the time is for historians to debate.

A reproduction Colossus machine was eventually built at TNMOC. The source of information amounted to just a handful of drawings and photographs, and personal recollection of a few individuals who worked on the machine.[10]

Combined Cipher Machine (CCM)

With the Allies working together there was a need to have a degree of compatibility between cipher systems and machines. This was achieved in a number of different ways, including modifying the US SIGABA design to work with the British Typex machine. Typex was a British copy of an Enigma machine. This modified SIGABA became known as the Combined Cipher Machine, or CCM. It was in use from late 1943. It was one of three different solutions, but CCM proved to be quite expensive to produce and only a limited number were made.[11]

Cyclometer

A Polish-designed and built machine that was the idea of codebreaker Marian Rejewski. It was established in the mid-1930s to attack the Bombe rotor permutations, and appeared a bit like an old mechanical calculator. It used a card catalogue to list the permutations. This may also have been termed Bomba.

Direction-finder equipment

Various direction-finding equipment was used during the war to locate enemy transmissions and messages from agents. One type was a GPO-built device, the Tester WL-53400 unit. Other examples were Quante, PE 484, RZ 301, Soyka, etc. Some were Russian built. The principle of using direction finders revolved around at least two, preferably three, D/F listening stations homing in on the transmission source and where the lines intersected would locate the source. Both the Allies and enemy used these techniques, sometimes with fixed D/F stations and also mobile units in trucks. The advantage of a mobile unit was that it could move around to a different location to make a new plot of the radio or Morse code transmission. However, this assumed the transmission was on air long enough to enable the truck to relocate and set up again. Some transmissions were purposefully short in duration to limit the risk of being detected as to the location. See also Y-stations.

Duenna

Another US-built specialist machine for the Navy called the Duenna was used for breaking Enigma keys on a clue or crib when the wiring of Reflector D of Enigma was unknown. It was a small Bombe unit recovering unknown settings of a pluggable reflector.

Enigma machine (three-rotor)

Although there had been a Dutch patent for a rotary encoding machine in 1915, it would be February 1918 until one was filed for the Enigma encoding machine. In 1926 the Poles and British studied the commercial Enigma as it was readily available to the public in the early years. This availability was stopped when the German military realised it could be of value to them. The three-rotor Enigma was the most popular machine before and during the Second World War. Rotary-based encryption machines were not new, but Arthur Scherbius, the designer and inventor of Enigma, would make his machine work well on the whole. A series of removeable wheel rotors with twenty-six positions, one for each of the letters of the alphabet, were provided in a box and rotors were inserted near the upper part of the machine, sometimes with a separate hinged lid. The rotors made electrical contact to enable the signal to be passed through wiring, and the route from the pressed key on the machine would be determined via the positioning of the rotors and the wired plugboard at the front. Notches in the rotors determined the position of turnover, which affected adjacent rotors. The setting positions for the rotors were decided by reference to a Nazi code book, and the rotors were given Roman numerals. Five rotors were initially available, this being later expanded to eight to improve the number of permutations and security on more advanced versions. Three rotors alone would then give a total of 17,576 possible positions, based on twenty-six letters to the power of three. But this would only form *part* of the possible Enigma settings permutations. Rotors would be kept in a neat wooden box and operators instructed to take particular care of them. They would be wired up in a specific sequence to form part of the decoding operation.

In February 1936, the Germans changed the rotor order monthly, but for added security they would change them daily by October that year, and this would become the norm from then on. By December 1938 there would two additional wheel rotors to supplement the original three, making five rotors in all and increasing the permutations and security. A reflector in the Enigma would effectively reflect the signal along the wiring back to increase the permutations and enciphering of the letters, making it more of a challenge for those who tried to break the cipher code.

The Enigma had, generally, no provision for printing the encoded or decoded message on the actual machine. Instead, a bank of letters above the keys illuminated one at a time on a lamp board as each key was pressed. No key could have the same letter illuminated, so a letter 'K', when pressed on a key, could never illuminate as a 'K'. Inside the machine would be numerous wires, a reflector to further scramble the letters and systems to move the wheels along to another position depending upon circumstances.

In later years, a plugboard of sockets would appear at the front of the machine, and pairs of letters would be connected with short black, flexible cables, much like a telephone exchange with its plugs and sockets, but on a reduced scale. Back in 1927, one early Enigma model showed a counter of the length of a message. It could also include a wheel turnover to run in reverse, which was useful for correcting mistakes. A standard German keyboard layout would be used from 1926.

While the Enigma 'Model A' cost around 1,000 Reichsmarks, later models would be around one eighth that, making it more economic, and it became much more portable, together with a significant reduction in weight. Numerous models and variations of Enigma would be developed, some with the aim to further improve security. The Enigma was contained within a hinged wooden box. It was designed to be portable, so it could be used anywhere from the battlefield in a dugout hole, to a U-boat, on a battleship, in a tank, or even on a bomber aircraft. The machine would not only be used by the German armed services and Abwehr but also the German railways, with some acquired by the Swiss. Italy, Hitler's principal ally, also used Enigma machines for confidential communication, with assistance from the Nazis.

Enigma could be operated by one person, but it would be relatively slow and cumbersome, so two or even three personnel were preferred. One read the message and pressed the keys, a second wrote down the illuminated encoded letters one by one in banks of five, and a third sent that encoded message by Morse code. The more people who were involved, the more possibilities there were for errors or mistakes to be made. If there were gaps or mistakes in the messages, that made it more difficult for the Allies to decipher them. Strict rules had to be followed by Enigma operators to ensure the system was not compromised. The message settings, crucial to the preamble of preparation prior to starting to send an encoded message, would be changed at one minute past midnight by the Germans, to make it even more of a challenge for the Allies to break the cipher. In practice, this meant that working on a series of daily messages to crack the Enigma settings was only effective until the next set of messages were transmitted after midnight, when the settings completely changed. The Germans and military personnel understood that if an Enigma machine was captured by the enemy, it was only really a security threat if the rotor wheels and code books were captured at the same time. That is why U-boat commanders would throw their Enigma rotor wheels and code books overboard if their vessel was being boarded by the enemy. They could not afford those items to fall into enemy hands, but on a very few occasions they did, and Bletchley Park staff were able to study them. Some of the Enigma models were:

Enigma H 29
Enigma A
Enigma B
Enigma C
Enigma D A26
Enigma K A27
Enigma I (with plugboard)
Enigma M2 (with plugboard)
Enigma M3 (with plugboard)
Enigma M4 (with plugboard)
Enigma Zahlwerk A28
Enigma G 31

Enigma T A27
Enigma Swiss K A27
Enigma Railway
Enigma Z Z30

Various accessories were available for some Enigma models such as the Uhr attachment. A printing facility could be used on some as an attachment. There would be around nineteen or twenty variations of the Enigma in all.

The *Abwehr* used some Enigma G models (counter version) which had no plugboard, but relied on the security of the irregular stepping system of the rotor wheels. Bletchley Park was able to decrypt this traffic in late 1941. Some plugboard Enigmas were allocated by the Germans to their allies. This was mainly because those countries tended to use simpler hand ciphers that were relatively easy to break. See also Enigma four-rotor.

Enigma machine (four-rotor)

The four-rotor Enigma was one way of increasing the permutations of message settings and improving security. The fourth rotor needed a different version of Enigma to be designed to fit the additional rotor and it was fixed, unlike the others, which could be taken out and inserted in a different sequence. U-boat commanders used four-wheel Enigmas, which upset the activities of those codebreakers at Bletchley Park for a period of time, and prevented the cracking of the settings for several months.[12] Attempts were made by the British to modify the three-rotor-based codebreaking Bombes to cope with the fourth wheel, but with limited success.

If selecting three rotors from a possible five was the main yardstick for a standard Enigma, then increasing the choice of selection of rotors to five out of a possible eight massively increased the permutations of rotor settings. The numbers became huge, particularly added to the other settings and variations possible. Some of the modifications introduced by the Allies involved attaching huge auxiliary machines with multiple cables and wires to the basic Bombes at the outstations. These were known as Cobra, and were installed in Outstations Stanmore and Eastcote. The codebreakers eventually successfully attacked the new four-wheeled machines, breaking the message setting codes, and the USA designed and build their own version of the four-wheeled Bombe and located them in Washington to attack the U-boat threat in the North Atlantic.

The principal four-rotor Enigma model was the M4. The extra rotor was added between the fixed reflector and the first left hand rotor. When set to position A, it was backwardly compatible with a three-rotor Enigma, for convenience. This rotor did not move during the enciphering operation and was not interchangeable with the other rotors. The German Navy had letters of the alphabet on each rotor wheel, whereas the Army incorporated twenty-six numbers on the rotors.

Enigma copies

Even before the war commenced there were Enigma copies made and secretly manufactured in Poland. Some were made by the AVA company and passed to Polish cryptographers. It is likely that Bletchley Park ended up with a copy of an Enigma machine. The Typex machine used by the Allies as the last stage to expose a decrypted message was a copy of the Enigma but with certain improvements, and it was used extensively at Bletchley Park. Typex machines were abandoned in Dunkirk at the withdrawal by British troops, and elsewhere, but the Germans appeared unconcerned and still considered Enigma unbreakable. During wartime there was no real concern or thought for countries infringing copyright of a design, and both sides would make copies of technical equipment. The Germans were unaware that the Poles and the British were making Enigma copies, albeit with certain improvements and design changes. Had they been aware, they may have added additional special features or changes to make using the machines far more difficult in practice. See also Typex.

Experimental cipher machine

A prototype cipher machine was developed around 1908 by Admiral Percy Scott for the Royal Navy, although it was rejected by the service. It was a mechanical machine intended to replace multiple code books in use at the time.

Fialka (post-war)

A Soviet-based rotary encoding machine used from circa 1956. This would be used post-war, mainly in the 1960s and 1970s, during the Cold War period. It had ten cipher wheels and they moved in both directions, which was unusual, and introduced irregular wheel-stepping. The wiring of the rotors could be removed and changed to reflect different settings of letters. Each rotor wheel had thirty electrical contacts, and that corresponded to thirty Russian characters. Fialka was only declassified in 2005, and the Russians had kept the machine secret. The name is roughly translated as 'Purple', which was the wartime Japanese enciphering system. The Fialka machine had a printer, a paper tape output, and it accepted punched cards as well. It was a much more sophisticated version of the Enigma machine, with many more wheel rotors, and substantially increased permutations of the settings. However, it was much heavier than Enigma, almost 50lb. Reports have indicated that the starting configurations were in excess of 604 quadrillion, a huge number. Later modifications and improvements of rotors and changed wiring gave 403 trillion, trillion, settings! The machine design did not allow for individual rotor removal and all had to be removed together, so it was complex. One feature enabled the equivalent of an Enigma plugboard or steckerboard to further increase the permutations, but relied on a 'day key' that was presented on to a punched card. The United States eventually decrypted and cracked Fialka intercepts using computers in the 1970s. Unfortunately for the Russians, Fialka came too late to have a significant impact on encryption as rotary-based machines were becoming more familiar to cryptanalysts as the war ended. New methods of encryption were being discussed in the 1980s, 1990s and at the turn of the century by experts in the field. Computers would be used as a useful tool in attacking ciphers by most nations with intelligence departments.

German radio aerials

It is worth mentioning a number of German radio aerials, many of which were on mobile trucks, armoured cars, and other wheeled or tracked equipment. These were used to receive and transmit radio messages and Morse, with the Morse range often different to that of radio signals, although in some cases similar in range.

Looped high-frequency antennae were used by the Wehrmacht on armoured cars with a dropped or dipped front part of the aerial to the leading edge. This aerial and the transmitter were used to communicate with aircraft and was positioned horizontally, parallel to the top of the vehicle. The design function of the dropped leading edge of the aerial is unclear. There were also 'frame' or cage-type antennae. Some examples of various transmitters/receivers were:

FuG1 receiver, used in command vehicles, and equivalent to R442 receivers.

FuG2 receiver, with a 1.4m rod aerial, and standard receiver equipment for armoured vehicles.

FuG4 Artillery command set with a 2m star-type design aerial.

FuG5 A 10-watt transmitter with 2m rod aerial. Range was 50km for voice or Morse. This would be used as a ground to air communication set.

FuG6 20-watt transmitter with similar 2m rod aerial, with ranges of 8km for Morse and 6km for voice. Used in early command vehicles.

FuG7 20-watt transmitter/receiver with 50km range for voice and Morse code.

FuG8 30-watt equipment. Early models had a frame antenna. Later on, a winch would be used to erect an 8m-high mast.

FuG10 30-watt. A range of 40km for Morse and 10km for voice transmissions. Used in reconnaissance vehicles.

FuG11 High-powered 100-watt transmitter with a frame antenna. Later versions had a 9m-high mast. They would be used as a command link to reconnaissance vehicles. The range was 50km for Morse code and 10km for voice transmissions. The 9m-high mast extended the range to 200km for Morse code and 70km for voice.

FuG12 High-powered 80-watt transmitter, with 2m rod aerials. A range of 200km Morse and 70km voice.

FuG13 20-watt power, and similar to FuG6 equipment, with two receivers used in low-level command vehicles.

FuG15 Assault gun unit transmitters, with limited range of 8km for Morse code and 6km for voice.

The use of the equipment depended upon avoiding hills and obstructions in the path of the signals. Engineers operating the equipment needed to understand about the radiation patterns and how to obtain the most efficient signal strength in the topography. The taller the mast, the more risk of enemy planes and observers identifying it as the enemy and attacking the unit. Clearly, an 8 or 9m-high mast winched in position was more vulnerable than low masts, which did not need a team to erect them, and they were relatively slow to erect. Some equipment was also used for direction finding. Two, or ideally three, mobile receiver units could be used to pinpoint an enemy, or enemy agent's radio or Morse code transmissions, using triangulation on a map of the locality.

Giant

A 'super-Bombe' machine comprising four separate individual Bombe machines, built at BTM in Letchworth. It was built on a massive steel frame and was so large and heavy on completion that it could not easily be transported. Eventually, it was decided to break it into the four separate Bombes and distribute them. Some went to outstations such as Eastcote, and at least one went to Bletchley Park. A high-speed version was operated at the factory from around June 1944, but under the control and the guidance of Bletchley Park. This was not operated by the Wrens due to its location. A smaller two-Bombe-machine combination was also built, called 'Ogre'.

Giant remained an experimental machine in use at the Letchworth factory, but there would be other developments that would be far more efficient for helping to break enemy message settings. The fact that the machine could be split into the basic Bombe machines was later considered to be a bonus as there would little waste, just the engineers' time in dismantling and reconnecting them for distribution. Lessons would be learned from this ambitious enterprise, and perhaps applied to other systems in development.[13]

Goniometer

A technical device used to aid direction finding of radio or Morse code transmissions, such as at Knockholt Y-station, in Kent, during the war. Essentially, it was based on two coils of wire that were used to identify and measure the bearing of a radio transmission. They were used in conjunction with radar plotting by Y-stations as well as naval and RAF uses.

Grenades

These were various attachments for finding machine settings when the wheel order, stecker and ring setting of the Enigma were known.

Headphones

An essential part of the Y-stations or listening stations was the need to use headphones connected to the wireless receivers. This enabled several personnel to work alongside one another and to concentrate on their reception of radio and Morse signals without being distracted by a blaring loudspeaker. The headphones used were basic and the earpieces often made of Bakelite material, with a metal headband. They were not be comfortable to wear for lengthy periods of time. The gain of the receiver could be controlled with a volume knob and the signal amplification increased where required. The frequency response of the headphones would be limited compared to modern headphones, although this was not a problem at the time as the transmissions were human speech or Morse. Whistles and static interfered with the clarity of the signals, and atmospheric conditions played a significant role in the quality of reception. Reception was in monophonic audio and not stereophonic. There was no advantage in having stereophonic equipment, and the technology would need to develop in future years. There are reports of some listeners multi-tasking by listening to codes in one ear and direction finding in the other. This was tricky, but was sometimes done abroad in the Pacific listening stations.

The patent for 'modern' twentieth-century headphones was granted to Nathaniel Baldwin of the USA in 1910. The internals varied, but some included Mica diaphragms, or phenolic diaphragms. Mica diaphragms are the more sensitive of the two and were preferred. In the 1920s a pair of Baldwin headphones as sold to the US Navy cost the equivalent of $250, a lot of money at the time. The flexible electrical cord connected and terminated at a jack plug, which is even used today for equipment, although now there is a stereophonic version as well. The unplugging of the headphone lead from the receiver could allow the receiver to be heard through a loudspeaker if required. Modern technology has introduced more powerful neodymium magnets and even noise-cancelling technology, brought about by the need for military helicopter pilots to communicate effectively with observers in noisy environments. Listening for hours on end on a shift by Y-station operators for enemy signals and Morse code would be exhausting and very uncomfortable, due to having an antiquated pair of crude, Bakelite headphones and a metal headband strapped to your head.[14] The effect on one's hearing of listening to loud, high-pitched signals for long periods would probably have resulted in a degree of hearing loss over time.[15] Health and Safety of workers and risk assessments were just not relevant in wartime. In the tropics, using headphones had the added complication of sweat running down your brow and forehead, and the annoyance of flying insects. On one Pacific island, a rare caterpillar could cause permanent paralysis of a human if bitten. Better to not be aware of such challenges when working abroad, perhaps?

Hagelin

An encryption rotor-based machine designed by Boris Hagelin, a Swede. He moved to Switzerland and at the beginning of the war convinced the Americans to use it for encoding and decoding messages. The company was Crypto AG or Hagelin Crypto Company. Hagelin became very wealthy selling his encoding machine, and it was widely used in the war. A specific model was the M-209, but there were many others, such as the C35, C36, and C37. Russia made its own copy of the Hagelin B-211 called the K 37, code-named 'Crystal'. After the war, the company was secretly sold to the German BND and the CIA in the 1970s. Machines were sold on to various governments, but with modifications that made them apparently vulnerable. Around twenty or more models of Hagelin machines were produced.

Hebern rotor machine

A single-rotor cipher machine combining some specific component parts from a traditional typewriter with that of an electric typewriter. It was connected with a scrambler, with drawings and prototype construction commencing in 1918. Rotor-based machines formed the basis of more advanced cipher machines and the German Enigma became the most famous, probably manufactured in the largest numbers. Early patents applied for innovative cipher equipment by Edward Hebern were from 1912.

HEC

The Hollerith Electronic Computer (HEC) was built by BTM in Letchworth, the same company that developed and built the codebreaking Bombe machines for Bletchley Park in wartime. The Model HEC 1 from the early 1950s incorporated around 1,000 valves. The original is now in a museum in Birmingham. The HEC 2, HEC 2M, and HEC4 models were advanced versions from 1953 onwards. These were sold to commercial companies. ICT was formed with the merger of BTM and Powers-Samas, and made versions with an ICT prefix but based on the HEC 4 model.[16]

Hellschreiber

A German teleprinter and facsimile-based system invented in 1929 by Rudolph Hell. Sometimes used in conjunction with Enigma messaging, it employed strings of vertical text on paper tape. Transmission was either via radio or by landline, which utilised scanning technology to convert text into on-off pulses and used an audible-based signal. Non-Morse messages were received by the British in 1940, but again in the early part of 1941 when *Hellschreiber* transmissions were intercepted via listening stations. Reports indicated that the *Hellschreiber* signals intercepted included special signs or symbols, including a triangle, square inverted 7, inverted 4 and two other signs. It was established that these and other symbols represented special functions of teleprinter transmissions, such as carriage returns, blanks, spaces, line feed, etc. The intercepts indicated that there were several months of *Hellschreiber* transmissions, interspersed with teleprinter transmissions.[17]

High-Speed Keen

The principal UK four-wheel Bombe machine, which was much faster than the basic factory-built BTM machine, with the fast thirty-six wheels added at the right-hand end. Bombe Registers indicate HSK for High-Speed Keen machines. The High-Speed Keen versions were developed in 1943 as configured four-wheel Bombe machines to attack the *Kriegsmarine* four-rotor Enigma encoding machines used in large numbers by German U-boats.

Hollerith tabulator

Hollerith was an American company that licensed the British Tabulating Machine Company (BTM) in Letchworth to market and sell its equipment throughout the British Empire. These were sorting machines using punched card technology, advanced for the time. BTM was keen to make its own equipment to avoid steep licensing fees, but for several years before the war used Hollerith machines to manage census processing both at home and abroad. These were electro-mechanical machines and not computers, although some of their applications used processing that could be attributed to computers later. The machines came in different versions and operated mainly by women in large rooms with several machines for sorting data and processing it for database storage. The first machines were used as far back as 1890 in the USA for census purposes, and Herman Hollerith, the inventor, was able to demonstrate they were as much as ten times faster to store and recover data as were rival competitor systems. The name most associated with Hollerith is the Pin-Box tabulator.

Hollerith machines were used in wartime at Bletchley Park on a large scale, and eventually the operation became so big in terms of the number of punched cards used that it had to be relocated to Drayton Parslow some miles away, where hundreds of personnel operated them. The operation at the new site was run by BTM manager Freddie Freeborn.

In modern times, the activities are carried out by a personal computer using a hard drive or SSD storage, hardly taking up any space. Software allows speedy recovery of data and filtering, such as using Microsoft Excel or Access. However, during the war a huge room was needed for the much larger and heavier Hollerith machines, plus the personnel who operated them, the punched cards themselves, plus storage cabinets and shelving. The processing of data was largely developed through census processing for countries such as the USA and Egypt.

In tabulating new data for say, a population census, census information was transferred from sheets with census schedules to paper punched cards using robust punches and pantographs. The census bureau clerks then punched each card to mirror specific data on the census information schedule.

Clerks using pantographs could prepare approximately 500 cards per day. To operate the mechanism, the operator positioned the punching stylus over the desired hole in a punch card template. Each hole in the template corresponded to a specific demographic category. Pressing the stylus into the template created a punched hole in the paper card that was read by the Hollerith tabulator's reader.

Each Hollerith tabulator was equipped with a card-reading station. The manually operated card reader consisted of two hinged plates operated by a lever. Clerks opened the reader and positioned a punched card between the plates. Upon closing them, spring-loaded metal pins in the upper plate passed through the punched data holes in the cards, through the bottom plate and into wells of mercury beneath. Pins that passed through the punched card completed an electrical circuit when contacting the mercury below. The completed circuit energized the magnetic dials on the Hollerith tabulator and advanced the counting hands. Upon completion of the electrical circuit (signalled by the ringing of a bell), the clerk transcribed the data indicated by the dial hands.

The 1890 Hollerith tabulators consisted of forty data-recording dials. Each dial represented a different data item collected during the census. The electrical impulses received as the reader's pins passed through the card into the mercury advanced the hands on the dials corresponding to the data contained on the punch card (i.e., responses to enquiries about race, gender, citizenship, age, etc). When the bell signalled the card had been read, the operator recorded the data on the dials, opened the card reader, removed the punch cards, and reset the dials. A sorting table was positioned next to each tabulator. After registering the punched card data on the dials, the sorter specified in which drawer the operator should place the card. The clerk opened the reader, placed the punched card in the designated sorter drawer, reset the dials, and positioned a new card to repeat the process. It is recorded that an experienced tabulator clerk could process eighty punched cards per minute. Adaptation of this process for recording, storing, and then retrieving enemy decrypted messages was seen as an important advancement for Bletchley Park, as the data could be recovered relatively quickly with a formal request to the Hollerith Section. There would be management challenges between Bletchley Park and Freeborn's Hollerith base at Drayton Parslow as regards the perceived priorities for sorting and recovering message-based data, but this was eventually largely resolved. The civilian uses for Hollerith machines would become quite limited as time elapsed post-war, and when computers began to be developed.

In the late 1940s, the United States Census Bureau commissioned the first electronic computer designed for civilian use. Developed by J. Presper Eckert and John W. Mauchly, UNIVAC I marked a major improvement in data processing. It was the dawn of the computer age. First used to process results from the 1950 decennial census, the machine was able to tabulate 4,000 items per minute, double the amount that electro-mechanical tabulating machines could process.

During the 1950s, the Census Bureau and the National Bureau of Standards developed a system called *Film Optical Sensing Device for Input to Computers* (FOSDIC), which took census and survey questionnaires that had been photographed on to microfilm, 'read' blackened dots opposite the appropriate answers and transferred that data to magnetic tape. These tapes constituted the input for the Census Bureau's computers. One important result of this process was the elimination of most discrepancies in data records sent for processing. First used to process 1960 census results, FOSDIC played an integral part in the Census Bureau's data processing system into the mid-1990s.

Optical character scanners were used to process returned questionnaires for the 2000 census. The scanners recognised handwritten responses, as well as filled-in ovals or boxes. Using complex software, the scanned images were processed and translated into American Standard Code for Information Interchange (ASCII). These responses were then transmitted electronically over secure lines to census bureau headquarters for statistical processing and analysis.[18]

It is interesting that various systems used some form of 'reading' holes or marks to sort, store and recover data, and this was relevant to non-Morse messages, the Robinson and Colossus machines, the use of optical sensors and improvements in modern technology. Punched cards were also used on a large scale in the 1950s and early 1960s for commercial and industrial computers, prior to the use of magnetic tape and magnetic disc storage systems. They were but an important stage in computer development and in advanced data processing. BTM would go on post-war to also develop its own business computers, and the company when merged with others, had links with IBM.

IBM was active in providing a Model 80 card sorter machine to aid the processing of punched card data in wartime. Around thirteen vertical card slots permitted the punched cards to be sorted in the machine, driven by a substantial electric motor at the bottom of the unit. Some of these machines would probably not pass health and safety inspections for workers today, with the motor drive belt exposed and unguarded. High noise levels nowadays would require risk assessments by employers, and possibly the issue of ear defenders. Almost twenty years before the end of the war, the early model of the IBM Model 80 could process and sort

450 punched cards per minute. This was considerably faster than the Hollerith equivalent sorter at the time.[19]

Hollerith machines were also in use post-war, at GCHQ Eastcote, and later RAF Eastcote. One woman explained that her mother worked in a room at Eastcote in the 1950s, working with punched cards and fed into a Hollerith machine. Her mother also took in local paying guests, including young women arriving with American communication receivers and who could speak Russian. Her daughter also later worked at the Eastcote base until she emigrated to New Zealand.[20]

Working in the Hollerith section at Bletchley or later, Drayton Parslow, was often a boring job for mainly women. They transferred filtered punched cards from one Hollerith machine to another, sorted them, stored them, took them from store and loaded them into the noisy machines. However, their work made a difference in areas such as traffic analysis, and during wartime it helped gain a bigger picture of the Nazi war machine.

Hollerith Equipment used at Bletchley

The equipment within Hut 7/Block C was:

Model 20 key punches and verifiers
Electric alphanumeric punches and verifiers
E6/6 tabulators
405 tabulators
Horizontal sorters
Reproducing punch machines
Card collators
Decimal cross-footing multiplying punches
Detachable plugboards

Most of this equipment would later be at Drayton Parslow, some distance from Bletchley Park.

Horn loudspeakers

Horn loudspeakers were efficient acoustically to convert electrical signals into sound. They were mounted on military trucks and used by the American 'Ghost Army', part of the US Signals detachment, to broadcast military noises such as tanks and trucks moving, and bridges being erected by personnel, to confuse and deceive the enemy. These were enormous, huge fluted, curved, metal horn speakers mounted to be raised vertically and then aimed at an enemy target position some distance away. The technology was secret, so that the trucks containing the horn speakers and amplifiers were pre-mined with explosives to destroy them if they were captured by the enemy. The horn speaker was probably of German origin, with Werner von Siemens taking out patents in 1877, although later patents through American companies such as Western Electric and others refined the design. Edison also used horn speakers for many of his projects.

The use of projected sound as a deception technique during the war by the 'Ghost Army' was secret technology, using physics and atmospherics to project transmission distances using tables and tests, along with monitoring weather conditions and barometric pressure. The other advantage of using horn loudspeakers was that the sound remained extremely clear over long distances, which was important for the military use of deception techniques. The American unit used their mobile audio horn-projection system throughout the assault across Europe, and it remained secret until relatively recently.

HRO receiver

A robust American valve-based radio receiver used on a large scale by the Allies and at listening Y-stations for monitoring enemy radio transmissions. They were manufactured by the National Radio Company, which had originally supported GEC in the USA to design a radio to fulfil a Government contract. The HRO receiver was the first of a series of radios that was designed in 1934 and shipped in March 1935. The basic receiver cost around $233, which was quite expensive at that time. It had an unusual design because to listen to certain radio frequencies one had to have a set of individual coil sets to plug into the front of the equipment. There were four basic coil sets, A, B, C, D, together with the frequency ranges marked on them. A further nine or so coil sets were later made available for special purposes. The frequency range provided by all the coil sets was 0.05MHz–30MHz. There were nine valves in the early HRO models, and the steel case was dominated by a large circular tuning dial, sometimes with an inset frequency indicator. Post-war, some models incorporated twelve valves.

Around 10,000 HRO receivers were ordered and used by the British during the war. The operators included shipping, Y-stations, as well as some amateur radio enthusiasts if they could afford them, although several would be allocated to Voluntary Interceptors via Lend-Lease arrangements with the USA. The design of the receiver was so successful that it was copied in part by the Germans and the Japanese. German manufacturing companies in wartime included both Siemens and Korting, the former producing a model R4, and Korting the KST radio.[21] Bletchley Park used various versions of the HRO but most often the HRO-M model.

The receivers were typically approximately 440 × 220 × 300mm and weighed around 14.5kg, the external power supply and coil sets being separate. The units were also used for direction-finding purposes in mobile vehicles such as trucks. It was easy to maintain the receiver as the top lid was hinged and could be lifted to inspect the components and change the valves. Controls at the front included the micrometre-type tuning dial, signal meters, phasing, selectivity, RF gain, CW oscillator, AVC, volume, and phones connector output. An external speaker was required and a transformer to drive it, unless one then listened on headphones. The metal meshed tuning capacitors were positioned at right angles to the tuning dial, so some form of geared worm mechanism turned the dial function, and this was considered as precision engineering. The physical insertion of the separate coil sets made electrical contact with a series of aligned copper 'fingers', which made connection with the metal studs on the coils. The reason the costs were designed and manufactured as separate units, was that they helped reduce the physical size of the receiver, and one could be selective as to which individual costs were needed for the task in question by the operator. It also meant the radio was less heavy to move without the coil sets in place.

The term HRO was thought to be a humorous abbreviation for 'Hell'uva Rush Order', as the US Government could not get enough of the units and instructed the National Radio Company to keep manufacturing them until told to stop. Many units came to Britain under Lend-Lease. Y-station operators would often listen to the receivers on headphones in the Continuous Wave mode, for Morse code, and in varying atmospheric conditions, for hours at a time. They would log the information on special log sheets identifying time, call sign, frequency, and relevant information, which was then passed to Bletchley Park.

Model types available of the HRO series of radio receivers are listed as follows:

HRO-SPC
HRO-B (Battery Version)
HRP-JR (1936–43)
HRO-M (Late 1941)
HRO-MX (1942)
HRO-5 (1944–45)
HRO-W (Signal Corps version of HRO-05)
HRO-5A (Early 1946)
HRO-5A1 (March 1946)
HRO-5TA1 (May 1946)
HRO-6 (Early 1947)
HRO-7 (1947–49)
HRO-50 (1949–50)
HRO-50T1 (1951)
HRO-60 (1952–64)
HRO-500 (1964–72) solid-state version
HRO-600 (1970–72)

The above listing is courtesy of www.cryptomuseum, with some others added to the list by the author. See also RCA AR88 Receiver.

Invisible ink

Used by spies and the SOE during wartime, invisible ink was used in letters between the visible text so as to appear normal to the reader. The application of either a chemical or gentle heat to the letter exposed the concealed text. Some letters written by double agent *Garbo* used invisible ink when communicating with his Nazi handlers, although the bulk of his later communication was via encoded radio messages. Materials used for invisible ink included lemon juice, milk, phenolphthalein, and iodine. The concept had been tried years before the Second World War and was a stepping stone to using much more sophisticated methods such as microdots, which could be concealed within a book or a toothpaste tube. Such methods became popular in the 1950s and '60s. George Washington is reported to have used invisible ink during the American War of Independence. In the First World War, British agents hid their messages using an ink powder chemical in something like a shaving stick, and the message was exposed when iodine was applied to the paper.[22]

Jumbo

A version of the Bombe machine but designed to work with weak Menus. They may not have had the indicator unit fitted to the right of the machine. An electric typewriter was attached to print out listings of some possible Bombe rotor 'stops'. Apparently, the operating machine with relays and selectors sounded not unlike a machine gun, being extremely noisy. Around thirteen of these versions of Bombe were built.

Loudspeakers at Y-stations and similar

Although personnel at Y-stations used mainly headphones for listening purposes on the radio receivers, from time to time there would be the need to switch to loudspeakers for more than one person to listen in to a message or transmission for monitoring purposes. Speakers were also used at military command bases, communication hubs, airfields, naval shipping vessels, factories, recruitment, and training sites. The design of the loudspeaker was largely based on a voice coil and fibre/paper cone, and the need for electrical amplification to produce an audible signal. *Tannoy* speakers were common and used in civilian and military sites, but there were many other makes, too. The speaker would usually be enclosed in a box to help amplify the sound and provide bass frequencies, with a metal or wooden grille for protection. Each speaker would have a measured impedance in ohms, which was relevant to the amplification provided, and determined the gain or loudness, to a degree. Some speakers could often be run in groups or arrays in series, and others in parallel on an electrical circuit.

The RCA-designed MI 22201 speaker was used in RAF and Y-stations and was often used in conjunction with the American AR88 radio receiver. The speaker had a metal steel casing with painted crackle finish, with a fretted steel grille, a speaker aperture of between 17.5cm and 20cm, and the cabinet measured 29cm × 15cm × 26.5cm. The fretted grille could either have the RAF letters or RCA letters across it. They would be manufactured in the 1940s and contain a transformer inside the case.

Specialist speakers would be a completely different design and could be based on 'horn' loudspeakers, which were extremely acoustically efficient in comparison to conventional models.[23] That is, a relatively small, amplified signal could produce a very loud output. Horn loudspeakers were used on mobile armoured tracked vehicles by the US 'Ghost' army for deceiving the enemy and broadcasting sounds and noise that could carry several kilometres, and to cause confusion as to where an attack would be coming from.

After the war, horn loudspeakers were developed further for high-tech industrial PA systems and high-fidelity sound audio, but tended to be physically very large and heavy. Modern conventional loudspeakers are still largely based on voice coils, but the speaker cones are often made from stiffer synthetic materials. Magnets have improved substantially with neodymium magnetic poles, and computer software analysis has revolutionised the quality of the speaker designs, often including multiple voice coils, electronic crossovers, and other advances. Even so, paper fibre is still regarded as a suitable material for good-quality loudspeakers at the budget end of the commercial market. Paper fibre-based speaker cones are relatively stiff, lightweight, responsive, and relatively inexpensive to manufacture. A flexible surround around the perimeter of the cone such as rubber or synthetic rubber is required in more modern speakers.[24] That was generally absent in wartime speakers. The purpose of the grille to the speaker was principally to prevent damage of the vulnerable speaker cone. Horn speakers generally do not have a protective grille, as their construction is completely different.

Lorenz SZ40 and SZ42

Hitler was convinced he needed a special extra secure communicating cipher machine so he could pass orders to his generals and field marshals. The result was a suite of special enciphering teleprinter attachments based on multiple wheel rotors, but far greater in number than with Enigma machines. The Lorenz attachment enabled the transmission of non-Morse messages to and from the generals and was relatively efficient, with the need for only one operator at each end. It was a machine and system the Allies had not seen and were initially unaware of until transmissions were intercepted at Denmark Hill listening station, south London, and investigations commenced. This new machine and system of communication posed a major challenge to the Allies, as they had no solution to it. It would take time for the British to analyse the transmissions and special listening stations were established in England to intercept the non-Morse messages. The progress for the Allies was largely down to a young British mathematician and codebreaker, William Tutte. He managed to analyse the Nazi machine and its configuration without ever having seen it. The SZ40 and SZ42 were initial models, later to be superseded by even more complex machines.

The introduction of Lorenz meant that there were at least two separate, parallel encoding/decoding systems being used by the enemy. The initial challenge was the Enigma, and that was largely dealt with using the Bombe codebreaking machine. Now, there would be Lorenz, using a completely different encryption system, the Turing–Welchman Bombe being incompatible with it. It is relevant that the quantity of the Lorenz machines used would be a fraction of the Enigma machines, but both were of importance and neither could be ignored by the Allies. More advanced machines would be developed by the Nazis, called secret writers, which were highly secure in comparison to Enigma, but even those were eventually cracked by the Allies. Codebreakers in Sweden were briefly able to break into the advanced Nazi teleprinter attachment ciphers and obtain valuable intelligence, alongside those at Bletchley Park. Bletchley concentrated on cracking Lorenz, as the intercepts were mainly based on radio transmissions from Europe.

The SZ40/SZ42 machine was termed *Schlüsselzusatz,* or special attachment, by the Germans. The machine was effectively copied in principle by staff at the Post Office Research Station in Dollis Hill, and the 'Tunny' machine was constructed by them to check the message output once the settings had been established. These machines were kept within the Testery at Bletchley Park, and were quite large compared to the original Lorenz machine. Setting the machine up using countless switches and controls would have been laborious.

Madame 'X'

Three-wheeled Enigma-based Bombes used telephone switching relays instead of rotors. One was built by AT&T for the US Army and was used for research.[25]

Mammoth

A four-wheel Bombe version with high-speed relays to sense stops. It was sometimes referred to a Keen-type High-Speed Bombe. Indications are that fifty-seven of these were built. (See High-Speed Keen).

Mobile Lorenz caravan

The Allies captured a caravan of German equipment and vehicles at the end of the war near Berchtesgaden, and these turned out to be a mobile Lorenz teleprinter enciphering attachment complete with a complement of operators and crew in adapted trucks. The SZ42 Lorenz attachment was large and heavy, and not really designed to be mobile. However, the German high command saw the advantage in having a mobile unit in the field, which could send and receive encoded messages using non-Morse communications via teleprinter, to and from Hitler and his generals in Berlin. Each of the vehicles contained radio transmitters, aerials, radio receivers, and the encryption equipment. There were sleeping bunks in the trucks for the driver and the assistant operator. It was the communication device for OB West to Berlin. The entire vehicles, equipment and captured Nazi operators were transported back to England, where they were interrogated and the equipment studied in detail. It was turned over to the Target Intelligence Committee (TICOM), with Major Tester and Lieutenant Levenson accompanying the vehicles back to Britain. They left Austria on 16 May 1945 with sixteen diesel trucks and twelve prisoners of war. Along the route back home and via Belgium, locals threw objects at the men and the trucks as there were no 'capture numbers' visible, which would have indicated they had been formally captured. The trucks were then loaded on a landing ship in Ostend for the journey to England.

This may have been the first opportunity for Bletchley Park codebreakers to study the Lorenz machine. However, the war had already ended in Europe. Whereas the Enigma machine was small and light enough to be transported across battlefields by one or two men, and was valued for its portability, finding Lorenz in a caravan was a surprise to the Allies.

M9 Bombe checking machine

An American machine to analyse Enigma decrypts. It would be used to determine missing rotor wheel order sequences, and missing plugboard/'steckerboard' positions. The M9 was used by WAVES personnel, and short messages could be decrypted on the machine. WAVES could also use it against other messages that were problematical and required more time to analyse. The equivalent machine used in England would be the four-wheel checking machine, although the M9 may have been more sophisticated.

M101 Emerald

A Russian encryption machine created in 1942, which was very reliable in enciphering high-level messages of great importance.

Morse keys

A hand-operated switch to generate Morse code messages electrically, and send the signal down wires to a receiver station. Trained operators would reach very high-speed Morse key rates, and could take down Morse messages transmitted at high speed by the Allies or the enemy. Early Morse keys were used in the First World War, and by the Second their use was widespread both at transport communication hubs and for the military. Some people suffered a type of repetitive strain injury when using the Morse key for long periods of time. The Morse tapping key would be pressed and released at high speed, and pivot, causing a 'make and break' electrically, with a series of short dots and longer dashes to a particular standardised pattern, so as to represent the alphabet. Listening stations, or Y-stations, would have listeners on headphones intercepting Morse code messages, which would be passed to places such as Bletchley Park. A series of practice Morse keys were designed to help train military personnel, such as those for the Air Ministry.

The United States military used Morse keys such as the J-38 and J-47 models, produced by the Lionel Corporation and McElroy, or Warren Manufacturing Co., under licence. The bases of the keys were Bakelite material, and that was also often used for the Morse tapping knob. The average sending speed would be around fifteen words per minute, but in some cases could be exceeded to around twenty, although the key design of the J-38 limited the ultimate speed compared with other designs. German military hand keys such as the T2 model, were built in substantial numbers by the Lorenz company.

Some Allied Morse key models were of 'flameproof' specification, to protect areas where there was volatile fuel adjacent, or other potential hazards nearby. There would be a sealed chamber to enclose any possible sparking from the Morse key operating, with only the key exposed. British-designed 'Bath-Tub' Morse keys were flameproof sealed units, often used in bomber aircraft during the war. The US had its own flameproof, enclosed sparking chamber designs. See also Y-stations.

N-530 US naval Bombe

See Bombe naval USA (four-wheel) N-530 and N-1530.

Ogre

This Bombe machine involved two Bombes connected together and used for breaking messages using the pluggable Reflector D.

Photographic cameras for recording

Cameras and photography were used extensively during wartime to help gather intelligence, and build a picture of the enemy activities, resources, troop movements, supply lines, etc. Aerial photo reconnaissance was a tool used by both sides in the war. High-resolution lenses were developed that could resolve detail from a high altitude. These images were then examined in great detail, and some were stereoscopically photographed, too. The Germans had quality precision cameras from Leitz and lenses from Leitz, Zeiss, Contax, Rollei, Voigtlander, Siemens, and others.[26] Models could include the Super Ikonta, also used by the British, as well as Rolleiflexes, Leicas, and others. British makes of cameras and lenses included Corfield, Microcord, Ross-Ensign, RAF F24 aerial cameras, etc. The Rolleiflex was a twin-lens reflex camera, with a viewing lens and a separate taking lens, and was extremely reliable. Movie cameras were used extensively, some with interchangeable lenses and others with fixed ones for wide-angle and telephoto work. Journalists and military photographers recorded action on the battlefields. Lenses were also needed for military rangefinders, to range and assess targets, as well as for binoculars, tank periscopes, etc. The coating of lenses was at a relatively early stage but was useful on cameras, binoculars, and telescopes, inasmuch it avoided internal reflections and could cope with a certain amount of glare while still recording the images. The value of the photographs could sometimes be the confirmation of activities or events that had been messaged earlier via Enigma and decrypted by the Allies. These were tools to gain military intelligence in a range of different forms and formats.

The speed of processing intelligence photographs was crucial, and multiple photos were developed and processed on long rolls of film when aircraft landed from a mission over enemy occupied territory. The time delay between taking the photographs and examining them had to be as short as possible to be of any real value, as things could change rapidly in wartime. Resistance fighters in occupied countries and agents would risk their lives photographing enemy installations, railway stations, harbours, geographical features, buildings, sites, and troop movements to pass the information to the Allies for analysis.

For clandestine operations some agents used Minox sub miniature cameras of a small size that meant they could be concealed. These specialist cameras used a specific size of film, 9.5mm, with images of 8mm × 11mm, being much smaller than conventional cameras with 35mm film and a negative size of 24mm × 36mm. The brand evolved in the 1930s before the war. The Minox became famous in the 1950s and '60s for use by spies, and they were seen in TV programmes and feature films of the era. It was a high-precision engineered camera, with several different versions over the years. In later years, a commemorative gold-plated version was produced.

It also should be recognised that processing film required large amounts of photographic chemicals, powders, and liquids to develop and print the photographs. Water for washing prints and films would be needed in large quantities. Sodium thiosulfate was used for fixing the images. Supplies of this, and of developing agents, would have to be obtained without interruption, this being challenging in wartime. Hydroquinone was another important ingredient in film processing.

Machines could process long runs of film and negatives, but had to be maintained and repaired when they went wrong. They also needed skilled staff to operate them, and women had to step in here if men were fighting in occupied countries, or training for action in the services. On clandestine operations, tiny microdots would have to be processed and enlarged to view enemy drawings or images of military hardware. That was specialist work. The technique would be further enhanced and used in the Cold War era.

Stereo photogrammetry was adapted from land surveying for survey mapping and used by specialists ,who would view overlapping photographic images to obtain the height or depth of targets, using shadows caused by natural sunlight. Thus, it was often possible to gauge the height of a building or a V2 missile in preparation on a launch pad using such techniques. Much of the specialist photogrammetry equipment was acquired via Switzerland, a neutral country. Germany monitored the activities in and around Switzerland, and the British had to be careful not to give too much away to the enemy when they were acquiring specialist equipment from Europe. Colour film was not used that extensively during wartime, partly due to its expense and partly due to the added complexity of processing, as it took more time to develop involving many more stages compared to monochrome work. Black and white images would be the default for most work, but there would be exceptions, particularly in cine work for record purposes, and colour film was used in the latter stages of the war, particularly in the Pacific against the Japanese.

Today wartime cameras used by the Nazis, particularly those with engraved swastika emblems, can be worth thousands of pounds if in moderately good condition. Several models of Leica had such embellishments. The Leica was such a good 35mm camera it was copied extensively by many nations, including the British, Russians, and Japanese. However, the quality often suffered when it was copied. Several wartime German companies still exist, such as Leitz and Zeiss, but some have been transformed commercially with various mergers and acquisitions.

The Rollei company made a range of cameras including the twin-lens reflex design until around the 1990s, but digital photography changed the market completely and many traditional manufacturers fell by the wayside. Jersey used to have a Rollei camera museum at one of its larger hotels, but this closed some years ago.[27] Jersey was one of the Channel Islands occupied during the war. While Rollei did venture into single-lens reflex film photography in the 1980s and '90s, and later, digital photography, it could not compete with its competitors and fell by the wayside. The German Leica brand is still sought after at prices that many consider eye watering, but there are few competitors for the quality of design and construction of their range of cameras and high-precision lenses.

Portable transmitter/receiver

A portable receiver and transmitter was necessary for use in wartime in battle situations, for reconnaissance and for direction finding in trucks to locate enemy targets where radio transmissions were being sent from. They would need to be robust and reliable as they tended to be subject to vibration, impact from localised shelling and mortars, and from inclement weather and damp. Electrically based instruments and equipment are not compatible with dampness. Extreme hot or cold weather also takes its toil and can cause malfunction and reliability issues. Dust is an enemy of radio equipment in the desert. Valves would need to be protected, and if equipment was used externally, some degree of weatherproofing was required. A protective water-resistant cover with a weatherproof flap cover was sometimes utilised by the radio operator.

Portable radio transmitters were also used by agents and double agents in the field. These were often contained in a medium-sized suitcase or large briefcase so as not to attract attention from others. Direction-finding equipment targeted such equipment. The penalty for listening to the radio in occupied countries was imprisonment or the firing squad. A civilian being caught with a radio transmitter by the enemy meant certain torture and death, as they would be considered a spy.

The United States Army relied on the SC300 walkie talkie backpack for military communication in the field. Spares had to be carried by the support unit in case a valve failed. Valves were relatively expensive in wartime, but fortunately the Philips valve company had managed to bring tools and equipment to Britain just before the Nazis raided the factory in the Netherlands when occupation of that country commenced.

Probemaschine

An early Enigma test machine from around 1918. This was an early predecessor of the 'Glowlamp' Enigma.

Radar

Radar was a British invention that was developed by both sides in wartime. Britain established a comprehensive network of radar stations across the country, monitored by radar operators to interpret the signals on display screens. Information would be fed to Fighter Command posts, naval commanders and to observers watching for the Luftwaffe. The use of radar on warships was also significant. It is strange that the Germans did not appear to use radar to quite the extent of the British, and that put them at a disadvantage. It was not that they did not have radar, but perhaps were not as experienced in the application of how it could be used to the best advantage of the armed services strategically and tactically.

It would be Doctor (later Professor) R.V. Jones, among others, who would move forward radar and its associated systems to significantly benefit Britain and its allies. Jones was a physicist, and became involved in developing an approach to obtaining intelligence using specialist equipment and processes to deceive the enemy, and to track them using what was modern technology for the time. It was most unusual and unorthodox for a scientist to be attached to the intelligence service of the country, so this was a pioneering approach. Jones and Joan Curran developed the Window or chaff confusion tactic using strips of aluminium foil of a pre-determined length in great quantities that was dropped from aircraft to cause mass patterns of radar disturbance on the enemy radar screens. While both sides knew of the impact of Window, it was the Allies that used it effectively.

Jones was also involved in the 'battle of the beams' during wartime, studying enemy tactics using radio waves and developing equipment to identify the specific frequencies used and distort or bend the Luftwaffe tracking beams, called *knickebein.* The Nazi aerials for this special navigation guidance system were huge, typically 100m across by 10m high. A jamming technique was also utilised against the Nazis. The British scientifically based attack on the *knickebein* system was most successful, and must have impressed Winston Churchill as it was he who had to give the authority for RAF aircraft to search the skies for the Nazi navigation beams.

While Jones worked for a time at Bletchley Park in the early years of GC&CS, he relocated back to London to continue with his technical and scientific research. He discussed options with Commander Travis at Bletchley, and learned of the challenge of the Enigma encoding machine. Travis introduced Jones to Alan Turing; two great minds conversing together. This intercourse was of benefit to the cryptographers at Bletchley and to Jones in understanding better each other's problems and approaches to their work. Codebreaking machines were discussed at length between the two parties. It is possible that the conversation might even have given Turing some ideas about the forthcoming codebreaking Bombe design.

Jones' study of SIS files and research identified a list of potential threats from the enemy to consider. These included bacterial warfare, pilotless aircraft, long-range guns and rockets, new torpedoes, and 'engine-stopping rays', among others. His published book, *Most Secret War*, 1978, gave a detailed account of British scientific intelligence in wartime, and became an iconic reference, written as it was by one of the most effective innovators and forward-thinking scientists to have lived in the twentieth century.

The German *Würzburg* radar was captured by British paratroopers near Bruneval, France, and components taken back to TRE in Dorset, for detailed analysis. However, there were concerns over Luftwaffe reprisals, so TRE was rapidly relocated to Malvern in Worcestershire. This was less exposed to enemy attacks, and would become the largest engineering factory in Europe during wartime, with thousands of staff, engineers, and support personnel. TRE provided technical support for a number of the codebreaking machines, and Dr Charles Wynn-Williams made valuable and significant contributions to their development. See also TRE.

RCA AR88 receiver

A general-purpose communications receiver designed and built by RCA in America. These were exported from the US and Canada to Great Britain in their thousands. They were used by Voluntary Interceptors working for the Home Office, also the Y-stations and elsewhere. The design was extremely reliable and robust. Much of the design was based upon the earlier costly, marine and military communications receiver, the model AR-60. The AR88 would be ready for production on a large scale by early 1941.

The AR88 was a 14-valve-tube superheterodyne, and the frequencies were 0.54–32 Megacycles in coverage, with six tuning ranges. The electronic design was by Lester T. Fowler. The sensitivity was unparalleled compared with other wartime communications receivers. Both Great Britain and Russia benefited substantially from AR88 imports in large quantities. The Lend-Lease agreement between Britain and the US opened the doors to equipment not generally available before the attack on Pearl Harbor. Organisations such as the SOE in the UK used AR88s to communicate with agents dropped in occupied territory in Europe. Wireless Receiving station STS 53b operated in Poundon, Oxfordshire, supporting the SOE. The Portsdown Tunnel communications centre used AR88s, many operated by Wrens, while other versions were produced for specialist purposes. The AR88LF was for low frequency reception (70kc–550kc and 1.5mc–30mc).

The total number of receivers produced across all the different versions was up to 25,000. This included RCA models AR88D, AR88F, AR88LF, and CR91. Sadly, after the war ended, many usable wartime radio receivers were dumped as the US did not want them back, preferring payment for them. Some were sold off as war surplus.[28]

The AR88 was an extremely useful receiver unit for the Allies for radio and Morse code communications.[29] See also HRO receiver.

Rhombic aerials

Y-stations required large aerials for listening in to the enemy's radio transmissions and Morse code. Non-Morse advanced transmissions were also of great interest as the war progressed, and Knockholt in Kent, a specialist Y-station, had an array of rhombic-shaped large aerial arrays at an elevated position. These would be aligned to obtain the most effective reception, having regard for the local atmospheric conditions.[30] Some Y-stations were able to pick up Japanese transmissions thousands of miles away using such equipment.[31] See also Knockholt.

Robinson

This was the intermediate-stage machine to help crack Lorenz and similar advanced, enemy encoding machines. Wrens used to call it 'Heath Robinson', or 'Robinson', as it appeared to have been thrown together with a range of components and parts, looking somewhat of a mess and like an afterthought. The designer William Heath Robinson played no part in its design. The constructors included Wynn-Williams of TRE, and the Post Office Engineering station, which built elements of it. It was not particularly reliable but did work and it obtained results.

One of the problems was that it relied upon the operator carefully synchronising two completely separate reels of punched paper tape to be read by a photo-electric sensor or magic eye. Paper tapes often broke apart and had to be glued together by the Wrens with a hot glue gun. It was a nightmare to set up with numerous pulleys and the tape reels spilling coils of paper. Some valves were used in the construction and it was built on a large frame.

Robinson could only achieve a throughput rate of about 2,000 characters per second, which was much slower than the later advanced Colossus codebreaking machines. Thomas Flowers, of PORES, who worked on it was critical of the design and later would go on to build a much better, more sophisticated, and faster machine. A Mark 2 Robinson machine was also developed. The National Museum of Computing built a machine that is now installed in the Heath Robinson Museum in Harrow, west London, for children to learn about codebreaking machines. Clearly, it is not a true 'Robinson' codebreaker, but looks impressive in its Perspex case and is termed 'Just William'. Operators who answer all the correct questions win a sweet!

The designer and artist William Heath Robinson was unaware of codebreaking machines and died during wartime, so only his name was used for the Robinson machines at Bletchley Park. See also PORES.

Russian teleprinter attachment

During the war, the Russians were using a modified Hagelin B-211 encoding machine for communication. This was the K-37 or 'Crystal' equipment. The cipher teleprinters were the B-4 and M-100. The B-4 was constructed in the 1930s and used in the Spanish Civil War. A modernised version, the M-100, was built in 1940. In 1943, a more compact version of the M-100 was built, the M-101.

Radio-teletype traffic was used by the Russians from the early 1930s but the Germans had intercepted and printed this from around 1936. Three German sections intercepted the traffic, one of them being the *Forschungsamt*, which reported back to Herrman Goering. They informed the German Army Ordnance, Development and Testing Group Signal Branch Group that they had successfully reconstructed a Russian cipher teleprinter. This was used to communicate encoded messages between the Russian fronts and Moscow. The German Army Inspectorate, 7/VI, also set up a unit to intercept and analyse the Russian teleprinter traffic in some detail.

The Russian machine had six wheels, five of which encoded the Baudot pulses. The final wheel was the motor drive, moving the wheels according to a strict pin-based wheel system. Apparently, the scrambler in the machine was based upon a Lorenz SZ40/SZ42 teleprinter attachment designed by the Germans, so the Russians were clearly copying enemy technology. Around summer 1943 a copy of the Russian attachment was used productively by the Nazis. There would be at least eight teleprinter links between the Russian front and Moscow, as well as several Russian Air Force 'Fish' communication links. This is of interest as Bletchley Park was separately and secretly decoding Lorenz teleprinter attachment non-Morse messages, and building machines to help with the task, while the enemy was building copies of the Russian teleprinter attachment, which was based to a degree on their own Lorenz encoding attachment. It was a game of cat and mouse, but done in secret, to find out what the enemy was doing and planning. So much expertise, time and resources was put in by the Germans, British, Russians, Poles and Americans to crack the ciphers, many of which originated via 'Fish' or 'Tunny' communication links, or in the case of the Germans attacking Russian ciphers, with a system known as 'Bandwurn', and identifying weaknesses in the design and operation of cipher machines by an enemy.

Scrambler telephone

In 1937, the General Post Office introduced a scrambler telephone system based on a 300 series telephone handset. The intended use was for the Government and the military. Early models were unreliable and could only deter a casual eavesdropper. The scrambler unit was positioned under a desk and connected to a telephone, with 'Secret' and 'Normal' buttons on the front. When one pressed 'Secret' and the other end recipient did the same, the scrambler electronics would come into play. However, the electronics were valve-based and consequently had to warm up before becoming effective to generate noise and avoid eavesdropping of the conversation. King George VI used such a device, but HM Queen Elizabeth II told GCHQ that the King became very frustrated waiting for the equipment to warm up and was unimpressed. A chosen frequency would be inverted and generate noise to block out anyone who tried to listen to the private conversation. The scrambler part of the circuit was known as the 'privacy unit', and was built by the Telephone Manufacturing Company (TMC) and by Plessey. As the war progressed, the units became much more reliable and effective. Winston Churchill used them but also employed SIGSALY equipment. This was a completely separate and highly complex voice encoding system using Pulse Code Modulation (PCM) technology and recorded noise on record playing equipment, designed by the Americans, and it was installed in the basement of Selfridges. It was linked and wired into the Cabinet War rooms in Westminster as well as to the American Embassy in Grosvenor Square.[32]

The Science Museum in London possesses a scrambler telephone and privacy unit, called the Secraphone. Their unit is circa 1941, and is referenced as '2004-184 Privacy set 6AA (GPTN) Diagram SA5061'. The telephones have a dial with text stating 'Telephone calls are not secret'. The same advice could be applied to modern-day social media, perhaps, and even many emails that may be less than secure. A scrambler telephone is also situated in the Westminster Churchill Rooms, coloured red, and may have been used by Churchill and senior staff. See also SIGSALY.

SCR-284 Receiver

This receiver was used by the Allies during Operation Torch in North Africa and elsewhere to communicate between the US fleet anchored off the coast of North Africa and the beach where troops were gathering for the multi-pronged assault. The principal use during the operation was to direct naval gunfire on to enemy positions. Around 50,000 pieces of radio equipment of this model were made for *Operation*

Overlord, the invasion of France. The receivers weighed more than 100lb, but fortunately could be divided into sections to transport them. Another transmitter, the BC-654, was difficult to carry around by personnel while in combat situations.

A total of 63,972 SCR-284 receivers were produced. After the war, many war-surplus units were purchased by radio amateurs. See also RCA 88 receiver, HRO receiver.

Secret writers

A development of the non-Morse Lorenz machine, the secret writer, or *Geheimschreiber*, was a more sophisticated and secure machine used by the Nazis as a teleprinter attachment for sending and receiving high command messages. This meant the permutations of message settings were greater than those of Lorenz. The Siemens T-52 was one secret writer model. While there was similarity between the T-52 and the Lorenz S40/S42, there were also important design differences to improve security. See also Lorenz.

Siemens relays

Siemens was a major German engineering company that manufactured equipment and component parts for the military. Its design of relays was particularly advanced as compared to those in Britain. This was noticed by engineers at the British Post Office Research Station, and as a result a version of the Siemens relay was made and tested in Britain. It proved to be more efficient, so it was put into production and installed in Bombe machines that went to the larger codebreaking outstations. Hitler would probably have been angered by this copying of German precision engineering if he had been made aware.

Siemens' computer branch merged commercially with the Fujitsu company in 1999, to be known as Fujitsu Siemens Computers GmbH, which is ironic as Fujitsu was originally ICL, which was born out of various mergers of BTM, the factory that built the Bombes.[33] The merged company became Fujitsu Technology Solutions in April 2009, having bought out Siemens' share. Fujitsu, a multinational company, based in Japan, was involved in a twenty-first century Post Office scandal involving its Horizon accounting software.[34]

Shlusselgerat 41Z

This machine was introduced by the *Abwehr* in 1944 as a potential successor to the Enigma Model G. The SG 41 was a mechanical pin-wheel cipher machine, and similar to the Hagelin C38. A hand crank gave it the nickname *Hitlermuhle* (Hitler Mill). It had a numerical keyboard in the front of the machine and a hinged flap to view the rotor readings and settings. A large drum with a reel of tape was situated in the base.

SIGABA

The SIGABA was an American enciphering machine also known as the ECM Mark 2 that was in use by 1941. Different references numbers were given to models used by the US armed services. Thus, naval versions included the CSP 888/889 and CSP 2900, while the Army named it M-134 Converter. One of the advantages of SIGABA over Enigma was the random method to rotate the wheel rotors, avoiding predictability. It incorporated a modified paper tape reader within the machine. Naval intelligence made modifications and design changes just before the war commenced, and produced the Electric Code Machine Mk II. There were three sets of five wheel rotors to encode and decode messages. About 10,000 SIGABA machines were made during the war. The downside of the machine was that it was very complex to operate, not as robust as the Enigma, and not as practical in use. Unlike Enigma, it was prone to malfunction if mishandled by the operator or while transporting it.

SIGSALY

This encryption/decryption machine enabled secure transatlantic conversations in wartime between Churchill and Roosevelt. It was designed and constructed in the USA, and the first version installed in the Pentagon in Washington. The second machine was offered to Britain and was located in in the deep basement of Selfridges, the famous London department store, hidden away from prying eyes.[35] This huge machine weighed over 50 tons and required air conditioning for ventilation. It used modern technology including PCM, and used recordings on records that were played to add noise to the conversation at one end. At the other end, across the Atlantic, the machine and system was duplicated, and by playing the duplicated identical 'noise', one could subtract it from the conversation to reveal clear, intelligible speech. This was a highly secure 'scrambled' encrypt/decrypt speech system, which was never broken by the enemy.

Churchill would enter a long room at the Cabinet War Rooms in Westminster on his own and pick up the telephone to speak to Roosevelt, and later Harry S. Truman. The 'noise' records that formed part of the scrambling system only lasted twenty minutes, so an hour's conversation required three of them, each one duplicated on the other side of the Atlantic, and synchronised to the microsecond. All equipment was operated by US Signals engineers on a shift basis. Extra security was applied to the cable runs between the Selfridges SIGSALY machine and the Cabinet War Rooms and the US Embassy in Grosvenor Square. This included monitoring pressure gauges in cable ducts that were gas-filled, and the pressure strictly monitored for any interference by third parties. The equipment was all dismantled after the war and sent back to the US. The general public at and around Selfridges would have completely been unaware of the existence of the machine, the US operating personnel, and its significance to the war effort.

Sobol-P

A Russian enciphering machine used at the front and, according to historian Dmitry Larin, having no foreign equivalent in terms of design. Initial supplies were sent to Stalingrad. The transmissions could be radio-based, and therefore not affected by the destruction of fragile telephone lines. The value of cryptographers in the Russian Army was recognised by senior officers and particularly the top Soviet commander, General Georgy Zhukov.[36]

Teleprinter

Teleprinters were used to communicate data and information back to Bletchley Park from several of the outstations and Y-stations, and were significantly faster than using dispatch riders. They worked off GPO engineering landline cables between the sites. Some teleprinters may have worked using Cable and Wireless infrastructure in the early years. Speed in wartime was crucial in processing encrypted enemy messages, so teleprinter data was particularly useful to the traffic analysis team at Bletchley. Teleprinters were also used for the Tunny machines for printouts of messages and support data.

Early teleprinters were invented by a group of separate individuals in different countries, via telegraphy and the tele-typewriter. It was effectively a marriage between telegraphy and typewriters, but the design was automated to print out the text. Companies that became involved before the war included the USA, Britain, and Germany, the latter including Siemens and Halske, which would later develop the teleprinter attachment, T52, the Nazi secret writer encoding machine.

While teleprinters were invented and used many years before the Second World War, gaining ground in the 1920s, their use was expanded in wartime to take advantage of the speed of sending messages and reports across long distances. This could be plain text or encoded messages, sometimes using the Baudot system, which was the basis of the Lorenz teleprinter attachment used by the Nazis. The teleprinter consists of a typewriter-like keyboard, a printer, and a motor. It is connected by a series of clutches that enables the operation to start printing. Key strokes on the typewriter keyboard trigger a series of electrical pulses. These are routed through a transmission system and electronic switching to the destination. The receiving teleprinter decodes the electrical pulses to print out the text at the other end. Modern ASCii-coded teleprinters can generate 150 words per minute, compared to half that quantity for those using the Baudot code.

Teleprinters were used by the London underground rail network during wartime for communications, via the Down Street disused station near Dover Street, a wartime central operations centre.[37] See also Vernam-Baudot and Lorenz teleprinter attachment.

Thyratron Chassis

The US Navy four-wheel Bombes had rotors that rotated so quickly they would overrun their stop positions due to the momentum of the drum rotors. They would rotate three and a half to four times past the stop position before stopping. A brake was needed to slow the wheels down and a 'memory' had to be designed so that the rotor could reverse to the correct position. Joseph Desch designed a circuit using a Thyratron Chassis to make this work. This demonstrates some of the challenges that the designers had with the codebreaking machines. Each problem had to be identified, thought through in some detail, and solutions found. One advantage of the high-speed rotors was that the Bombe run could take as little as twenty minutes.

Tunny

A machine designed to emulate the Lorenz advanced encoders used by the Nazis, and located in Bletchley Park in the specialist section termed the Testery. 'Tunny' has two meanings: first as a physical specialist machine used at Bletchley Park, and second as the Nazi Lorenz teleprinter attachment for the communications network used by the Nazis across Europe with 'Fish' links, i.e. names designated as Fish, such as Gurnard, Bream, Stickleback, etc. 'Tunny' comes from the tuna fish. Note that the terms 'Fish' and 'Tunny' can be interchanged when talking of Nazi communications links based on advanced enemy encoding machines.

The British Tunny machine could not be built until William Tutte, a mathematician and codebreaker, had analysed and established the Lorenz machine configuration on paper. This took several weeks of intense work, analysing a machine he had never seen, and based on the non-Morse encrypted messages coming into specialist Y-stations. This was a mammoth task and a formidable achievement for the young codebreaker, which moved Bletchley Park forward in its aim to design machines to help attack Lorenz and the advanced secret writers that had eluded its codebreakers.

The Tunny machine at Bletchley Park was quite large, and built on a frame. It was built at Dollis Hill by the PORES team, including Gil Hayward. Tunny used a teleprinter for the input and the output to produce clear text. A large proportion of the equipment was based on use of British GPO telephone exchange equipment, including relays and uniselectors.

The Tunnies were installed within the Testery and operated by ATS women.[38] There are reports there were around ten machines within the Testery as the war progressed, while one or two may have been in the Newmanry next door. Although the Newmanry was the section that dealt with the machines, they were located within the Testery as they were used in the final stages of Lorenz message decryption after most of the hard work had been done by the codebreaking machines and the codebreakers. Some advanced features would be incorporated within the Tunny machines later installed in the Newmanry. For comparison purposes, WRNS personnel operated the codebreaking machines such as Robinson and Colossus, whereas ATS staff worked on Tunny. This demonstrates the reliance of Bletchley Park on utilising women in wartime to support its operations in the team effort of codebreaking and decryption.

Typex

The Typex, or Type X, machine was originally produced by the RAF and was used extensively to carry out a final stage of testing the message settings derived from the Enigma decryption. Development of the design commenced in 1934, with a sample produced for the Air Ministry in 1935 by Wing Commander Oswyn Lynwood. A quantity of machines were later dispatched for use in 1937. This would officially become the 'RAF Enigma with Type X attachments'. The attachments were printing facilities, and enhancements for plain text output. The message would appear in front of the operator, usually in the language of the sender of the message, (e.g. German), if the correct message settings had been determined and entered. It was an improved version of the Enigma, with five rotating wheels, instead of the three or four wheels on Enigma models. Bletchley Park and other locations had rows of Typex machines, with operators producing the final message, which then needed translation into English.[39] The conversion process involved identifying the Enigma message settings, based on an equivalent Enigma machine with several modifications. There were two large drums either side of the typewriter keyboard containing paper for printing the messages. Translators would be required to translate the German message text into English, before it was read and prioritised, and allocated to military commanders. It was essential to obtain the decoded message settings before one used the machine, otherwise the message could not be read. There are some reports by women operators of Typex that the equipment and keys were sometimes stiff, so wooden stick pieces were used to make them easier to operate in practice.

Some Typex machines were used in the Far East by British outposts and a few listening stations. The Germans had seen a British machine abandoned at Dunkirk, but thankfully did not pursue it further. Some initial attempts were made to evaluate it, but the German team became frustrated and were not prepared to allocate the resources to a further evaluation.[40] Had they progressed to an analysis of Typex by German cryptographic experts they would have realised it was a substantially improved emulation of the Enigma, and a potential threat to their security. That may have then resulted in a change to the way the codes for Enigma were structured, and further changes to the machine itself.

Different versions of the machine were produced during the war, and some post-war:

Typex Mark I (1937)
Typex Mark II
Typex Mark III

Typex Mark IV
Typex Mark 22 (Post-war model, circa 1950)
Typex Mark 23 (Post-war model, circa 1950)

While a machine prototype was produced in 1935, the first issue of production models of the Mark I was in 1937. These initially went to the RAF, principally as the designer was working for the RAF and for the Air Ministry. Later, portable models were produced, with the Army also going on using it. Bletchley Park, GC&CS, had a whole section in a hut with multiple Typex machines to expose the decoded messages following manual or machine-based decryption. Technical development of Typex enabled better security features in the later models. Powers-Samas, a competitor to codebreaking-machine manufacturer BTM, manufactured many of the wartime Typex models. Some modern versions were used by other countries until the 1970s.[41] There are reports of Typex being supplied to Russia, due to an earlier Anglo-Russian agreement of cooperation, although one assumes the message settings of messages would have to be passed to them unless they had decoding expertise on advanced Nazi machines.[42] A Typex machine can be seen in the Bletchley Park Museum. See also Enigma copies.

Valve tubes

Electronic components as valves were extensively used in radio receivers, transmitters, radar equipment, and the more advanced decoding codebreaking machines such as Colossus, during wartime. It would be the latter part of the war before engineers such as Thomas Flowers at PORES would experiment with incorporating valves within codebreaking machines as digital switches. Flowers had an interest in valves and valve technology before the war, and had done much reading and research. Of course, valves were used for many years in radio receivers and transmitters before they were considered by Flowers.[43] The quantities of valves needed for codebreaking machines was very large and the Mark 2 Colossus would need 2,400, which generated a lot of heat and used a great deal of electrical energy. Breakdowns and failures were minimised by keeping the valves switched on for as long as possible. The Philips company had managed to transfer a great deal of valves and manufacturing equipment to England from the Netherlands before the Nazis occupied its factory.

Valves were expensive to manufacture, and shortages would result in higher priorities for certain equipment over others. It would be years before solid state technology would overtake the use of valves, and the transistor would then dominate modern electronics. The United States manufactured wartime valves and exported them to Britain and allied nations, including the Acorn 955 Triode valve, followed by the 954 and 956 Pentode valves. The Mullard EF50 valve would be used in radar equipment. The Colossus computer incorporated the GEC GT1C valve, amongst others. It worked as an Argon-filled electronic switch, and was much faster than older electro-mechanical relays of the period.

Valve tubes are still used today, even in a world dominated by solid state electronics, transistors, and microprocessors. They are popular with audio and hi-fi enthusiasts for audio amplifiers and pre-amplifiers, even some recording studios as part of the audio-mixer design as they possess certain audio qualities, including a 'warmth' to the sound.

Valves were used in the US Navy Bombes constructed in Dayton, Ohio, instead of the relays that were used by the British. The British generally only used valves for their advanced codebreaking machines. See also Colossus Mk1 and Colossus Mk2.

Wheel rotors for Enigma

Metal-toothed wheel rotors were used in Enigma codebreaking machines and were removable. They would be inserted before setting up the Enigma machine, in a sequence dictated by a Nazi code book. There would be mainly three rotors, although there was a choice of selection from five and later up to eight rotors for four-wheeled Enigmas. Without the rotors, the Enigma was a relatively useless piece of metal and wires. Rotors were given Roman numerals to designate their unique number, and the code book would list the numbers and date for the operator to select them and install them in a specific sequence. If the receiving station did not follow this exact protocol then they would never be able to decipher the sent messages.

The *Kriegsmarin*e would equip its U-boats with four-wheeled Enigmas and there would be a greater choice of rotors to select from, usually kept in a neat wooden box with a hinged lid. Any U-boat captain being boarded by the enemy or captured would promptly instruct personnel to ensure that both the rotors and Enigma machine were sent to the bottom of the ocean. The rotors must never be captured, neither the code books, as it would give the Allies a distinct advantage to help break the Enigma ciphers. There are various tales of gallantry and heroism in wartime reports and citations involving Royal Navy personnel capturing U-boat Enigma wheel rotors and code books, and having them transported to Bletchley Park for analysis. They took extreme risks capturing enemy equipment under difficult circumstances at sea. Wheel rotors were seen as a prize for the Allies, even more than a captured Enigma machine without rotors.

One should not confuse the wheel rotors of the Enigma machine with those of the codebreaking Bombes. The former were rotors selected and inserted in the Enigma machine for encoding/decoding purposes and communication, the latter being much more complex drum rotors to emulate the Enigma, fitted by operators manually on a Bombe decoding machine developed and used by the Allies. A simple table here gives some information on the wheel rotors in different versions of the Enigma machine, and it is these that were the challenge for the Allies to analyse.

Rotor	Year	Model	Remarks
Rotor I	1930	Enigma I	
Rotor II	1930	Enigma I	
Rotor III	1930	Enigma I	
Rotor IV	December 1938	M3 Army	
Rotor V	December 1938	M3 Army	
Rotor VI	1939	M3 & M4 Naval	M4 used by U-boats in North Atlantic
Rotor VII	1939	M3 & M4 Naval	As above
Rotor VIII	1939	M3 & M4 Naval	As above

Note: Early Enigma rotors were introduced in 1924 as the IC, IIC, IIIC. A special Beta and a Gamma rotor were introduced in 1942.

Not all Enigma machines had the choice of eight wheel rotors. The more rotors available, the greater the quantity of permutations to set up the machine and the higher the security. The top of the machine had to be lifted up to insert the rotors before the lid was closed and the rotor settings were aligned and set up based on the code books available. Rotors were wired in a particular routing of the electrical wires, to help route the signal when a key was pressed on the Enigma keyboard. Bletchley Park needed to work out the wiring of each rotor wheel and the sequence of installation of the wheels. Electrical current is passed through the rotors, then around a reflector, then back out the rotors again. Just by moving, say, the right-hand rotor one single notch, the routing will change and the letter illuminated above the Enigma keyboard will also have changed. Within each rotor, the wiring is hard-wired to the contacts and that makes each rotor unique, due to the wiring diagram and connections. Rotors had turnover notch positions that would advance the next rotor to a particular letter when the key was pressed. These were built into the rotors, and later rotors had an advanced two turnover notches, to step the rotor positions. The nearest that could be compared to is an odometer in a car, which advances when 999 miles is exceeded to move the display to make 1,000, with the nine numerals moving to zero and the 1 appearing at the front of the numbers. That might appear to be fairly simple, Enigma rotors were much more sophisticated in comparison. On wheel rotor II, if the rotor steps from E to F, then the next rotor along is advanced. This process increases the security of the system by making it largely unpredictable, unless one understands that the turnover points are fixed for each rotor. See also Enigma.

Wire recorders

Before tape recorders were used, the military would occasionally make use of magnetic wire recorders, which could record sound on long spools of steel wire of a relatively thick gauge. These were certainly used by US Army Signals personnel to record the assembly of Bailey bridges, tank and truck movements and other sounds. This was part of the art of sonic deception. The sounds would be mixed together to create a part of an overall detailed and managed deception plan, with large horn speakers broadcasting the noise of military activity across considerable distances to confuse the enemy. The horn speakers were acoustically very efficient compared with traditional box enclosed speakers. The wire sometimes used to break and had to be re-joined so that it could pass smoothly over the magnetic recording head. Some of the wire spools could be over half a mile in length, but shorter lengths were used, too. Sometimes the spools were transcribed to a record disc, but these were generally too fragile to be used in the field. The wire recorder was a good compromise, although the valve tubes for the audio amplifiers and preamplifier were delicate and had to be protected from damage in a truck. Some wire recorders were used in wartime aircraft for recording cockpit conversations. They were relatively compact at the time.

The first commercial magnetic recorder was made available around 1903 in the USA. However, the first wire recorder was invented by a Danish engineer a few years before in 1898, under the name 'Telegraphone'. While wire recorders existed and were further developed after the war ended, magnetic tape recorders became the norm in the 1950s as these proved to be more reliable. The main improvement would be based upon the new magnetic tape technology, with oxides carefully applied to a flexible, thin, polyester base, which was put on spools to pass across the magnetic heads for recording and erasing. Tape would be used for speech as well as music post-war, and studio recordings would often use professional tape speeds of either 15 or 30in per second to maintain quality and reduce background noise. The magnetic nature of tape or wire would need the heads demagnetising with an electronic specialist demagnetising tool from time to time, to keep background noise and hiss low compared to the audio signal output. Early tape recorders, around 1948, were too expensive commercially for the general public, until technology was improved and mass production brought down costs. See also Deception.

Deception

This chapter is about the combination of deception techniques and codebreaking for the gathering and processing of enemy intelligence. There are, additionally, references made to more conventional forms of deception. While aspects of deception relevant to codebreaking have been mentioned previously in the other volumes of the glossary, this is an opportunity to bring certain aspects of deception together, with specific examples to illustrate them. Deception was used as a tool in warfare hundreds of years ago before codebreaking came into being. It was a way or method of confusing and tricking the enemy into taking physical military action they would not otherwise take. That could just be relocating to another position where they thought the enemy would be. The wooden horse of Troy is perhaps the best-known story, in which a wooden horse was presented as a gift to the enemy but actually concealed soldiers.

The art of deceiving the enemy has become far more sophisticated over time, applying a variety of different methods and techniques. The creation of a fictitious army on D-Day and the planting of a corpse in the sea off the Spanish coast with secret papers in a briefcase handcuffed to its wrist were both to mislead the enemy into believing an attack would come from a particular direction. The relevance of codebreaking and intelligence gathering to this is that it enables one to listen in to enemy conversations and orders of a strategic nature, decode them, and see if the deception tactics are being taken as bait. It is ironic that the advanced communication links were known as 'Fish', and yet the Allies would be preparing the bait for the fish to swallow hook, line, and sinker.

The amount of work that went into preparing a deception plan could be considerable. It involved advanced planning, identifying the particular and specific resources needed, the specialist equipment, trained staff, adding some factual information to make the story viable, and monitoring the whole event from a distance. With codebreaking, it is important to realise that as the war progressed there were different but parallel encoding and decoding systems in use, and both would be of importance. Tactical intelligence would generally come via Enigma, whereas strategic intelligence was far more likely to be intercepted via Lorenz and the Nazi secret writers, teleprinter attachments that encoded the messages, although it was not impossible for some strategic clues to come via Enigma. There were many more Enigma machines as compared to Lorenz, so more opportunity for the Allies to intercept Enigma messages and add two and two together. However,

US Ml-Enigma Analog five-rotor encoding machine, machine No 17 stamped 43. This used SIGABA rotors to determine Enigma messages after the message settings were identified. A Cryptanalytic device. Size 18″ X 8″ X 7″ high. (*Courtesy of National Cryptologic Museum, Maryland, USA*)

Above left: The four-wheel American Cryptologic Bombe, at the National Cryptologic Museum in Maryland, USA. This machine along with the others operated from Washington. (*Courtesy of National Cryptologic Museum, Maryland, USA*)

Above right: The commemorative plaque at St Edmunds Church in Northwood, London, referring to Wren *Cecilly Bruce Benjamin* who was formally in charge of Cipher Wrens from Scarborough, and travelling from Liverpool to Gibraltar via a merchant ship, had a large part of the convoy sunk by German U-boats, including the *SS Aguila*. The loss of the ship and occupants is commemorated in at least five separate locations across Britain, including the National Arboretum where a sculpture of a Wren bird is displayed to reflect the WRNS personnel lost in world war two. (*Ronald Koorm, with kind permission by the Vicar of St Edmunds Church, Pinner / Northwood*)

American four-wheel Bombe used for attacking Naval Enigma machine cipher messages to find the message settings. These were organised via US Naval Department OP-20-G and built at the NCR factory in Dayton, Ohio, by a team of specialist workers including female WAVES. (*Courtesy of National Cryptologic Museum, Maryland, USA*)

Previous page – lower image: Enigma codebreaking machines from a private collection. Note these are three-rotor machines with the indicators at the top for setting up the rotors. The illuminated lampboard is seen directly below the rotors, then the keys, and at the bottom is the plugboard or *steckerboard*, with cables to be plugged into the sockets to pair various letters. Not all models had plugboards and more advanced and secure Enigma's had four rotors, with the ability to choose four from a total of eight-wheel rotors to increase the permutations of the rotor settings. Each rotor was wired differently. (*Courtesy of Mr Damien Horn, Curator of Channel Islands Military Museum at St Ouens, Jersey, CI*)

Right: Enigma encoding machine-A12370 from a private collection. Flap for rotor wheels can be seen to top of the machine with indicator panels. (*Courtesy of Mr Damien Horn, Curator of Channel Islands Military Museum at St Ouens, Jersey, CI*)

Colossus Original Component made into a formal presentation in 1986 from The Director of GCHQ to The Director of the NSA for the 40th Anniversary of signing the UKUSA agreement in 1946. (*Courtesy of The National Cryptologic Museum, Maryland USA*)

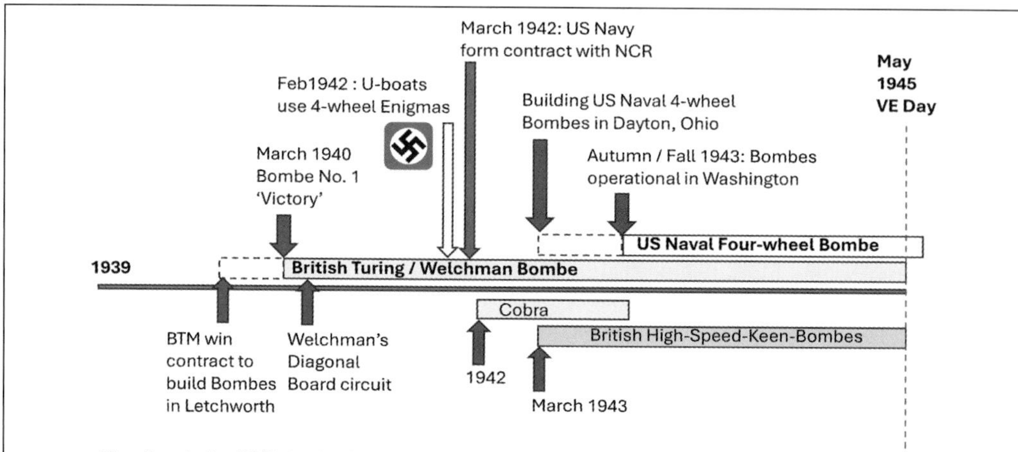

Timeline during WW2 for the Attack on Nazi Enigma encoding machines showing how four-wheel Enigma's affected allied codebreaking machines

The diagram illustrates a simple timeline of WW2 and the development of British and American Bombe codebreaking machines to tackle the Nazi Enigma. When Admiral Doenitz decided to use four-wheel Enigma's for his U-Boat fleet, the number of permutations increased dramatically for the Enigma settings and this caused a problem for the allies. Various solutions were tried and the Americans built their own version of the Bombe with improvements. (*Copyright ©2024- Ronald Koorm*)

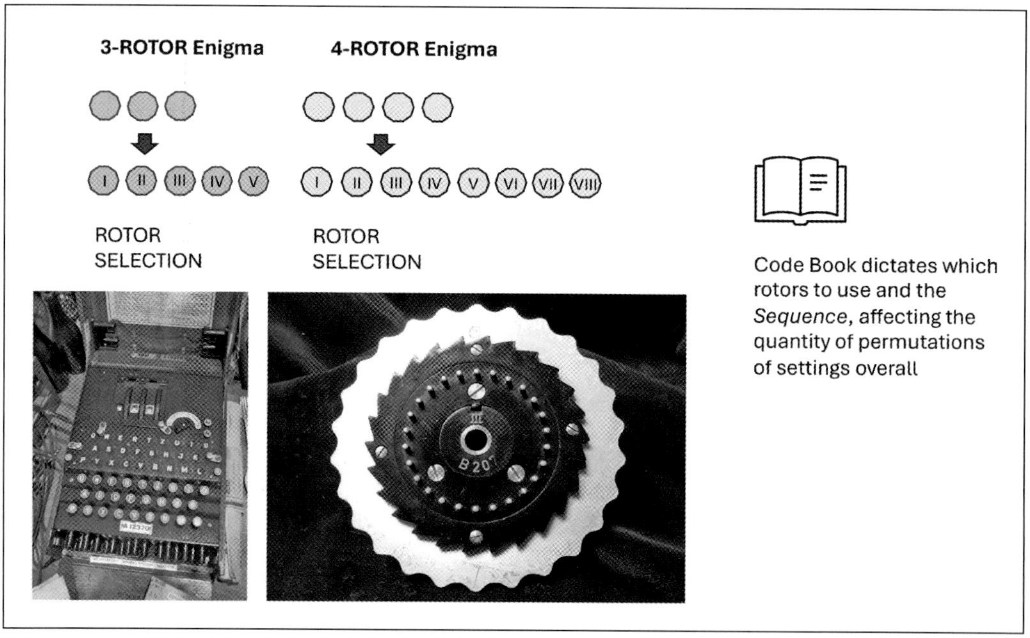

Illustration of Differences between 3-wheel and 4-wheel Enigma's and selection or wheel rotors for setting up the machines. Note the rotor shown is marked as rotor III. Each rotor would be wired differently, presenting a different route to the signal and wiring circuit when the key was pressed on the Enigma. (*Copyright ©2024- Ronald Koorm Photos courtesy of Mr Damien Horn (Enigma) and National Cryptologic Museum (Rotor wheel)*)

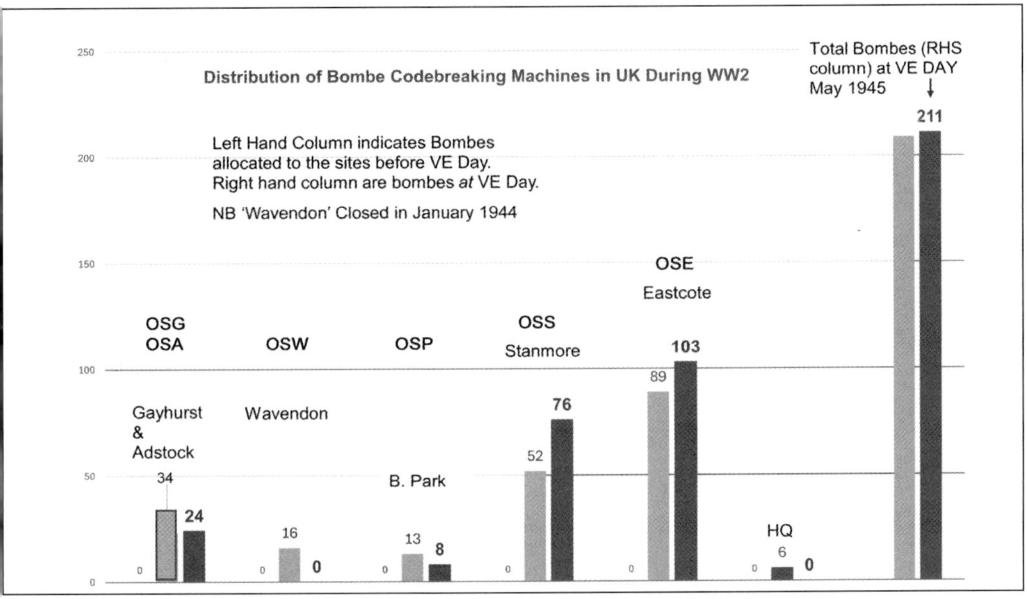

Bombe distribution chart illustrating the spread and allocation of UK codebreaking machines across Bletchley Park and the outstations during WW2. Some machines were transferred from the country house outstations to the newer, larger outstations at Stanmore and Eastcote as the war progressed. Data source from The Official Bombe Registers. (*Chart diagram – © Copyright 2025 Ronald Koorm*)

Colossus at Bletchley Park operated by Wrens (WRNS), to tackle the advanced Nazi Encoding machines such as Lorenz and Secret Writers. Note punched paper tape on pulley wheels read by optical sensor. (*Copyright © GCHQ, By Kind Permission of the Director of GCHQ*)

Outstation Stanmore after the war ended. Inset photo- Wrens in front of huts at Stanmore. The second largest codebreaking outstation during the war, and designated O.S.E. It would have many Bombe codebreaking machines transferred to it from the country house outstations. (*Creative Commons*)

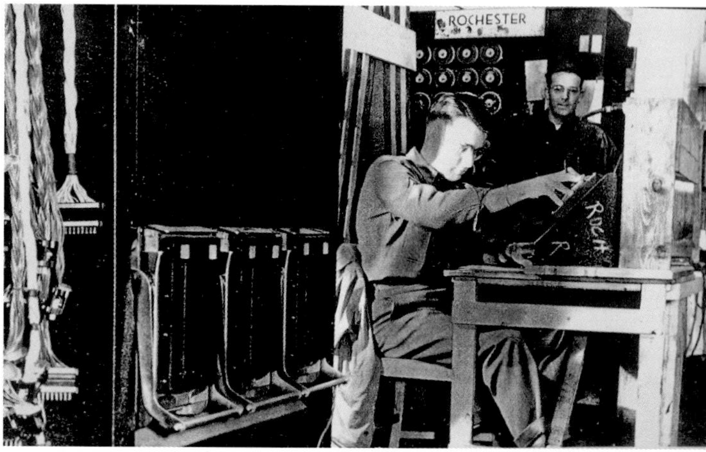

Above left: German *Schlusselgerat* 41Z encoding machine, used by the Abwehr and nicknamed *Hitlermuhle* (Hitler Mill). (*Courtesy of National Cryptologic Museum, Maryland, USA*)

Above right: 6812th US Signals Engineers working on a checking machine at Outstation Eastcote, Middlesex, England, in a Bombe room. The machine at the back, ROCHESTER, was one of ten Bombe codebreaking machines that were under the control of the American engineers, to crack Enigma message settings. (*Courtesy of National Cryptologic Museum, Maryland, USA*)

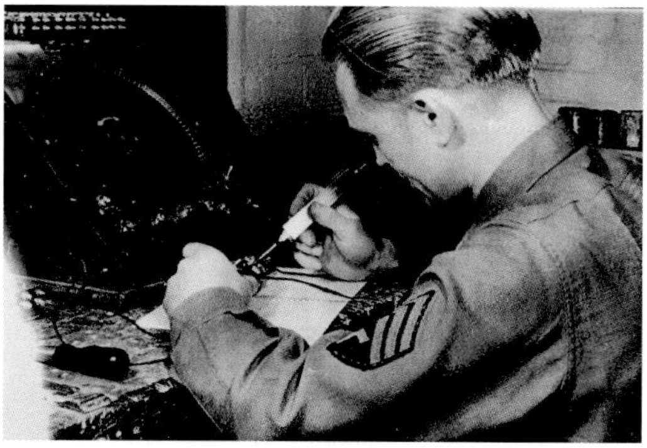

Above left: US Signals Engineer testing and repairing components at Outstation Eastcote. The engineers were encamped in Ruislip Woods for a time. (*Courtesy of National Cryptologic Museum, Maryland, USA*)

Above right: General Rommel greeting allied Italian officers and soldiers. (Supplied by courtesy of Mr E.W. Pearce, Royal Engineers)

Left: German soldiers operating Enigma and writing down the encoded letters for morse-code transmission. (*Courtesy of National Cryptologic Museum, Maryland, USA*)

Ultra intelligence memo referring to J.I.C., SHAEF, and the First US Army Group in January 1944 outlining the communication protocol for special intelligence from 'Station X' i.e. Bletchley Park, known also as GC&CS. (*Photo taken by author and is Courtesy of the National Archives*)

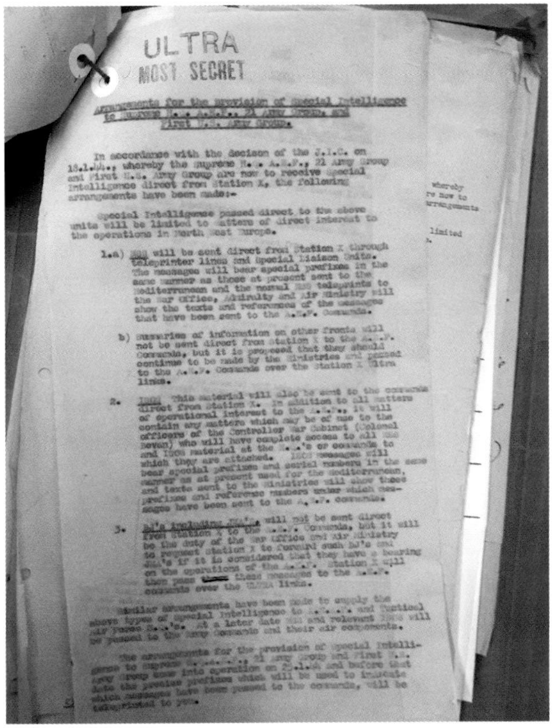
ULTRA
MOST SECRET

Arrangements for the provision of Special Intelligence to Supreme H.Q. A.E.F., 21 Army Group, and First U.S. Army Group.

In accordance with the decision of the J.I.C. on 18.1.44., whereby the Supreme H.Q. A.E.F., 21 Army Group and First U.S. Army Group are now to receive Special Intelligence direct from Station X, the following arrangements have been made:-

Special Intelligence passed direct to the above units will be limited to matters of direct interest to the operations in North West Europe.

1.a) [illegible] will be sent direct from Station X through teleprinter lines and Special Liaison Units. The messages will bear special prefixes in the same manner as those at present sent to the Mediterranean and the normal [illegible] teleprints to the War Office, Admiralty and Air Ministry will show the texts and references of the messages that have been sent to the A.E.F. Commands.

b) Summaries of information on other fronts will not be sent direct from Station X to the A.E.F. Commands, but it is proposed that they should continue to be made by the Ministries and passed to the A.E.F. Commands over the Station X Ultra links.

2. [illegible] This material will also be sent to the commands direct from Station X. In addition to all matters of operational interest to the A.E.F., it will contain any matters which may be of use to the officers of the Controller War Cabinet (Colonel Bevan) who will have complete access to all [illegible] and [illegible] material at the [illegible] or commands to which they are attached. [illegible] messages will bear special prefixes and serial numbers in the same manner as at present used for the Mediterranean, and texts sent to the Ministries will show these prefixes and reference numbers under which messages have been sent to the A.E.F. commands.

3. [illegible] will not be sent direct from Station X to the A.E.F. Commands, but it will be the duty of the War Office and Air Ministry to request Station X to forward such [illegible] if it is considered that they have a bearing on the operations of the A.E.F. Station X will then pass these messages to the A.E.F. commands over the ULTRA links.

Similar arrangements have been made to supply the above types of Special Intelligence to [illegible] and Tactical Air Force [illegible]. At a later date [illegible] and relevant [illegible] will be passed to the Army Commands and their air components.

The arrangements for the provision of Special Intelligence to Supreme [illegible], 21 Army Group and First U.S. Army Group came into operation on 2[illegible].1.44 and before that date the precise prefixes which will be used to indicate which messages have been passed to the commands, will be teleprinted to you.

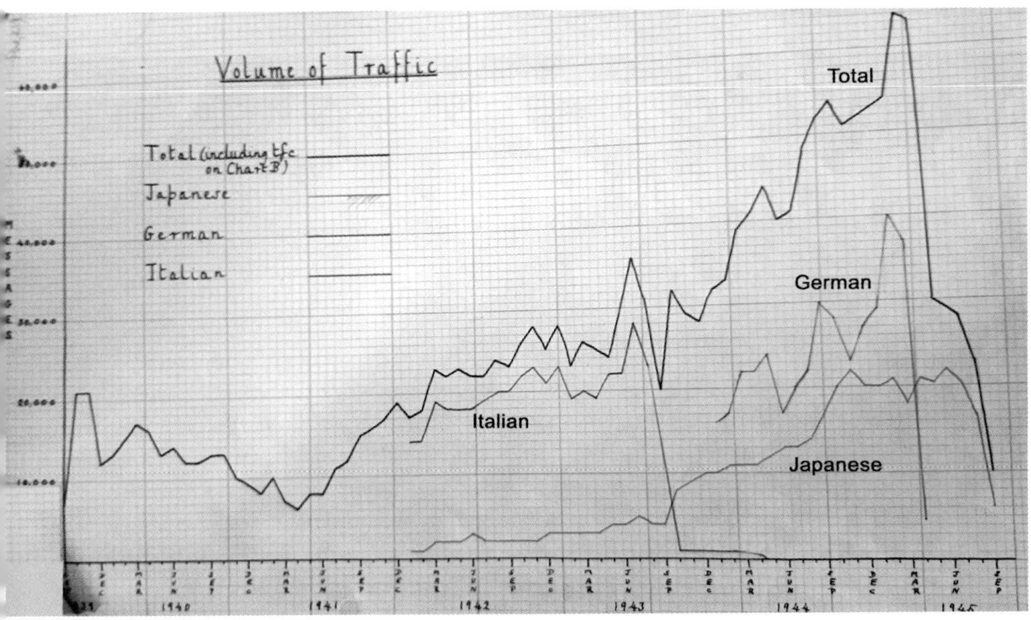

Graph of enemy intelligence traffic gathered by listening stations over time, with dates at the bottom and volume of messages intercepted to the vertical column. It is thought this information was related to *Flowerdown* Listening Y-station for at least part of the intercepts, splitting the Italian, Japanese, and German intercepts as shown. Note the increase in traffic intercepted as the war progressed. (*Picture part-annotated / taken by Ronald Koorm, and courtesy of The National Archives*)

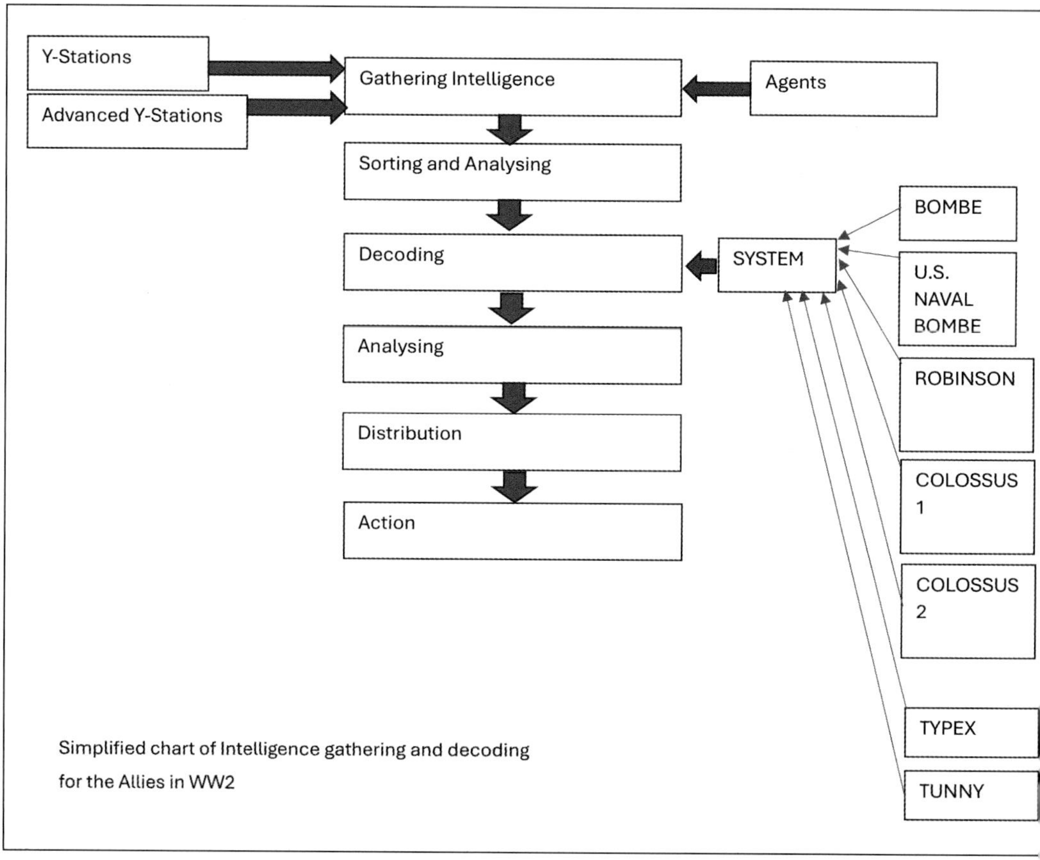

Simplified chart of Intelligence gathering and decoding for the Allies in WW2

This chart outlines the range of tools that could be used to process and decode enemy messages either based on the Enigma machine or the more advanced Lorenz S40 / S42 machines and Nazi secret writers. Some may have assumed that the output of codebreaking machines would be the deciphered message itself, but that was often not the case. 'Message settings' remained the key. Manual codebreaking would also play a part in the process, either using cribs, menus, or similar, or work in the *Testery* at Bletchley Park following use of the Robinson or Colossus codebreaking machines. (*Diagram copyright of the author, Ronald Koorm*) when 'Fish' or 'Tunny' intercepts came through to Bletchley Park via the specialist Y-stations, the codebreaker recipients knew that the information could be of major strategic importance and value. This was because some of the messages were sent on behalf of Hitler to senior military officers, including generals and field marshals. The Allied prize would be to deceive the Nazi leadership, and perhaps even shorten the war. Evidence of deception and trickery gave a degree of comfort to the Allies when planning operations.

The processing of decrypted messages did introduce much trivia, or less interesting intelligence. This was inevitable in wartime. It is the equivalent of a newspaper journalist waiting for a groundbreaking news story, which comes into his lap only rarely in practice. There are lots of minor stories and events, but the one that sells newspapers in large volumes is the unusual event: a major plane crash, a multi-million-pound bank robbery, or perhaps a senior member of the government exposed as a spy and a traitor. The codebreakers and intel traffic analysts are looking out for 'orders of battle' and instructions from the top, which the Allied commanders could benefit from to save lives and use resources more efficiently. If there is some confusion in the ranks of the enemy because of a trick or deception tactic applied by the Allies, then that is a positive result. But we need to establish to which degree that deception has caused orders to be changed at the top to really gauge the impact, and that is not always easy to achieve. There are many different examples of using deception during the Second World War and post-war to deceive the enemy. A few of these are listed below and they are discussed in some detail here:

- Operation Torch
- Operation Mincemeat
- Fortitude North
- FUSAG/Fortitude South
- D-Day
- Pearl Harbor
- Midway, Pacific Ocean
- Barbarossa
- Use of Window against the enemy
- Eavesdropping on prisoners of war
- Distortion of *Knickebein* radio navigation beams
- Battle of Matapan
- A mysterious convoy
- Berlin – Tapping into Russian military telephone lines post-war

Operation Torch

These were the Allied landings across North Africa to surprise Rommel's forces. They began on 8 November 1942, and the resulting fighting was largely between 8 and 16 November. In response, the Nazis sent troops across from Sicily to Tunisia.

The Allied assault was in three sectors: West, Centre, and East. General George Patton landed in Morocco as the Western Task Force, General Lloyd Fendenhall in Algeria as the Centre Task Force, and General Charles Ryder as the Eastern Task Force. A Polish intelligence unit collected military intelligence on North Africa from 1941, and this was useful to the planning of the invasion. This organisation operated Agency Africa, and was organised by Major General Rygor Slowikowski. Torch became the first combined Anglo-American attack using seaborne troops. The Nazis reacted speedily when the landings occurred. Before the Allied landings in Tunisia there were around 11,000 Axis troops present, but within six weeks of the landings there were some 47,000. The battle would be bloody and protracted but Tunisia eventually fell on 13 May 1943. There are reports that the Axis powers suffered five times the Allied quantity of casualties.

Deception tactics were used, with reports of troop convoys tasked for the Mediterranean from the Clyde, in Scotland, sent via double agent Garbo, known to the Nazis as *Arabel*. The information, sent by air mail, intentionally arrived too late to be of any military use, but the Germans were pleased with Arabel's apparent attempt to inform them of the troop movements. This was all about building the Germans' trust in their agent to increase the chance of success of future deceptions.

Operation Mincemeat

A daring deception by the British based upon a submarine placing a body in military uniform in the sea off the coast of Spain to be found by locals and hopefully investigated by the Nazis. In a locked briefcase on the body, attached to the man's wrist, would be maps and key secret documents that would indicate that the Allies would attack in the Mediterranean in Greece and Sardinia, whereas this was a trick to deceive the enemy to locate their resources away from the true point of attack in Sicily. Operation Mincemeat would be part of the wider deception in the Mediterranean under Operation Barclay. The plan to use the body was largely devised by Captain Ewen Montagu RNR. Churchill approved it and advised that General Eisenhower should be informed.

The body was of a man with no living relatives, and he unwittingly played an important role in the deception. He had been a homeless labourer who had died suddenly from ingesting rat poison. The deceased would be difficult to trace, and there was little possibility that anyone would come looking for him in England; a perfect scenario for the deception team. He was given the created identity of William Martin, a major in the Royal Marines, with false papers.

Various items were placed in his pockets, including personal things such as ticket stubs, love letters, photos of a girlfriend, and a receipt for an engagement ring, to make him appear to be credible. When the corpse was picked up by a fisherman, the Spanish government shared these documents with the *Abwehr*. The Nazis at senior level fell for the trick, although it took some time before his body was eventually moved to Berlin for detailed examination following an initial autopsy in Spain. Not all the German officers involved were convinced, but they were overruled by more senior staff. The invasion of Sicily was a significant success in July 1943, and surprised the Nazis. Two separate feature films were made about Operation Mincemeat, one being released in 2022. The original film was *The Man Who Never Was*, released in 1956 in monochrome. It is quite incredible that the enemy fell for the deception trick, which took considerable resources in planning and organisation.

Fortitude North

The Allies tied down Nazi troops in occupied Norway by creating an illusion to convince them that they would be mounting an assault, and therefore the coastal defences needed reinforcing and adequate resources. The Allies had no intention of mounting such an attack, preferring to concentrate on the invasion of France on D-Day. However, they wanted to improve the chance of success by keeping the Nazi forces in Norway from being transported to France. Radio transmissions would help convince the occupation forces that a build-up of men, equipment and supplies was already occurring in Scotland, ready to cross the North Sea at any time. A plan was established known as Operation Skye to provide radio transmissions based upon deception and this was operational by 6 April 1944. In spring 1944, there were Allied attacks on industrial infrastructure in Norway and increased naval activity in the area, giving the impression of preparatory work prior to an invasion. Hitler would have been informed of this activity, and had no intention of allowing the Allies access to Norway, where materials and resources were supplying the Third Reich. A captured Nazi map of the United Kingdom after the war showed Allied divisions in Scotland that were part of Fortitude North. This confirmed that the Germans were convinced there would be an assault on western Norway and that they had to maintain a robust defence.

FUSAG/Fortitude South

The First US Army Group, or FUSAG, was a brilliant idea, in 1944, to convince the enemy that a large army force was in south-east England waiting to cross the Channel near the Pas-de-Calais. However, it took enormous efforts and organisation by a number of different organisations and a foreign double agent to make it happen. Some Nazi generals would be less convinced, but the stubborn character of Hitler meant that advice from many of his senior generals was swept aside. A more well-balanced commander and leader may have acted more cautiously. While some detail of this is contained in the author's earlier volumes in the Glossary, we set out some of the key points here also.

The establishment of FUSAG was approved by Eisenhower. Anything that could buy the Allies time at D-Day was worth a gamble. Tying the Nazis down by keeping the Panzer divisions awaiting an attack in northern France would be extremely valuable. Making the deception work required a great deal of planning and resources; including the provision of numerous false radio transmissions, inflatable tanks and lorries, mock-up inflatable landing craft, and misleading shoulder flashes on American uniforms. In addition, close monitoring of the Nazi response via double agents and 'Ultra' intelligence, using both Y-stations and Bletchley Park, would be needed.

A significant part of the deception under Fortitude South came from the double agent Juan Pujol Garcia, code name Garbo. Pujol Garcia was a Catalan who hated the Nazis and had built up contacts in Portugal, feeding information to them to gain their trust. When he eventually came to Britain, MI5 was not impressed, but he persevered and over time the British realised he had important links back to the enemy that could then be exploited if he was handled carefully. He had taken risks while in Portugal, buying shipping publications and basing his reports to the Nazis on the movement of Allied shipping purely on what he read in them. Fortunately, he was not found out. Sending numerous messages to Portugal and Madrid from a residential house in Hendon, north London, he built up a rapport with his Nazi contact, and was able to feed him a mixture of facts and lies. Part of this was the existence of FUSAG, the First US Army Group, based in southern England and commanded by General Patton. Garbo's work became more significant as D-Day approached and even in the days following D-Day, convincing the Germans that the main force would come any day soon, and to be ready for the attack in northern-western France. Garbo then disappeared to Venezuela, fearing for his life if the Nazis realised he had been leading them on a merry dance of deception on behalf of the Allies.

Pujol Garcia had been awarded the Iron Cross by Hitler for his services to the Third Reich, evidence of how much he was valued and believed by the enemy. He was also given an MBE by Britain after the war had ended. He was an extraordinary character, who probably gave his MI5 handler a heart attack when he sent a bold message to the Nazis criticising them strongly for not responding quickly when his message warning about D-Day was sent in the early hours of the morning of 6 June 1944. Garbo had received special authority from Eisenhower to send it, a measure of how much he had become trusted by the Supreme Allied Commander. Pujol Garcia became probably the most successful double agent in history, and certainly in the Second World War.

D-Day

While the deception for D-Day revolved largely around Operation Bodyguard and Fortitude South, a range of misleading Allied reports were circulated that were planned to fool the Nazis about when and where it would take place. The Germans were fully aware that the Allies would open a front in France at some stage, so this is principally why the reinforced Atlantic Wall was established, taking years to construct and plan. The problem with the Atlantic Wall concept was that there would always be relative weak points in the continuous defence system. Rommel was aware of this, as was Field Marshal von Rundstedt. There were constant inspections to identify weak points and shore up defences to plug the gaps. A chain is only as strong as the weakest link. The intelligence gathering system for the Allies was particularly interested in the Normandy area but obtaining information had to be carried out in such a way that it would not give the game away to the Germans that Normandy was a priority. Therefore, a series of bombing and other raids would occur at various locations in France, and particularly around the north-west coast of France near Calais. This would pass for softening of the German defences prior to an invasion of some force.

The use of the weather in June 1944 proved to be almost accidentally fortuitous for the Allies. The summer weather in the Atlantic was very changeable and unpredictable. Storms and rough seas would be a barrier to a large invasion force, and the Germans knew this. They monitored the weather reports as much as the Allies did. A coastal station on the west coast of Ireland sent in advance weather reports, as the weather came in off the Atlantic. The deferment of D-Day from 5 June to 6 June would catch the enemy unawares. Rommel was convinced the weather was so poor that no real threat from the Allies would be forthcoming at the time, and it would be an opportunity for him to go to Berlin to meet Hitler, as well as purchase shoes for his wife's birthday.

The decision by Eisenhower was touch and go, but on reflection he made the correct one, based upon data and reports from his meteorological advisers. There was a small break in the weather, and an opportunity to get across to Normandy before it deteriorated again. For days, men were waiting patiently in their landing craft, support ships, and vessels, not knowing when the signal to go would occur. Many would be seasick, even in harbour. They could see how rough the weather was. The Supreme Allied Commander knew if he made the wrong decision, the impact of the poor weather at sea could result in significant losses to craft and personnel, which could result in failure. Taking the decision to go on the morning of 6 June 1944 was a brave one, albeit with a high degree of risk to the operation. It caught the enemy by complete surprise. How could the Allies have risked their ships and personnel at a time when the weather was so unpredictable? Rommel would rush back from Berlin to take charge. Hitler assumed that it would be straightforward to drive the Allies back into the sea at Normandy. However, by the time the Panzers were organised in the area, the Allies had established a substantial bridgehead, with the Canadians making the most initial progress. This would be the beginning of the end for the Nazis and Hitler. The actual personnel losses at D-Day amounted to around one quarter of what had been predicted, which was of much relief to the generals, to Churchill, and Roosevelt. However, the penetration of the assault landings would be hard fought and bloody. The intelligence from the landings would be fed back to the military leaders and to Churchill and to Roosevelt. There was a sense of relief when all the sections of the assault were moving inland. The supply operation to reinforce them would be huge and continue for months.

Pearl Harbor

We have mentioned Pearl Harbor in some detail in other parts of this book, so will concentrate here on the surprise of the attack on 7 December 1941 and whether or not it was intended to be a deception on the part of the Japanese. The diplomatic service had been sending messages between embassies and Tokyo in a number of encoded parts. The Americans had been intercepting these and knew something was going to happen, but when and where was inconclusive. Admiral Yamamoto said his information was that the attack on Hawaii at Pearl Harbor would come around fifty minutes prior to the Japanese delivering their ultimatum to the Americans through official channels. He understood this would be seen by the Americans as a slap in the face, and gave them no chance to be on alert for military action. The US had only broken Japanese diplomatic codes, and not Navy codes.

While there was the intention for the Japanese ultimatum to be served officially on America at 1pm Eastern Standard time, this was actually delivered twenty minutes after the attack occurred in Hawaii, where it was morning on Sunday, 7 December. The poor communication at the time through official channels via the US security services and the American Navy added to the calamity and confusion. When intercepted messages indicated the Navy should be on alert at all bases, telegrams were sent instead of using the radio, and these were sent commercially with no degree of urgency. Add this to the fact that a radar base report of a large number of mysterious planes approaching the island early on Sunday morning was dismissed as false by an American officer, who took no action. The official declaration of war on the USA was some seven and a half hours after the attack. In any military conflict, surprise is the tool that an enemy will use effectively on another party to inflict severe damage and weaken them. This is true of Hitler moving into Poland, and into Russia, later. It is a form of deception, and Stalin could not believe what Hitler had done once Operation Barbarossa had commenced. One can state that the action by the Japanese Navy was carefully planned and a strategic blow against the Americans that crippled the Navy for a time. However, no American Aircraft carriers or submarines were attacked, and these were used effectively to attack the enemy in months to come. Furthermore, the fuel depot and repair facilities at Pearl Harbor had not been seriously damaged or attacked, and were back in action soon after.

Battle of Midway, Pacific Ocean

Ever since the attack on Pearl Harbor, the US Navy had been trying to gain control over the Japanese Imperial Naval code, and with a mighty blow. American intelligence officers were aware of the Japanese using their own encryption equivalent of Enigma, nicknamed 'Purple'. The Japanese Operational code JN-25 was cracked by the intelligence services on a regular basis.

The Japanese Operational Naval code JN-25 was complex and involved syllabic writing or 'Kana'. Latin letters were used in a substitution to make sending it practically possible. A five-digit code number in a message was modified by adding a different five-digit number from a cipher table, and that had around 100,000 permutations and combinations. The sender would transmit those messages with a numerical key, which would then indicate the location and position of the cipher numbers from a table. An American naval intelligence unit, Hypo (Project Hypo), was established based at Pearl Harbor with Captain Joseph Rochefort in charge and including a crypto analyst, Elvin Urquhart, to assist in the codebreaking team. They worked night and day on the Japanese codes, using some trial and error to guess the word for 'ship', and other military words of interest. Another significant codebreaker was Commander Thomas H. Dyer, who was brought in to work alongside Rochefort.

A mistake by the Japanese meant they delayed changing their codes on 1 May 1942, which gave the codebreakers an opportunity to read some messages. These established that a major invasion was planned by the enemy at location 'AF', which the Americans had identified as Midway. To confirm this, a false message was then broadcast to Pearl Harbor from Midway Island to state that they were running low on fresh water, which was not actually the case, but a deception, looking for a response. The Japanese then transmitted a coded message reporting this and inserted the letters 'AF', which enabled the Americans to confirm it was their code for Midway Island. The Project Hypo team managed to read around one third of the JN-25 code by April 1942 and with perseverance broke into more enemy messages over the next few weeks. They eventually established the intentions of the Japanese, indicating that Midway was planned for attack, and even the date and time. The intelligence gained allowed Admiral Nimitz to take a calculated risk and position his aircraft carriers 300 miles north of Midway Island, setting a trap for the Imperial Japanese Navy.

The trap would be set to attack the Japanese when they were close to Midway, but the input of spotter planes was crucial in identifying the exact location of the Japanese fleet. While Midway island was attacked heavily by Japanese planes, they managed to resist the force, and maintained occupation of the island long enough for the American fleet to attack Yamamoto's carriers and battleships, which caught them completely by surprise. The use of codebreaking in the build up to the event was a key factor in favour of the Americans. The main Battle of Midway took place between 4 and 7 June, with overall success for the US Navy and its air support operations. (See Pearl Harbor).

Barbarossa

Adolf Hitler had previously made peace agreements with Russia before the war, non-aggression pacts in exchange for flexibility in acquiring land in adjacent countries.[1] Stalin was convinced that Germany was no longer a threat to the Russian people.

How wrong he was. Not content with invading Poland, France, Belgium, Holland, and other countries, Hitler had his eye on invading Russia, but needed the timing to be right to fit in his plans. Hitler hated the Bolsheviks, hated communism, and saw the Russian people as an underclass who needed to be eliminated. Russia was home to many Jewish people, and their extermination was an added incentive to invade. Hitler instructed his senior officers to show no mercy. The prime objective would be to obtain more living space, *Lebensraum*, for the German people.

Vyacheslav Molotov, who became effectively Stalin's number two, had information from agents that Germany was planning to invade Russia, but Stalin would hear none of it. He could not conceive that Hitler would invade, and rebuffed Molotov, telling him he had no proof. Hitler understood how Stalin worked and used this to his advantage by spreading rumours and false information indicating that other nations were the real enemy of Russia, and that Germany was on his side. This was done in a combination of ways, using the press, radio, meetings, agents, and other means.

When Hitler felt the time was right for the attack, he assembled his generals and gave them clear instructions. The aim would be to attack in three forces: Army Group North, Army Group Centre, and Army Group South. The centre group would go for Moscow. Hitler's challenge initially was to put his armies on his side of the border with Russia, and yet not raise alarm. This was achieved by informing Stalin, Molotov, and others that this was a training exercise and that Hitler's real intentions was an invasion of Britain in the west, where many German forces were assembling. Molotov had clear reservations about this information and approached Stalin to convince him that invasion was imminent and he must now act and prepare for war with Germany.

However, Stalin was a stubborn character and once again dismissed Molotov. He could not conceive that Hitler would attack his country. To do so would go against the non-aggression pact the two countries had signed, and it would not make sense in his eyes as he knew Hitler was serious about Operation Sea Lion, the invasion of Britain. It surely would be inconceivable to attack two countries on different fronts simultaneously? Stalin was in self-denial about the horror that war could bring to the Russian people. Hitler's deception to spread rumours and doubt, and support the notion that it was other nations who were the real threat, was working.

If we move forward to late February 2022, Russian forces in Belarus on the border with Ukraine were also supposed to be carrying out a 'training exercise'. This was nothing more than a ploy to put off the adjoining NATO countries and Ukraine, but few, if any, were convinced this was anything other than an impending attack. The only intelligence gap was in trying to ascertain the date that the invasion would begin, and the scale of it. World leaders met President Putin to plead with him not to commence an attack on Ukraine, which would have devastating consequences. Putin, of course, ignored all of them.

In 2022, the world had excellent communications, social media, instant news coverage, computers, smartphones, military satellites, and advanced intelligence.

In the Second World War they had none of this, which was to Hitler's advantage. Communications were spasmodic and unreliable at times, and it could take many hours or even days for crucial information to get back to central command if an incursion occurred.

Operation Barbarossa started on Sunday, 22 June 1941, with Germany invading Russia with millions of men, thousands of trucks, tanks, support vehicles.

This table lists some of the quantities of various equipment used in the campaign:

Item	Quantity German Lead Troops*	Quantity Russian
Soldiers	4,136,000	3,300,000
Reservists	Unconfirmed	500,000
Aircraft	4,006	10,775
Tanks	4,919	15,470
Trucks/vehicles	629,200	173,000
Field Guns	45,096	58,000
Anti-Aircraft Guns	4,496	5,833
Horses	680,000	700,000

* Including Finnish, Hungarian, Italian, Romanian, and Slovak troops.[2] The Germans would have nineteen Panzer divisions for the assault, and overall around 150 Army divisions.

The quick progress in penetrating western Russia delighted Hitler and his generals, with little resistance to their forces. When Stalin was informed of the invasion, he could not believe it and became temporarily impotent in issuing orders and directing his team. It would be his colleague, Molotov, that would take over temporarily and then convince Stalin he had to take the reins of leadership again, to act constructively against the enemy using his generals, and to regain the trust of the Russian people.

Whilst Hitler's invasion of Russia was ultimately a catastrophic move, and arguably led to the downfall of the Third Reich with loss of millions of men women and children, the build-up to the invasion was seen as a complete success by Germany's leader. Hitler's key generals, Commander in Chief Walther von Brauchitsch and Army General staff Chief Franz Halder, who planned Barbarossa with Hitler, were wary of the invasion, but when they reported the progress of penetration into Soviet territory, all were convinced that everything was going according to plan. However, plans have a habit of falling apart if they have not been thoroughly and completely evaluated, setting out the risks and the opportunities in a pragmatic way. Hitler only saw success, and failure was not an option in his mind. Millions of German troops would later die in the cold Russian winter, where they lacked winter clothing even though this was requested by the generals in good time.

Russian losses were huge in Barbarossa, with more than 10,000 aircraft and 12,000 tanks destroyed, and more than 2 million prisoners captured.[3] The Soviet Union suffered greater losses than any other country in the war, a staggering 27,917,000 people, which was a combination of both military personnel and civilians.

Window and use against the enemy

Window or chaff were long strips of metal aluminium foil arranged to trigger enemy radar screens on certain selected frequencies and cause confusion for the enemy. Both sides knew of this system, but it was Britain and its allies who would use it on a large scale, dropping mass quantities of foil strips over the Channel, France, and the occupied countries as bombers approached on their runs. Window was the invention of Joan Curran and Dr R.V. Jones, with initial development at the Telecommunications Research Establishment (TRE) in Malvern. That site was the largest research engineering factory in Europe during the war, and was visited by the King and Queen, but without disclosing the location to the public for reasons of security.[4] It would take until the early part of 1942 to perfect this radar-jamming tool. The strips were 250mm long and 25mm or 50mm wide. These dimensions were calculated by physicists to have the maximum effect on the enemy radar reflections.

Dropping large amounts of foil at the appropriate time could deceive the enemy radar operators that large convoys were approaching the shores of France, or that massive air forces were overwhelming the skies, with little or no information about the true direction or numbers involved. Some German radio-based equipment was found to be immune to Window, and it was Dr Jones' job to identify which types of radar or radio systems were unaffected, when they were used, and how to possibly and practically overcome them. Tests were carried out in early 1942. In July 1943, 40 tons of Window, around 93 million foil strips, were dropped against the enemy. An enemy radar operator would have been both confused and flustered, trying to make sense of his or her radar screen, and trying to contact other nearby radar stations to compare notes.

The relevance to codebreaking here is that Enigma Morse code transmissions were sent between sectors and divisions to warn of impending attacks, and the Allies needed to understand from high-level Ultra German intelligence to what degree the radar deception was effective and how it impacted upon the organisation of enemy resources. One of the negative aspects of using Window from bombers was that it was possible for the enemy to home in on the bomber dropping it, with fighters carrying modified, appropriate receivers.

The principle of Window is based on resonance, and the length of strip or wire cut to a length of half the wavelength used by the enemy radar station. The strips resonate and re-radiate the radio waves, causing mass confusion on the radar display. The foil strips were 10in long, about 250mm. As they would fall from a great height and be relatively light, the effect on radar screens would last for many minutes, possibly half an hour or even longer. Wind speed and atmospherics would affect the fall rate of the foil and its distribution. If the bomber release of foil strips was staggered, there could be hours of radar disruption for the enemy. By summer 1943 Window was approved to be used on a relatively large scale against the enemy. To arrive at this decision, it had taken many months of reports, arguments, and counter-arguments between technical people, military officers, and even politicians.

The use of Window during D-Day and the period around D-Day was significant in that Allied planes would fly specific patterns across the Channel dropping the foil strips en masse, and allowing planes behind them to take over, so there would be a virtually continuous dropping. The consequence of this is that the enemy radar operators were convinced there was a large amount of shipping and aircraft in the Channel approaching France, their screens displaying a confusing mass of noise. Some observers thought that if the Nazis had used Window themselves, it would have resulted in the reduction of Allied night-fighter defences against Luftwaffe attacks. Window was a well-organised deception technique, but eventually its effectiveness reduced over time. See also Radar.

Eavesdropping on prisoners of war

Eavesdropping was carried out by all the major participants in the war, from prisoners of war camps to Gestapo cells between interrogations. But sometimes the process was relatively scientific, involving numerous hidden microphones, recorders, and banks of human listeners translating German into English and taking copious notes in remote rooms. Various degrees of success were obtained, but the Allies used eavesdropping on German officers in England to obtain effective and promising results. Tests were carried out during the war at the Tower of London, where selected prisoners were held. Locations such as Trent Park, Latimer House, Wilton Park Estate, and Farm Hall near Cambridge were used for eavesdropping on senior prisoners of war, including some generals. Some captured scientists were also recorded secretly. At Trent Park, secret microphones were hidden in light fittings, furniture, walls, ceilings, billiard tables, and plant pots, and wired back to a remote room where the monitoring listeners and recorders were set up, often in a basement a good distance away from the recorded rooms. No wireless technology was around at the time so everything had to be wired, and those wires concealed in the room to be bugged. Portable disc recorders were also used, and possibly some wire recorders, which preceded tape recorders. Reports indicate that fifteen RCA 88A pressure microphones were used. Disc recorders used 12in, double-sided, acetate-coated metal discs, and some of the equipment came from the USA. Both the BBC and the Post Office Engineering Research Station were involved in organising the technology, wiring, testing of microphones and recorders. American equipment came via the Lend-Lease American agreement, which became so crucial during wartime.

The 'M' rooms stood for 'miked rooms', those with hidden and concealed microphones. One incident recorded and transcribed indicated that a Luftwaffe pilot was awaiting orders in Germany and had some free time, so he was invited to join a colleague in shooting some Jewish men near a mass grave. They then shot several Jews in cold blood, as though it was some type of killing sport. The majority of transcripts of conversations processed were not as horrendous as this account, thankfully.

The organiser of the operation, T. Kendrick, used displaced personnel from occupied countries and refugees who spoke good German to eavesdrop. Some were Jewish, and they had to listen to discussions of the methods of torture and mass murder of Jews by German officers, a difficult scenario for anyone in that situation. One wonders what long-term effect listening to such horrors on headphones for hours upon hours had on their mental health? Kendrick had previously managed to help many thousands of Jews escape extermination from Austria. He was effectively another Schindler, helping people to escape and risking his own life, but he was not really recognised for his brave and selfless actions in history.

The output resulted in around 100,000 detailed transcripts of recordings. Some implicated the Nazi officers and military men who were eavesdropped on in serious crimes against humanity, but none were prosecuted, which was a political decision from high up. One of the reasons for this may have been that to do so one would then make it known the Allies had the technology to eavesdrop on a large scale, and this would then not be as effective post-war. The security services decided to keep their powder dry, and perhaps use the techniques in another operation. Some of the eavesdropped recordings gave the Allies information on the development and siting of the V1 and V2 Nazi weapons launch areas, including one near Calais.

Knickebein

The Nazis used technology and radio beams to help guide the Luftwaffe bombers on to their targets in England. The Allies managed to identify the source of the beams and develop equipment at TRE in Worcestershire to locate and distort them. This meant that major Allied targets could sometimes be saved from major and significant attack, with the bombs dropped by the Luftwaffe landing relatively harmlessly on open fields or less built-up areas. Double agents could also be used to inform the Nazis they were bombing a particular target too short, and to fly further north-west, again wasting their bomb load when the track was further 'corrected'. Dr R.V. Jones was instrumental as a physicist and scientist in helping to develop numerous radio-based wartime systems to either deceive the enemy or provide an advantage to the RAF on bombing raids, such as Oboe.

Matapan

This was a deception revolving around the gathering of encoded intercepts via Y-stations, and passed to Bletchley Park for analysis. Mavis Lever, a codebreaker at Bletchley, managed to crack the Italian message advising of the attack on the Royal Navy fleet in the Mediterranean at the Cape of Matapan. The information was promptly passed to the admiral in the area and used to create a trap for the Italians, resulting in the considerable loss of its warships. Without the cracking of the Italian coded message, the outcome could have been very different. The early intercept of the message by GC&CS in England was effectively concealed from the enemy, with an Allied reconnaissance plane in the area becoming the reason for how the Italian fleet's movements were observed. It is essential in wartime and peacetime to have a plausible cover story so as not to give away the fact that the enemy's ciphers and codes have been intercepted and passed on for decoding at Bletchley Park. Admiral Cunningham used the intelligence to the advantage of the Royal Navy, to defend merchant shipping convoys supplying British forces near Greece and mount a trap for the Italian Navy. What added salt to the wound was that the Italians and Germans had incorrect information and intelligence about the Allied naval strength in the area, and assumed there would be no aircraft carriers present. However, they were wrong, with HMS *Formidable* being a key player. The Italians termed the opening encounter the Battle of Guado.

The mysterious convoy

A Bletchley Park intercept of a Nazi message made clear and specific reference to a British convoy that started its journey in Liverpool, then travelled down the Irish Sea to the Atlantic, across into the Mediterranean and then to Malta to replenish much-needed supplies. The problem was the British could not identify which specific convoy this was in the planning logs for convoys and it became a mystery. With further investigation it appears this was a fictitious convoy of five ships that was reported to the Nazis by a double agent. It transpired that a search patrol of military Nazi naval ships and planes went to pursue and locate the convoy in the Mediterranean, also flying over Valletta harbour in Malta, wasting fuel and resources looking for a convoy that did not actually exist. This decoded intercept, and the investigation that followed, proved that the Nazis believed the reports of the double agent Arabel, code-named Garbo, based in Portugal at the time, but much later working under the direction of MI5 in England. It was valuable to have evidence of the enemy's trust of a double agent, but he had to be cautious to not alert the enemy and blow his cover. His message was the third of three to his Nazi handler, and while there was a convoy due for Malta from Liverpool in reality, the dates given by him for departure and the configuration and the numbers of vessels did not match up to the real one in any way, which was just as well to avoid risking an enemy attack on it. Garbo's explanation of the source was that the information about the convoy was from a sailor he had met in Portugal. The other messages were about his network of agents being gradually established in the UK. Later, Garbo would move to London to continue his deception and report on an expanding team of completely fictitious agents he claimed to have assembled to support him and provide information to be passed on to the Third Reich. So effective were his reports on the convoy that at the time the British thought they had a dangerous spy leaking information to the enemy, before they established the source. Most German agents had been caught by the British, but even one remaining could cause great damage to the Allies. They did not need to have concerned themselves as it turned out.

Berlin – phone tapping (post-war)

A daring clandestine post-war spying project organised by the Americans to tap into Russian and East German telephone lines in Berlin in the 1950s. This involved creating a long tunnel under part of West Berlin in the American sector, but extending into the East German sector, where a junction box housed Russian military telephone lines. British Royal Engineers would excavate some of the soil for the vertical shaft at the end of the tunnel, and work alongside Post Office Engineering technicians to tap the frail and poorly insulated telephone wires at the junction box. It was not only the Americans who tapped cables, the KGB had done the same to them elsewhere. But this was a much larger project, taking many months to excavate and dig the long tunnel by hand to avoid noise being transmitted to the enemy through the use of machinery. Amplifiers and communication equipment within the tunnel were state of the art at the time. Cost was not really an issue, as the benefits of the tunnel and phone tapping were considerable and gave the Americans much valuable intelligence of what the Russians were doing and planning. It would be exposed eventually by George Blake, the Russian spy who had worked for MI5, in 1956.[5] The tunnel was later opened as a museum by the East Germans to embarrass the Americans and the West. A souvenir illustrated booklet, *Tunnel Spies*, was provided for a small fee to visitors, and the tunnel was referred to as the Museum of USA Villainy. It became a major tourist attraction, attracting thousands of visitors. Surprisingly, the British did not get a mention, and escaped all the diplomatic fuss. Nikita Khrushchev, the Soviet leader, visited England in the same year that the tunnel was exposed, but it was apparently not discussed. He was far more concerned with the Americans at the time. It was the Cold War era, and the Cuban missile crisis would trouble the world until it was resolved with a stand down on both sides. An agreement to remove American missiles from Turkish soil formed part of the agreement with the Russians.

Many thousands of hours of tape-recorded telephone messages were recorded and analysed by the American intelligence services before the tunnel was exposed. Numerous Ampex tape recorders operated constantly, day and night, collecting and recording important intelligence to be further scrutinised by intelligence experts. It was fortunate that this incident did not escalate into the Third World War, and the UK came off extremely lightly for its part in the operation.

Deception tactics in wartime

A broad range of specialist tactics were used in wartime to deceive the enemy, and some are listed below:

- Smoke for disguising attacks and direction.
- Use of projected audio sound to confuse the enemy.
- Moving signposts and signs for confusion of orientation.
- Radio transmission broadcasts from fictitious military units.
- Inflatable tanks, landing craft, vehicles for use in a managed diorama or scene, to be photographed by the enemy.
- Dropping, firing, and exploding dummy soldiers from aircraft.
- Coastal attacks with diversionary tactics and Beach Jumpers.
- Voice encoding and vocoder techniques for transmissions of a highly secure nature.
- Sabotage in enemy occupied ordnance factories to ensure grenades did not explode.
- Creating road maps of occupied territory that were purposefully flawed, and inaccurate, to be dropped by air into enemy territory.
- Using graphics, matte paintings, and other methods to give a false illusion of a scene from a distance.
- False insignia badges on shoulder flashes of military uniforms.
- Fifth columnists introduced into the enemy lines to create confusion and commit sabotage.
- Radio broadcasts from military units, indicating fuel reserves and supplies were much lower than were actually the case, giving the enemy a false picture.
- Use of severely inclement weather and cloud cover to prepare an attack, or counter-attack, when it would have been otherwise considered unwise due to the severe conditions.
- Extending tank gun barrels with a false pipe or tube to give the impression these had much larger guns and greater firing ranges when seen by the enemy from a distance, e.g. to emulate a Sherman Firefly tank with a bigger gun, and which was much more powerful than the standard Sherman, and a threat to enemy Tiger tanks.
- Contaminating discarded fuel in abandoned fuel dumps, which would cause engine problems if the enemy used that same fuel in their tanks and vehicles.
- Booby traps to abandoned buildings, armaments, equipment.
- Creating false airfields with support buildings and vehicles, as seen from enemy reconnaissance planes at height.
- Tapping into phone lines to obtain intelligence.
- Use of enemy agents to blend in with the enemy local population, but at great risk to themselves, to gather intelligence.
- Concealing radio equipment, batteries, code books, cameras, weapons, ammunition, maps, etc., in a variety of secret locations hidden from the enemy, in occupied territory.

- Dropping leaflets from aircraft into occupied territory with a combination of factual information, but also misleading information that may confuse the enemy or the population to a degree. Effectively creating fake news.
- Providing information via radio or Morse code, implying that an important general was somewhere other than he really was, and that may have an impact on the enemy resources.
- Capturing code books from the enemy but using them sensitively, so that the enemy does not realise the codes have been compromised, at least for a time.
- Use of SOE forces to target specific enemy positions, objectives, and locations to have an impact on the progress of the war, using a variety of clandestine methods.
- Creating maps, documents and supporting information to be specifically acquired or captured by the enemy giving a false illusion of the 'order of battle' and positions.
- Radar-jamming devices.
- Anti-radar jamming devices.
- Using mini-submarines to sneak into harbours and plan an attack against enemy shipping.
- Use of trained double agents, who pretended to work for the enemy but were really working for the Allies.
- Concealing production factories underground in man-made caves away from the eyes of the enemy, or from bombing.[6]

The relevance of the above is that a number of these tactics were supported by the Allies listening for enemy Enigma transmissions or even Lorenz transmissions to confirm whether that tactic had been successful or not. The confirmation could sometimes arrive days or even weeks later, and needed to be matched to the specific deception tactic applied, which was not always straightforward. The provision and creation of dioramas or 'scenes' using inflatable vehicles was largely dependent upon the enemy using reconnaissance planes and taking photographs of such areas, but as the war developed relatively few enemy planes flew over England as the Allies commanded the skies in late 1944 and in 1945. Of course, spies could transmit information as to what they had witnessed or seen, but the Allies had exposed and eliminated the Nazi spies in the UK, and concentrated on using double agents such as Garbo to feed intelligence back to his Nazi contact.

The inflatable vehicle scenario was used countless times in occupied Europe, and Nazi soldiers using binoculars would often be deceived by the tanks, vehicles and equipment seen from a distance, even though they were nothing more than rubber, paint and bits of wood and metal. The attention to detail involved positioning tyre tracks and tracked vehicle tracks carefully in the mud to provide a degree of realism. From time to time, the vehicles and equipment would need to be moved. French farmers, seeing four American soldiers lifting up a Sherman tank and carrying it 100 yards or so, were aghast. 'The Americans are very strong!' came the response from one of them to another. In practice, the organisation and process of creating such dioramas of false equipment and vehicles was highly structured and taken extremely seriously. Even the American Signals sound projection equipment used on armoured cars with enormous acoustic horn loudspeakers had inbuilt explosive charges to destroy the evidence before the enemy could capture it and expose the engineered deceit by the Allies.

The origins of such specialist divisions of military illusionists came from a proposal by Louis Mountbatten, Head of Combined Operations, who tasked the Hollywood actor Douglas Fairbanks Junior, visiting England during the war, to come up with some deception techniques that could be used again and again to confuse and mislead the enemy. Fairbanks went back to the USA and helped to organise tests and experiments in using Hollywood motion picture and audio sound techniques to come up with a plan to be used by the Allies in war situations. The senior sound engineer who worked on Disney's famous *Fantasia* movie was used to help to provide technical advice to the military group involved in sound recording and techniques. This was, after all, state of the art equipment at the time. Technology in Hollywood sound stages was applied to a degree in creating illusions and deception that could buy the Allies time on the battlefield. Experiments using 300 American infantry troops on a beach proved decisively that projected audio sound through enormous 500-watt horn loudspeakers could completely disorientate the men if set up correctly. The beach at Sandy Hook, New Jersey, would prove to be a successful experiment in projected sound using real American troops. The US Army's Colonel H. Railey would become a master of these deception techniques and help to drive them forward. He had come from a background of military intelligence, and was appointed to his new role by the War Department Planning and Training Board in 1942.

Applied physics and mathematics had to be used to take into account both the current and forecasted atmospheric conditions, barometric pressure, humidity, elevation, and many other factors. Sound travelled variably under different circumstances, but could be scientifically predicted quite accurately if you knew the physics of sound, and the associated rules. Topography and the lie of the land profile was critical, and affected the distance of the sound transmission. Barometric pressure was also relevant, and height above sea level. Sound could be projected for many kilometres under the correct atmospheric conditions, and confuse the enemy. Across still water at night, the distances for sound transmission could be substantial. Sometimes, the sound may appear much closer than it actually was. The American 3132nd Signals Company, Special, would become expert in applying the physics of sound to the equipment and creating a military 'performance' aimed to confuse the enemy. Mixing the sounds became as much an art as a science to fool the enemy.

The acoustic efficiency of horn loudspeakers was many times higher than that of conventional speakers. Sound could travel over water at night for considerable distances and would be utilised for transmitting the sounds and noises of the erection of Bailey bridges and gantries, with grinding of metal against metal, chains, and hammering in of bolts, as well as personnel shouting, laughing, and giving orders. The illusion would be that modular military bridges were being erected to cross a river, or body of water with a view to transport tanks, equipment, and personnel. However, the actual crossing of the river would be planned elsewhere, perhaps miles away from the specialist sound broadcast unit team, to confuse the enemy. Recordings would be made back in the United States of a variety of activities, then catalogued and assembled on wire recorders. These sounds could be mixed by an engineer on site, almost like a modern DJ, to create a combination of sounds relevant to the situation. Steel wire recorders were more suited to being used in this situation, as compared to using record players. If the tactical military unit was fixed and not mobile then record discs could possibly be used. Shellac records were, however, brittle, easily damaged, and not ideal in a war situation. Recording on to records was carried out in experimental sites in the United States, with the intention to transfer them to wire. Speakers were sometimes referred to as 'heaters'.

Fairbanks Jnr also established the Beach Jumper naval group, to provide high-speed boats to assault coastal positions using projected sound amplification and other methods as a diversionary tactic. Smoke bombs, delayed ordnance explosives, and even the use of metal-coated balloons to confuse enemy radar positions, was part of the arsenal of deception tools for the Beach Jumpers. The unit was used in Operation Husky in July 1943, the invasion of Sicily, and was very successful. Fairbanks was made a Special Operations Officer, and coordinated deception techniques with the British. A total of eleven Beach Jumper units were established during the war, using air-sea rescue boats, PT boats, and versions of them for both training and for operations. Fairbanks also was involved in helping to coordinate assault boats under Operation Dragoon, which caused problems for the Germans around Genoa in Italy and up to Cannes in France. Fairbanks would become a highly decorated Navy officer and retired as a captain. Illusion and deception would officially form part of the military strategy and tactics for the Allies, but be kept under wraps to not give the game away to the enemy. Some of the Beach Jumper techniques were even used in the Cold War during the Cuban missile crisis. US Navy Seals would develop these from Second World War experience and feedback on operations.

Use of secret ink was used by both agents and double agents to conceal writing or maps from the enemy. This was used by double agent Garbo to send messages to the Germans in Portugal and Spain in the post. The ink would become apparent once exposed to the heat or warmth of a naked flame. Then there would be a range of items concealed in the heel of a shoe, or a concealed compartment in a case or trunk. The Enigma machine was too large to be concealed, but some thought it was a strange typewriter. It would be contained within a wooden box with a serial number. Lorenz was much larger still, as it was a teleprinter attachment, and there were far fewer of them. Code books were easily concealed in other books, secret drawers, or compartments in furniture or shelving. It must be recognised that code books had to be revised and updated from time to time and reissued secretly to key personnel. They were the equivalent of an examination paper that must be kept secret from students, as to make it available before the exam would give a distinct advantage to some compared to others who had not seen it. There would be different types of code books, and capturing them without the enemy being aware was considered a major success. U-boat captains and Enigma operators would have strict instructions to throw the code books overboard to destroy them before the enemy could access them. If anyone failed to follow the strict security protocol, then they would be in serious trouble from senior officers. However, operators of Enigma became sloppy over time, largely due to boredom, and left openings for the Allies to make use of the carelessness, making it far easier to penetrate the ciphers by breaking the message settings.

Inflatable vehicles, tanks, and aircraft

Part of the deception process included using mock vehicles made of wood or rubber to create a diorama or scene of a military encampment, or similar. These were often constructed around inflatable rubber vehicles, tanks, landing craft, trucks, field guns, ambulances, and similar. From a distance, and certainly from an aerial view, these could appear quite convincing to an enemy spotter plane or tank crew through binoculars. Even dummy aircraft were created and inflated to make false airfields appear realistic. The Americans became masters of this, using techniques from the art and film industry in Hollywood. A special 'ghost' army was established, recruiting artists, engineers, painters, and other specialists to design and construct the items for deployment in the battlefield. Adding detail such as tyre tracks or tank tracks enhanced the realism of the overall scene. The scene would need to be managed so it could have movement when photos were taken over several days or weeks. Experiments using hinged wooden and metal-profiled tanks were less successful, as they were more difficult to transport, and took longer to erect and dismantle than inflatable vehicles. Technical innovation such as use of compartmented rubber tanks would make inflatables more robust in the field, and more easily repaired if punctured or damaged. This system would be developed and improved upon by the Americans, using welded rubber compartments to create smaller airtight sections.

The 'Ghost' team of army personnel, revolving around the American 23rd Headquarters Specialty Troops, would need to move at a moment's notice, assemble their equipment and arrive at a new location by a specific time. Secrecy in the erection of the equipment was essential to avoid giving the game away. One problem for the Allies as the war progressed was that enemy planes became less frequent in the skies, so it was mainly land-based enemy spotters that would report back the scenes to their headquarters. However, some German planes did get through to report what they had seen on the ground, or took reconnaissance photos as evidence. Enemy radio transmissions could often be monitored by the Allies to confirm whether or not they had deceived the enemy. Repair crews would need to ensure the inflatable items were kept operational and appeared realistic. A deflated gun turret would hardly look convincing, even from a distance. Such activities and deception could divert enemy units away from other key positions, and spread the personnel much more thinly. They might have the impact of holding back certain Panzer divisions in reserve, at locations that were of little strategic importance to the Allies as they advanced.

Overall, the ghost army was extremely effective, although the turnover of personnel was relatively high as the work was not suited to everyone. Combining the deception techniques of long-range sound transmission as well, using large horn loudspeakers and recordings of tanks moving over land, the arsenal of techniques became quite sophisticated. The generals and commanders realised that it was another tool to be used effectively against the Axis powers, and could save lives if organised well. Due to the Allied air superiority approaching D-Day, it must be stated that few enemy planes over Britain saw the synthetic equipment intended to deceive the Nazis, but as the war progressed it would be of use and of considerable value in France and elsewhere.

Evidence of deception and MILDEC

It is one thing having a deception plan and putting it into operation, but quite another to identify intelligence of evidence that the enemy has fallen for the trap. Ideally, this is recorded via radio, or Morse intercepts and decodes of enemy messages, confirming their change of tactics arising from the deception. But sometimes it is in the maps or diagrams that are captured from the enemy either during or after the war. One captured map issued by German Intelligence shows the deployment of British and American divisions and forces in Great Britain, and particularly in the south of England, as of 15 June 1944. This was part of Operation Fortitude South, to deceive the Germans into thinking that the main attack in France would be at the Pas-de-Calais, and that any other assault would be a mere diversionary tactic. The deception was a combination of double agent Garbo's messages to Nazi contacts in Portugal and Spain, as well as Allied radio traffic pretending to be the US First Army Group led by General Patton. There would additionally be physical deception aimed at enemy spotter planes to enhance the plan. False roads leading into woods might imply they led to ammo dumps for the invasion. Lights on carts would indicate aircraft landing areas at night.

The consequence of this MILDEC, short for military deception, was that the Germans kept key Panzer divisions stationed around Calais, expecting the main assault by FUSAG, whereas they would never come across the Pas-de-Calais. The German 15th Army and its Panzer divisions could have been attacking the Allies in Normandy, breaking out after D-Day, but Hitler and certain generals were convinced the main assault was yet to come and they needed to be in reserve, and battle ready. Field Marshal Von Rundstedt was not totally in agreement with Rommel's positioning of Panzers so near the coast, preferring them to be in reserve to meet the allies, as they advanced further inland. The delay to moving reserve

Panzers to the Normandy area was partly due to the confusion caused by the allies with FUSAG and a potential crossing at the Pas De Calais. Additionally, it was influenced by Hitler's inflexibility in allowing his Generals the ability to move forces without his personal authorisation. Two Panzer divisions moving south heading for Normandy on 10 June 1944 were called back north, in anticipation of the Calais encounter. Not all German generals agreed with Hitler but those who did not were too scared to challenge the Führer, who could often go into a rage and become angry when challenged. The German 15th Army was kept stationed near and around Calais until several weeks into July. This was a bonus for the Allies, as realistically they had thought the deception would last at most a week or two at most following the D-Day landings. The result was that the size of enemy resistance, although strong, was a fraction of what it could have been had the 15th Army been around Normandy repelling the invaders.

Equally valuable was the Fortitude North Plan, which was a deception to convince the Germans that an assault on Norway was planned, and that forces were in place in Scotland to attack. Germany had many troops and divisions in Norway, and the last thing the Allies wanted on D-Day was the transfer of a large group of German divisions from there to France. That would have upset their strategic planning and could have been disastrous. In the event, Fortitude North also worked as a deception. So, in effect two large groups of enemy forces, one in Norway and one in France, were holed up and locked in place, awaiting assaults by the Allies that never came. The maps confirmed the trick had worked, although Bletchley Park had intercepted intelligence via the Y-stations and were aware of instructions being forwarded to von Rundstedt via the 'Jellyfish' non-Morse communication link from headquarters in Berlin.

The Germans had a problem fighting in the east against the Russians, and were losing in summer 1944. To supplement their Atlantic Wall forces in France, the Germans would introduce many foreign soldiers and put them into German uniforms. These would often be second-rate troops from Russia, France and other occupied countries, and they bore no comparison to the crack SS troops that Hitler preferred. Indeed, Hitler had given strict instructions not to dilute the German Army with substandard foreigners, but the generals and officers had little choice as men were spread thinly across several fronts. This is not to imply that the Allies had an easy time in Normandy and beyond; they did not. But the enemy had many less able soldiers in their path than could have otherwise been the case, and relatively poor communication, erratic supplies of fuel, ammunition, and reserves, would play into the Allies' hands. Some of the soldiers would be experienced but old, approaching retirement age, while others would not be able to speak German. Then there would be young teenagers, the Hitler Youth, who were inexperienced, but keen, and who could be potentially deadly with a rifle in their hands.

The premise that the Allies would come over the Pas-de-Calais would be based upon logical arguments. Firstly, the shortest route for an assault was to Calais from Kent. The Calais and northern area was also the location of several V1 and V2 missile launch sites, and it was the fastest route to the Ruhr and the industrial areas of Germany. An attack near Calais and the north of France would also separate the

German forces from the Mediterranean theatre of operations. Von Rundstedt was convinced that the Pas-de-Calais was the objective for the Allies, and that is why it was so heavily fortified. He had commented to others that if he was Montgomery, he would come across there.

In hindsight, it was too obvious as a target, and the Allies or any attacking forces knew if they chose this route the losses would be substantial due to the defences and reserves in place. After all, since the 1940 British Expeditionary Force Army incursion into France, and eventual withdrawal at Dunkirk, the Germans had taken years to build up the Atlantic Wall and their defences around Calais and the north-west of France. It would be a hard nut to crack. The provision of a purpose-made fuel line under the sea to France from England via the Isle of Wight proved to be a game changer, as did the floating Mulberry harbours for landing troops, fuel, supplies, and equipment. It gave the Allies a degree of flexibility that would assist them to keep their ships and vehicles supplied with fuel on an unprecedented scale. Keeping this secret from the enemy was essential.

Camouflage

Camouflage had been used in a variety of different forms and formats going back hundreds, if not thousands, of years. The word, camouflage, comes from the French *camoufler*, to disguise. It would be the late 1800s when two American artists adopted a scientific study of how plants and animals concealed themselves with tricks of nature, using protective colours and shapes, and the serious study of camouflage took a step forward.

In the Second World War there was a scientific approach to camouflage, with experimentation and testing in the battlefield and at research stations back home. A double agent was instructed by his Nazi handlers to sabotage a de Havilland aircraft factory in southern England, and a method had to be arranged whereby there was an impression of an explosion and physical damage. This was achieved by using local art students to prepare large sheets, which would be painted with damaged brickwork, featuring large, irregular holes blown through the walls, all hung carefully over the actual walls and roof of the building to create an illusion. When photographed from a distance, the illusion of a bomb explosion appeared quite convincing. Add in a brief local newspaper report with a few lines of text about an explosion at the factory, which was unexplained, and this gave further credibility to the sabotage. The Germans were convinced that the agent had done as asked. They were able to then provide other detailed tasks and instructions, trusting the double agent to carry them out. This was but one example of deception using paint, shapes, sheets, and materials. The use of art students was fortuitous as they did not ask too many questions about the project, and obtained valuable work experience in their college art course.

Camouflage is more traditionally used to conceal an enemy position, or movement of troops or equipment using paint or netting with foliage, patterned cloth, or other materials, and frequently used on military clothing, helmets, tanks, and armoured vehicles, as well as gun emplacements. Ships too would receive camouflage to their superstructure to help with concealment, which may have worked better in extreme weather and rough seas, by confusing a captain looking through a periscope from a U-boat at some distance. 'Dazzle' camouflage was experimented with towards the end of the First World War, with rather wild, zigzag patterns applied to warships. In the United States it might be referred to as 'razzle-dazzle'. It was invented by British artist Norman Wilkinson and virtually did the opposite of conventional camouflage as it used bold angular patterns that contrasted and highlighted an object to the background. The true effectiveness of such patterns is not really proven but gave the ship's crew some degree of comfort when exposed in the North Atlantic, with wolfpacks of U-boats in the vicinity. Some photographs of warships and merchant ships painted in the dazzle style in 1917 can confuse and disrupt the human brain optical processing to a degree, appearing rather unsettling to the viewer. Thick, angular black and white lines are offset at some positions, making ranging from a distance quite awkward. That was the idea, at least.

Around the same time, an American, William Mackay, experimented with using certain specific colours on a ship's hull to create an optical illusion. One experiment used an oil tanker, which at 3 miles distance 'appeared to melt into the horizon'. Colour combinations of shipping camouflage developed for the Second World War were called 'measures'. These were standardised to a degree and applied to principally warships and support tankers but some merchant ships, too. US Navy colours included Haze Gray, Pale Gray, Navy Blue, Deck Blue, Ocean Gray, and Black. Geometric patterns would be applied by painters slung off cradles to the sides of the ship.

Both Allied and enemy forces took advantage of using camouflage for troops, military vehicles, and armament. The German *Kriegsmarine* used dazzle camouflage for some of their shipping around Norway. However, it would soon change tactics and blend in the warships to the rocky background of the coastal physical features using their own version of camouflage paint. The battleship *Tirpitz* would have a special colour scheme of different shades of light and mid-grey, with darker grey near the upper superstructure. The Japanese took camouflage techniques very seriously and developed their own rules and protocols for using it effectively against an enemy. A US Navy camouflage pioneer and expert, McClelland Barclay, would be killed in action during the war, but later inducted into the Society of Illustrators Hall of Fame in 1995.

Netting over aircraft was used extensively when hangars were not available. Foliage from forests and woods would be taken to supplement camouflage. Aircraft in the Pacific theatre would often have bold camouflage paintwork across the wings and fuselage.

Snipers relied heavily on concealment while operating in the battlefield, and could take out enemy personnel at a distance of up to 1,100m in calm weather, and the right atmospheric conditions. They would arrange their clothing and helmet to be non-reflective and use twigs, branches, leaves, and moss to hide their position. Their faces would be blackened or use mud to darken their features. Use of khaki and green colouring on tarpaulins, netting and vehicles would make them difficult to detect at a distance. In Norway, troops would dress in white uniforms or overalls to imitate snow and ice. The North African theatre would have its own light khaki uniforms, and there would be artificial features made of sand embankments and similar to blend in with the surroundings, to hide radio positions or base units. Even some of the exploding dummies dropped around D-Day from aircraft had a degree of camouflage on them to make them appear more realistic as they approached the ground by parachute. Today, camouflage is used extensively around the world for military personnel and equipment. Some systems are classified for reasons of security.

Modern deception techniques

One may ask, 'To what degree have Second World War deception tricks and techniques filtered through to modern-day warfare?' A fair question. It is principally about pre-planning a deception to create an illusion, much like a scammer tries to control someone's bank account by convincing them they are from that same bank when they are really an imposter. The planning is critical to the success of the operation. Without careful planning, mistakes can be made, alerting the enemy to trickery. The 9/11 attacks in the USA were planned many months in advance, enabling terrorists to learn how to fly aeroplanes and gain sufficient knowledge to take over a commercial airliner in mid-flight. They blended in with other passengers across several different flights and their timing was crucial to make their plot work. Although a horrendous outcome, that operation was well planned and completely unexpected to the authorities and the US Secret Service. The planning may have taken a year or more to fine tune.

When planning deception strategies against an enemy, one looks for their weaknesses, their methods of communication, and the efficiency of their chain of command. Something like Operation Mincemeat was highly complex but paid off. It could so easily have failed or backfired. The preparatory phase, and making the 'officer' who drowned after an air crash appear credible, took many months of work back in England. Attention to detail was essential in case the Nazis checked back as to the validity of purchasing the London theatre tickets he was carrying at a particular time or date, or the rather unusual receipt for an engagement ring for his fiancée, carried on his person as a photograph by the officer, water damage being part of the trickery. Detail was used extensively under Operation Fortitude South and for the creation of the imaginary FUSAG force in England. These included providing special shoulder flashes on American soldiers' uniforms created for the deception, transmitting wedding announcements of FUSAG personnel over the radio, and transmitting supply requests for equipment and fuel on an increasing basis as D-Day became nearer. Also, making false landing craft visible from the air when they were but inflatable rubber objects made to appear like landing craft. It was all to create the illusion of the bigger picture by drip-feeding the enemy small trivial bits of information, some of which were reinforcing their ideas of an attack via the Pas-de-Calais. Of course, not all the Germans believed what they saw or heard, but Hitler's mind could not be changed, and that was a major advantage for the Allies at the time.

Double agents have been around for hundreds of years in various forms and agent Garbo was a prime example in the Second World War of how to feed a handler information to build up trust over time. He made several mistakes in his reports and accounts of being in Britain supported by his fictitious list of agents, but these were not picked up by the Germans. One came when he made a report on Glasgow, stating that 'the Glaswegians would do anything for a litre of wine'. Wine was probably not the main beverage drunk by Glaswegian workers at that time! It was fortunate that the Germans overlooked such slip-ups. His communications, often using secret ink, outlined the exploits of his network of agents, which Garbo had invented stories about. None were factual, but his Nazi handler in Portugal believed what he was sending through, and his reports became more interesting as D-Day approached and movements of troops, ships and equipment were included in those reports. Double agents were used during the war, also post-war and are almost certainly in use today.

Looking in more modern times, many years post-war, to the Falklands campaign back in 1982, there were few opportunities to deceive the enemy as the Royal Navy task force could hardly be cloaked in secrecy when the world news reported on the progress of the flotilla on a daily basis. The RAF's first Vulcan bombing attack on Port Stanley airfield was, however, a complete surprise to the Argentinians, but the logistics and resources used to achieve the objective were of humungous and complex proportions. The slightest malfunction and the whole operation would have failed. Just the refuelling of multiple aircraft alone en route to the target required thousands of gallons of fuel, and relied on pinpoint accuracy to coordinate the refuelling tankers with the Vulcan bomber on the seven missions. It was the huge distance away from Britain that caused the RAF such a challenge at the time. They were also completely at the mercy of the weather en route, which could be unpredictable, particularly in the South Atlantic. There were times when the bomber crew thought they would have to ditch in the ocean due to not having sufficient fuel to reach the tanker rendezvous point. That was a close call. To complete five of the seven planned Black Buck missions was a remarkable achievement, well executed, and did a great deal for British morale at the time. The financial cost of the operation would have been extremely high due to the number of planes required, the fuel, and distances to be overcome. The result of the runway bombing was probably of minimal impact in the bigger picture of things, but it did stop the Argentinians using the runway as a base, which was the main objective. The enemy were not expecting the runway to be bombed, so the first attack was a complete surprise and may have changed the strategy of their air support.

Drones in battle today can identify and participate in 'real-time' action, and leave little opportunity for elaborate deception plans. The operator has complete control of the drone and can see and record the situation of the enemy forces and equipment on the ground. Drones are now used extensively to replace what used to be the observer with binoculars or a rangefinder, to report back ranging errors for artillery. Some are the size of moderately sized commercial aircraft, others only half a metre across and difficult to spot. As they are pilotless in the air, any damage or loss is limited to the machine with no injury to personnel. Ukraine and Russia are using drones in their war at the time of writing, and allegedly Iranian-backed, Yemen-based terrorists are using drones against commercial and military shipping in the Red Sea. Drones are now changing and modifying military tactics, and are getting more reliable with much-increased battery capacity. It is possible to mislead the enemy by flying multiple drones towards a particular objective and dropping small ordnance, creating a diversion, while attacking from a different direction or route with other forces and personnel. A whole new group of skilled drone pilots need to be trained in their use in the battlefield and for military reconnaissance. The rules of engagement also have to be redefined.

Technology is a key part of modern warfare. There are reports that Iran allegedly once 'acquired' a stealth US drone flying to Afghanistan by convincing the software that it was in Afghanistan when it was really flying over Iran.[7] Apparently, the Iranians could not 'see' the drone due to its stealth technology but somehow managed to track its flight, using methods unknown. If this is true (and one needs to be cautious about such reports), technology is vulnerable to interception, 'hacking' and clandestine methods to fool military software and equipment in a similar way that countermeasures fired from a military fighter plane can mislead a missile targeting that object, allowing the pilot to escape. There will no doubt be dangerous actors out there who will, for a fee, obtain and supply technical details, drawings, and calculations of drone and stealth technology to foreign powers, using a variety of clandestine methods.

A whole new area of deception is being unravelled in the twenty-first century, this being based upon digital technology, including:

(a) 'Deepfake' reports imitating persons digitally, stating things that they did not actually say but appearing convincing.
(b) Hacking into 'secure' state computer systems, but concealing the activity for as long as possible to procure confidential data and information.
(c) Changing financial data electronically to attack the economy of a state and generate both confusion and an economic crisis, affecting the stability of that country or state.
(d) Using clandestine means to alter voting habits of a population or a sector of a population to bring about a different result.
(e) 'Phishing' for information from a senior politician, military officer or similar using digital activities or via social media to gain an information advantage for a state.

(f) Using the fear of a fictional pandemic or virus outbreak to alter military strategy.
(g) Destroying or modifying secure digital servers, including 'cloud' storage of digital data that a military power relies heavily upon to formulate their strategic planning in wartime.
(h) Using complex AI systems to attack an enemy encoded message or cipher system, learning quickly from different methods of attack and analysis of the cipher.

These above are just a few of the tools and techniques that could be used in the digital age. Some may have already been applied in practice. The gloves are off when one is dealing with a rogue state that intends to crash a stable economy or bring it into a war that it otherwise had no intention of becoming involved in. As the world has changed significantly in the first quarter of the twenty-first century and Europe is at war, alliances are clear between Russia, China, and possibly North Korea. The fragmentation of Europe politically and economically, and the hesitation of the United States to continue to support Ukraine in its fight for democracy and freedom, has shaken the European Union and NATO. Russia's President Vladimir Putin will use deceptive techniques to his advantage in a situation where he may consider he has little to lose.[8]

Deception can be used at almost any level, from heads of state, down to officers on the battlefield and the grassroots soldiers attacking a military objective. The planning of strategy is the key to it all. Implementing strategy can be complex, and forces must be prepared to change tactics as the situation develops. Fail to do that and the enemy will expose any weaknesses and take advantage of them.

Commentary

Introduction and background

Firstly, a recap on the complex subject of which German encoding machines were challenged by which Allied codebreaking machines as the war progressed.

Enigma was an encoding machine produced in various models by the Germans, well before the Second World War and refined over time to increase the security of sending messages for confidential communication. It was mostly for military use, but some were used by diplomatic staff, security services, the German railways, etc. The Allies challenged it with, initially, manual calculations to decipher it, and then via machines, first the Polish Bomba, then the British Bombe.

The four rotor-wheel Enigma was introduced, and this proved extremely difficult for the Allies as their codebreaking machines were all based on the three-rotor Enigmas. Modifications included the Cobra attachment with limited success and other systems. Manual codebreaking did eventually tackle four-wheeled Enigmas, but took considerable time and a great deal of frustrating failures.

Parallel to the Enigma/Bombe scenario, Hitler wished for something even more secure for him to message his high command generals and field marshals. The result was the Lorenz S40/S42 teleprinter attachments, which used a system based upon Vernam-Baudot code using punched paper tape and was designated by the Allies as 'non-Morse'. This used high-speed, semi-automatic transmissions over the airwaves, but could also be sent via landlines to a limited degree.

The Allies were initially stumped when trying to decode Lorenz non-Morse messages as they had not come across such an encoding machine, had no way of knowing how it was configured, set-up, operated, or how many wheel rotors it had. It took many weeks before a young Bletchley Park mathematician figured out the system using lots of overlapping paper with apertures and a mathematical mind. He had managed, single-handedly, to work out the structure of the machine, the number of rotor wheels, and how it was configured. This would be a first initial step, but progress would be slow to design and build a machine to crack it.

The first machine was the Robinson, completely different to the Turing–Welchman Bombe, and arguably more complex. This was eventually followed by the more sophisticated and reliable Colossus Mk1, followed by the Mk2. Only part of the decode was possible with the Robinson and the Colossus machines, but it saved valuable time and manual methods finished off the job. This was the time of intercepting ‘Tunny’, or ‘Fish’, enemy non-Morse messages across the communication network of Europe and the Mediterranean, into North Africa.

The Germans never rested on their laurels and produced a more complex version of Lorenz for the German high command, the secret writer. Even more permutations of message settings were possible than with Lorenz, but Colossus could cope if set up correctly. Two separate sections were established within GC&CS at Bletchley Park to deal with the decoding of non-Morse messages. It became an important Allied team effort under difficult circumstances. There would be several differences of opinion on the technical design of the codebreaking machines and their operation, but in the end it worked in the Allies’ favour.

The use of a large quantity of female personnel for a wide range of codebreaking and support duties would be instrumental in the success of the outcome of the war. A table and breakdown on the number of female personnel at some of the key organisations that were particularly relevant is provided within this book. (See Female wartime input and contribution, in this section.)

It is important to appreciate the difficulties the Allies had with parallel encoding and decoding systems at the time. The Bombe machine was not compatible with the advanced teleprinter attachments that encoded Nazi messages. The Allies had to design and build a completely new system to challenge the advanced enemy encoding machines. Attachments were added to some Enigma machines to increase security even further. The Americans became frustrated and designed and built their own codebreaking Bombes, based on four-wheeled Enigmas, which they based in Washington.

The above is but a brief simplified summary of the challenge that the Allies faced during the war, although there would also be developments pre-war and post-war, too.

Each of the chapters in this volume provides certain specific information on Systems, Equipment and Deception. It is appropriate to point out that these overlapped in many cases, so that a system or procedure involving traffic analysis of messages became critical in using and applying the intelligence decrypted from the codebreaking machines. Similarly, deception techniques and their effectiveness in practice during wartime could be checked and verified by intercepting and decrypting enemy encoded radio transmissions with appropriate codebreaking equipment, or the use of double agents. This overlap varied to a degree, dependent upon the system or procedure being applied. It is only by looking back in time that we can understand how this worked in practice. The vast amount of personnel and resources involved meant that in some cases there was little correlation seen between applying a procedure or protocol and arriving at a key bit of intelligence further down the line. There were so many different sections, divisions, teams, individuals, and with different levels of ability and skills. No wonder that at times there would be inefficiency, rivalry, poor communication, documents, and items lost or mislaid, wasting valuable time. But, on the whole, the system worked.

The organisation of the capturing of enemy messages and processing them so they could be read, and read promptly, required the organisation of resources on a very large scale. Just the coordination of collecting and distributing data from the listening stations would become a mammoth task in itself. There was also the need to ensure the people doing the job were properly trained, had the appropriate skills to listen to Morse code and take it down both quickly and accurately. New codebreakers and support staff needed to be encouraged and allowed to make minor mistakes and learn from them. Those at the top of the management tree at Bletchley and elsewhere had great responsibilities. Reports were prepared and issued to senior commanders and to the Prime Minister, outlining progress, achievements, problems and threats, resource levels, and future planning to keep up with the messages and intelligence. Technical issues were not of interest to the commanders; intelligence was the objective. Or rather, accurate and timely up-to-date intelligence. Identifying the orders of battle of the enemy were the true prize. At least the codebreakers were not being targeted for Luftwaffe bombing raids specifically. There were so many wireless listening stations around the country and abroad that the Luftwaffe had no chance to make a dent in the Y-station network, at least none that would be significant. The threat from the Luftwaffe reduced in southern England as the war progressed after the Battle of Britain. The only real problem would be the V1s and V2s, which were relatively silent, fast, and deadly. But their accuracy in hitting specific targets such as a potential codebreaking base would be severely limited. It was more of a worry that those missiles, and particularly the larger V2 rockets, could cause havoc to England's infrastructure, affecting roads, rail, communications, power supplies and utilities, and put a strain on the hospitals and medical staff. The factories such as BTM in Letchworth needed to be supplied with steel, components, cables, wires, plugs, sockets, and many other items to build the codebreaking machines and keep to their production targets. The same was true of the Post Office Engineering Research Station at Dollis Hill. They could not afford to run out of tube valves or of vital components that would slow down production.

One can follow the history of the establishment of PORES at Dollis Hill and appreciate that, at least initially, research was for the development of Post Office engineering technology to improve communication and systems. Their focus was on telephone exchanges, amplifiers, switchgear, etc.[1] It is unlikely that those working at wartime in the Post Office Engineering organisation could have perceived or predicted that they would be designing equipment to help break the Nazi enemy ciphers and encoding machines. War can radically change the function of organisations and resources to meet the need at the time.

Post-war they would go on to create and organise a substantial number of projects, including designing the National Savings ERNIE lottery machine in 1956, and even researching to help design hearing aids for the new National Health Service.[2] Without the expertise in working on machines such as Robinson and Colossus, it may be that ERNIE could not have been designed or built. Indeed, the same team of engineers worked on the design of ERNIE. The machine was dependent upon the randomness of the output, for fairness, and to avoid favouring particular numbers. This was achieved with the aid of thermionic valves and neon cold cathode equipment with random noise generated, and a detailed understanding of physics. Two separate random devices were within the design which generated pulses and the output was a series of numbers. It was scrutinised frequently by an independent actuary to ensure it remained random, at least within certain prescribed tolerances as part of the machine's specification and output. To check that the design worked in the early stages, a smaller Little ERNIE was built, which was later reproduced in TNMOC and demonstrated in 2017. A much smaller TNMOC-designed and built device was installed in the Heath Robinson museum in Pinner, Middlesex, for children and young visitors.

Female wartime input and contribution

The reliance on using thousands of women during wartime was common to both Britain and its allies, particularly the USA. The US equivalent of the WRNS was probably the WAVES. However, initially, while Wrens were volunteers, later they were conscripted as the war progressed. A selected few Wrens and WAVES worked on codebreaking machines. Six hundred WAVES were engaged in working on the American versions of the Bombe machines in Ohio. The WAVES were established in July 1942 and wore either white or dark blue uniforms, designed by fashion house Mainbocher in New York. This is a simple table of the number of WAVES personnel engaged in military duties:

Year	WAVES Officers	Enlisted personnel
End of 1942	770	3,109
1945	8,475	73,816

Source: Naval History and Heritage Command

From the above it can be seen that in excess of 82,000 WAVES personnel were in service, as compared to a total of 74,000 Wrens in Britain. Only a small proportion of these would work as WAVES codebreakers, or in building codebreaking machines. The main difference was that whereas the Wrens operated Bombes, Robinsons, and Colossus machines, a number of the WAVES helped to actually build their US Navy Bombes together with some male assistance.[3] There is no evidence that Wrens or other female military personnel built any of the British machines, or contributed to the build. However, women factory workers did assist in building British codebreaking machines at BTM and Spirella, also at many of the surrounding villages, where components were assembled such as cables and connectors. There are a few isolated photographs of women assembling the components, and also of a group of women who worked on the project. All of them needed to sign the Official Secrets Act and be trained to carry out their tasks. They had to be adaptable and flexible. Mistakes in production could be a serious problem, so quality control was a key factor and the checking of assembled work was ongoing. The components would then be transported back to the main BTM factory for final assembly as modules on to the large metal frames that made up the Bombes. Much of the learning was on-the-job training, as few women at the time had engineering qualifications. Yet, most would learn quickly and contribute significantly to many achievements, both tactical, and strategic during the war. The adaptability of women can clearly be seen with the example of them making corsets in Spirella, Letchworth, then adapting to making parachutes for Irvin's down the road. Then some would be utilised to supplement BTM's workforce on Bombe components, working to very fine tolerances and scrutinised quality control procedures. The delicate wire-brush assemblies for the Bombe codebreaking machine drums were made by women in the Spirella factory.

Many women were based in industrial factories, working on armaments, parachutes, tanks, aircraft, engines, and vehicles. Some were qualified engineers. A relatively small number of women made codebreaking machine components in secret. These are a few of the British wartime female-based organisations:

Organisation	Type	Remarks/numbers
NAAFI	Catering	110,000 employees
ENSA	Entertainment National Service Association	(Entertainment for the armed services) (men and women)
ATA	Air Transport Auxiliary – support for RAF and others	1,245 (both men and women)
WRNS (Wrens)	Women's Royal Naval Service – Royal Naval support	74,000 Wrens (of which 1,676 came under Special Duties X/ Pembroke V duties)
ATS	Auxiliary Territorial Service	250,000
RAF	Royal Air Force	See WAAF
WAAF	RAF support	181,835
QARNNS	Queen Alexandra's Royal Naval Nursing Service	Part of 1,244 military nurses
PMRAFNS	Princess Mary's Royal Air Force Nursing Service	498 (Date for this quantity uncertain)
QAIMNS	Queen Alexandra's Imperial Military Nursing Service – Army support	12,000 (including 1,244 QAIMNS and other nurses who served in France during the war)
QARANC	Queen Alexandra's Royal Army Nursing Corps	See QAIMNS (>10,404 end of the First World War)
ARP	Air Raid Precautions (Civil defence)	Note: Men and women were members of ARP
ROC	Royal Observer Corps	Air defence (men and women) 1,500–2,000
Women's Land Army	Women's Land Army support for agriculture	80,000

NB Overlapping with some of the above were the women working in the listening stations (Y-stations), across the UK and abroad. These included WRNS, ATS, and other personnel. The above is not a complete listing but outlines the principal relevant organisations. Nurses in the health service, the Wartime Emergency Medical Service, were also in significant numbers during wartime. The WEMS was launched shortly after war was declared in 1939.

Note that the ATS was superseded in 1949 after the war by the Women's Royal Army Corps (WRAC). The WRNS was amalgamated with the Royal Navy in 1993.

Selected numbers of WAVES had a dual role of helping to manufacture US Navy Bombe codebreaking machines and operating them in Washington. Strict security limited the extent of knowledge of personnel involved, and much was on a 'need to know' basis. All those involved in manufacturing components for the machines had to be specially trained in wiring, soldering, and assembling the many delicate parts.

Deception and its uses

The examples given of deception techniques during the war and post-war, are but a small selection of what went on at the time to gain an advantage over the enemy and to confuse it. Technology was used wherever possible to make deception tactics work, and this included use of radios, transmitters, receivers, codebreaking machines, acoustic devices, inflatable dummy tanks, vehicles and landing craft, misleading signage, specialist equipment to bend radio beams, and many more besides. The training of support personnel to make this work effectively was critical. In some cases, it involved actors, graphic designers, set designers, agents, and double agents, even corpses. Where an English aircraft factory had to be shown to be severely damaged by sabotage by an agent, the graphic designers, artists, and painters would make changes to make it appear that large holes had been blown into the external walls and roof. Of course, the Allies needed accurate feedback as to what degree the Nazis were being taken in by all of this. Enigma intercepts and others would help to provide confirmation in some cases. The intercepts, and the complex process of codebreaking arising from them, were just one tool in Britain's arsenal of intelligence, albeit an important one.

The idea of developing deception techniques such as use of projected audio sound to create an illusion and sound performance, was started off by the British but developed in practice by the Americans, which had the advantage of the Hollywood movie industry, sound recording, specialist microphones, etc. This was backed up by some expert audio engineers, technicians, recording engineers, and film animators. Douglas Fairbanks Jnr would go on to help develop this environment to exploit such opportunities, and use them against the enemy to the advantage of the Allies. Fairbanks Jnr would become instrumental in creating and organising the Beach Jumpers force, used in places such as North Africa, Sicily, and elsewhere, using sound, flares, explosions, lighting, and other means of deception when raiding beaches and enemy positions. He, himself, would become highly decorated as a Navy officer. There would be some resistance at first in spending time and resources to create a deception force in the military, as this was not seen as productive by all at senior level, and could just be an experiment. But tests using the techniques proved it could work. When in wartime, with many servicemen losing their lives to defeat the enemy, it is worth trying out new ideas to reduce potential losses. The Beach Jumpers was one idea that worked effectively using robust basic principles written down in an operation manual, and it was used successfully until the end of the war.

The use of camouflage battalions would further assist the deception strategy on the battlefield. Camouflage was developed into more of a science as well as an art, using experimentation. Whether you were a sniper up a tree or up a church bell tower, lying low in a field protecting a crossroads from enemy attack, camouflage could sometimes save your life. The Germans and Japanese were also good at using and applying camouflage to personnel, tanks, artillery, and military equipment. Use of camouflage netting was widespread to conceal unit headquarters, aircraft hangars and similar. It was also applied to warships, but with more limited success. Today, camouflage is used across all military forces in the world. The most effective camouflage is the use of stealth in fighters, warships, and drones to make them disappear from enemy radar screens.[4]

The success of using Window

As soon as radar was developed by the British experiments took place to see what would disrupt and block the radar waves. TRE in Malvern carried out a lot of research in this respect. While both sides of the war had Window or its equivalent, its use was far more widespread by the Allies, and organised on a huge scale. From a pollution viewpoint, it was not good, as much would end up in the sea or river estuaries, and wildlife would digest some of the foil strips. However, this was of little concern as the Allies were at war. Many tons of Window were manufactured and dropped over the Channel, over enemy territory and on the approaches to France. There was almost enough volume of aluminium foil strips dropped to largely cover the Channel in a continuous foil blanket if it was connected together. The use of Window, or 'chaff' as it is now referred to, is commonplace across most modern military air forces.

The arrangements for use of Window on the build-up to D-Day were extremely comprehensive, with different sub-operations identified for aircraft to drop foil strips over the Channel in a controlled way. They included operations Mandrel, Glimmer, Taxable, and others, choreographed almost as a ballet, or a rehearsed theatre performance to deceive the enemy via their radar screens. Some of these operations were more successful than others. Combined with the use of small boats towing radar-reflective balloons, the Nazi radar operators would have been confused, at least for a time, reporting approaching Allied assaults from the Pas-de-Calais and south off the coast of France, many of them false. The sequence and timing for aircraft was critical, to make the scenarios believable. This was part of the process, and the coordination of the various individual and separate operations on the day, with the timing, position, and movement, or track of aircraft dropping the stuff, was far more complex than even organising a Royal Coronation event. The famous 617 Squadron became involved in dropping the foil, with some modifications to its Lancaster aircraft to cope with the enormous quantities used. Much research had been carried out at TRE in Malvern (where Window was invented) on the foil strips and best way to deploy them. Dr R.V. Jones was writing reports as to how to configure them in practice and identified the strengths and weaknesses of using the system, understanding the frequencies and dipole characteristics of the strips and their reflective properties from a physics and scientific viewpoint. The Luftwaffe had also tested Window and was alarmed at how effective it could be in the right hands, classifying its use.

Conferences between leaders and political strategy

Conferences and meetings between world leaders should be an opportunity for openness, transparency, and useful dialogue in a relatively safe environment. Yet, at the Yalta conference in 1944, when Stalin, Churchill, and Roosevelt met in the Crimea near the Black Sea, the rooms of the UK and US leaders and their support staff were bugged with microphones. What was unexpected were the array of hidden microphones in the gardens, bushes, and landscaping outside the house where the conference was held. Stalin wanted to know the thoughts of his rivals to be in a position to obtain the best deal for the Russian people in his negotiations. His intelligence services had agents feeding back information and reports to Russia from America and England many months before the Yalta conference took place.

Those who gather intelligence secretly, and effectively, are in a much stronger position at the negotiation table. Russia would play a game of deception with the Western powers, particularly as Stalin saw the conclusion of the Second World War as part of the process of establishing world power. Churchill understood that Stalin could not really be trusted and that he would have to tread carefully, particularly as he had the integrity of the British Empire to consider. Decisions made by Stalin could impact adversely on the Empire. Poland, the entire reason that Britain went to war in the first place against Germany, was being carved up geographically and politically by the three leaders at the table, dominated largely by Stalin. It would be Stalin that had the most to lose if he could not acquire a 'buffer zone' of part of Poland to help protect the Russian people from a potential attack on Russia. This would have been embarrassing for Churchill in particular. Many Poles had fought with British soldiers against the Nazis, risking their lives, and the Polish Government in exile was in London awaiting the end of the war so it could return to Poland. The outcome of the negotiations would later shock them, and Stalin would gain the upper hand in dictating how Europe would be sliced up post-war. The intelligence reports and listening to private conversations would all be part of the tools for the Russian leader to help deceive the Western leaders. However, the intelligence gathering was just a means to an end.

GC&CS would also be deciphering messages and helping the British Government to spy on the Soviets pre-war and during wartime. They would stop for a time, when the Russians became allies after Operation Barbarossa, but continue when it was considered as both useful and productive to do so. Nazi Germany would spy on the Swiss and other neutral countries, too. Japanese agents reported shipping and troop movements at Pearl Harbor, before the attack on the United States. No one was safe in war or even in peacetime. Deception would remain part of the arsenal of governments across the world and is alive today in the twenty-first century.

The process of modern hacking of conversations, emails, and secret files on both electronic servers and computers has added a degree of complexity to the deception equation. While some of these intrusions are readily apparent and corrective action can be taken, others are clandestine and can go unnoticed for a good period of time, leaving governments and states extremely exposed and vulnerable to military, commercial, and economic attack. Bring down an economy of a thriving state and you are one step closer to weakening the country and its politicians, leaving the door open for third parties to step in with devious intentions. You may not even need your tanks, cruise missiles, and drones. The spreading of fake news by social media is another useful weapon, and now Artificial Intelligence can mimic a politician or world leader on screen quite convincingly, making untrue and false statements that can help change people's minds. The modern world is now full of a variety of deception techniques to supplement the old successful deception methods. Companies want your personal data more than anything else and it has become invaluable in determining trends. Access to data is fundamental to being in a position of power in modern society. The only defence and solution is for people to switch off their smartphones, laptops, tablets, computers, social media, and TVs, and disassociate themselves from the world. Few of us will be doing that anytime soon.

Coordination of Allied services, training initiatives, and output

The involvement of the Allies during the war meant that there needed to be a clear hierarchy, and coordination of the armed services and their support groups to become truly effective against the Axis powers. This was even more true of the build-up to D-Day. SHAEF was the focal point for decision-making at the highest level, via Supreme Allied Commander General Eisenhower. However, he relied on a network of teams and units to feed both him and his commanders accurate and timely information. Some of this was via the underground tunnel base at Combined Headquarters (COHQ) at Fort Southwick, near Portsmouth. Intelligence would be fed back and forth to give Eisenhower and his supporters the information that was critical to the success of D-Day. Everything from crucial weather reports to the state of the shipping in the Channel, the clearing of mines, and in reporting locations of enemy action. Hundreds, even thousands, of people would be doing their skilled jobs in secrecy, and some of this involved use of ciphers and codes. Meetings to arrange major events such as D-Day would be held sometimes years in advance, in Canada, and later in Britain. Stalin would be pressing for a second front to relieve the pressure on the Russians in the east. However, neither Roosevelt nor Churchill wanted to act prematurely, as D-Day would be a one-time event that could not afford to fail. Planning years ahead would pay dividends, and would leave no stone unturned. Stalin was disappointed and frustrated until 6 June 1944, when the largest seaborne invasion in the world opened a second front in France.[5]

Keeping the top brass informed so they could decide the correct conditions for the invasion was tricky, as the Allies needed reasonable certainty about weather conditions, the position and status of the Panzers in France, fuel reports and the readiness of their armies, navy and the air forces who would play their part at D-Day. Collection of military intelligence would, of course, involve Bletchley Park, the numerous Y-stations, home and abroad, the engineering part of the Post Office, and many others in a crucial support role. So much of the intelligence reports had to be kept secret, to avoid the enemy being aware of how exposed they were to the Allies. Lists of authorised personnel would be scrutinised to identify to which people specific intelligence reports should be circulated. Who had the authority to see a report on the Luftwaffe's recent activities near the Channel, or the fuel reports for the invasion? Sharing information was one thing, but acting on it brought differences of opinion between military experts, or even the weather experts looking ahead at the isobars coming in from the Atlantic as D-Day approached. Furthermore, D-Day would be but one stage, albeit an important one.

Following on from the main assault in Normandy, intelligence reports would be required daily on troop movements, enemy positions, the level of resources supplied to the troops, the rates of advancement, even the capacity of the hospital ships for the wounded. As the advance took place in June and July 1944, the Bombes at the outstations and at Bletchley were busy with the rotor wheels turning, deciphering message settings of enemy messages, and the output from Colossus would also be of great interest. Russia would still need to be kept supplied with armaments, across the Baltic Sea, much of it via the Lend-Lease US agreement. U-boats were still active in this region and a potential threat. The Americans were operating their specially designed and constructed four-wheeled codebreaking Bombes in Washington to neutralise the U-boats in the North Atlantic. Some degree of coordination with the British would be ongoing as regards deciphering the messages and locating the positions of enemy submarines. The use of centimetric radar developed by the British at TRE would help to locate the conning towers from a distance, as the U-boats came up to recharge their batteries. This would eventually prove to be very successful, resulting in fewer attacks by the enemy as the war progressed.

Back in France and Belgium, mobile caravans containing senior Nazi officers' Lorenz teleprinter attachments for encoding non-Morse messages were captured by the Allies and brought back to England for detailed examination. It was not expected that such specialist technical equipment for the German high command would be mobile for use in the field, but it was. Captured German operators were interrogated and gave useful information to the Allies. They probably realised that once the Allies obtained a strong foothold in France and advanced deep into the country, it was only a matter of time before Germany was defeated.

During the period before D-Day, commanding officers of several Y-stations had been asked to sacrifice some of their technical operators to assist Knockholt, the specialist listening station in Kent. Reports indicated a major shortage of women for support roles. Based upon the non-Morse committee, 144 operators were needed urgently, but only thirty-nine had been offered by other listening stations. Training was in force, but there were only forty-eight new operators on the course at the time. Also, many operators could only become efficient and effective after several months' experience on the job. It was reported that only radio operators who could put up with long night shifts should be considered. That further limited the resource capacity.

By August 1944, a couple of months after D-Day, the daily output of Knockholt would be around 250,000 characters of intercepted Fish messages. Professor Newman had estimated that with the arrival of the much faster Colossus Mk2s delivered to Bletchley Park, his department could manage some 320,000 characters per day and increase this further to 500,000 per day by September. Compare this to March 1944, when a Colossus Mk1 could just about manage fifteen messages a day, and one can see the progress made. All this work at Bletchley was happening behind closed doors in relative secrecy while troops and aircraft were penetrating ever deeper into the Nazi-occupied territories. Intelligence supplied for the commanders from Bletchley, or other valid sources, could save lives, and speed up the process of winning the war. The support staff for the Bombes, Colossus, Robinsons, Typex, and at the listening stations would be rather bleary-eyed, with long shifts, little sleep, and food that was only just edible. They would have to wait for a break until May 1945 for VE day, and then some exhausted individuals would be transferred to the Pacific, to help finish the job against the Japanese.

Soviet intelligence during the Second World War

The track record of Soviet intelligence is a tricky one for historians as much information was kept secret from Western journalists, historians, researchers, also from the Russian people themselves. Today, there is limited information available, but we can say that there were opportunities during the war to gain some advantage in intercepting enemy enciphered traffic, as well as direction-finding units to identify the locations of German positions. Before the war there were some instances of breaking into the codes of Great Britain, France, Germany, Italy, Japan, and others to varying degrees. Some involvement with China against the Japanese proved fruitful in gathering intelligence, and intercepts of diplomatic 'Purple' ciphered messages also revealed that Japan would not support Germany in attacking Russia. Before the war, ten Japanese cryptosystems were solved by the Russians.

Restructuring of the Russian intelligence services made it more difficult initially to predict that Germany would invade Russia, and Stalin did not believe such reports even when senior officials informed him that an attack by the Nazis was imminent. There was a shortage of key Russian crypto personnel. In 1941, the crypto service would become the 5th Department of the NKVD. The Red Army had its own intelligence division under the GRU, but it spent too much time monitoring its own armed forces for breaches of security.

Russia captured Enigma machines and code books supported by German documents. However, there is no evidence to suggest a Russian anti-Enigma deciphering machine was designed or constructed, such as the British Bombe machine. We have insufficient information as to whether hand deciphering methods by the Russians were successful or, if they were, to what degree.

There was much concentration on using direction-finding equipment and army teams to locate German radio transmitting stations and take them out. Reports to Stalin from GRU in late November 1942 set out the progress made in intercepts and deciphering messages. More than 220 keys had been analysed and more than 50,000 German messages read since the GRU's formation in February 1942. There was also talk of the 'possibility of solving German messages enciphered on the "Enigma" machine, with a start to construct equipment, speeding up the solution'. This is where the track goes cold in historical records, with no evidence of such equipment having actually been used. That did not mean the equipment was not considered by the Soviet cryptanalysts in some detail, or even designed. Any drawings, sketches, or similar of such decryption equipment would be of great interest to historians if it should become available for study.

The Germans broke low, mid, and sometimes high-level Soviet traffic. They also hacked into the Soviet internal radio teletype network. Using all the tricks of the trade, the Germans used military D/F techniques and traffic analysis to identify the Russian order of battle.

Restructuring the WRNS and other forces post-war

Post-war there were large numbers of military personnel being demobbed, a process that sometimes prioritised married women over others where possible so they could quickly return home to their husbands. Those out in the Far East and the Pacific would continue in their roles until VJ day, when they too would be demobbed after a period of clearing up, obtaining the necessary paperwork, and arranging transport home. Their service records would need to be kept up to date as to where they had served, their dates of service and rank. The demobbing operation started on 18 June 1945. During the war, some 523,000 women served in the auxiliary services of both the military and civil defence service. Many women waiting for their paperwork would be put on courses to help them to return to civilian life. Some of these would be as bizarre as ensuring they were able to prepare afternoon tea, although there were also lessons in childcare from the Mothercraft Training Society. Rationing would remain in force for civilians. At the end of the war some 74,000 Wrens would be spread around the world, many preparing for a homecoming, others wanting to travel and explore further in countries where they had been deployed for their wartime service. Of this 74,000, only around 2.26% of them were employed in Special Duties X work on codebreaking duties, a relatively small proportion given the specialist nature of the work.

In early 1974 the Ministry of Defence Study Group tried to evaluate the role of the WRNS for the next ten years and beyond. Bear in mind that the WRNS had been established many years previously and then disbanded at the end of the First World War, only to be resurrected for the Second. The WRNS became less relevant to the Royal Navy and in 1993 it was disbanded, with 4,535 women being integrated into the service. The final passing out parade at Greenwich for WRNS officers had occurred some years previously, in March 1976. The training base at HMS *Dauntless*, in Burghfield, closed in 1981, having trained some 30,000 Wrens. This event may be arguably seen as the start of the end of the WRNS as a separate organisation. From then on, Wrens trained alongside new Navy ratings and recruits. Falling recruitment in the 1990s triggered a strategy to encourage and permit Wrens to go to sea on active service. HMS *Brilliant* accepted the first tranche of such volunteer WRNS officers and ratings in 1993. This formed part of an equality strategy that filtered down to the other armed services in time, but the Navy were pioneers in this respect.

One should not forget the change in military policy by the Navy during wartime when a complement of Wren cipher clerks was killed at sea in a U-boat attack as they were being transported from England to Gibraltar. Twenty-one Wrens lost their lives with others on the merchant ship *Aguila*, when the convoy of ships was torpedoed at night on 19 August 1941. Twelve of the Wrens were based at Scarborough Y-station and on their way to take up a posting in Gibraltar. The Chief Wren, Cecilly Monica Bruce Benjamin, was only 20 years old when she drowned along with the others.[6] Eight merchant ships and two Royal Navy support ships were sunk and 400 lives lost in total in Convoy OG-71. (This was designated as such because it would be the seventy-first outbound convoy to Gibraltar during the war.) As a direct result of the sudden devastating attack and loss of life, Wrens to be transported by sea would later only be allowed on Royal Navy warships, and not on undefended merchant navy vessels.

Policies change for a variety of reasons over time. Thus, there would be a gradual evolution that culminated in an environment of equal opportunity, while respecting gender differences, bringing together males and females in respect of the range of duties, activities, and promotional aspects of service in the Navy. Young people nowadays expect equal opportunities in the armed services as a matter of course, and they would be surprised at the prejudice that occurred many years before, particularly against women, and with the class system impacting on careers significantly as regards promotional prospects.

But what of the codebreaking women who worked at Bletchley Park or the outstations? Many were demobbed and got married, and forgot about their secret work, only to have a proportion of it exposed in the media in the 1970s after much of it was declassified. Some went to work after the war at the new GCHQ at Eastcote for a time, and then later worked in some other unrelated field. Eileen Hughes, nee Lawrence, went up to Scotland, worked on a military base at Donibristle for a time as a 'writer', and was asked to join MI5 in London after the war ended. To an outsider that seemed an exciting career, even after the war. Many would not speak about their activities in wartime with their families or children, a certain background anxiety affecting them. This was also true of ATS and WRNS Y-station personnel. A listener/operator at Chicksands Y-station did not tell her family anything about her work, and probably went to her grave with her secret intact. From various reports, this was quite common, and there was a certain pride in the women's refusal to reveal their experiences. It was possibly seen by them as both loyalty to the state and to the Queen. It was their choice, of course, and some of their experiences may have been harrowing, so the individuals may not have wished to bring back those memories due to the distress that may have opened old psychological wounds.

Overlapping aspects of Second World War and post-war activities

It is relevant to state that some post-war activities evolved directly from incidents during the war. An example is the Russian clandestine operations that evolved into the *Venona* Project post-war. This was about the infiltration of Western intelligence and infrastructure across the embassies and security agencies of most allied states. As a result of suspicious activity being picked up by the West in Canberra, Australia, the Russians became the official enemy of the West, having allegedly probed into secret conversations and documents using a wide range of spying techniques. Russia had never trusted the West, even when it became an ally after the Nazis invaded in wartime under Operation Barbarossa. The feeling was mutual, with Roosevelt and Churchill putting up with Stalin for the sake of convenience. After all, during the war Stalin opposed the Nazis openly and was no longer a threat to the West, at least not for the time being. But even before the fighting had ended, Russia was looking to see what it could gain as the spoils of war, and carved up parts of Europe to its benefit. It was not just about acquiring territory, but exerting influence and power over Europe and beyond. Part of this involved the interception of intelligence by Russian agents to learn what the Western leaders were really planning. The consequence was a shake-up in the West, it having been severely compromised in security terms. A process had to be established to gather all the sources of information, going back years, to find how this could have occurred. Documents, messages, recorded telephone call, and communication would be scrutinised in their millions to establish the truth. This was wound down in the 1980s, but taught the Western powers the lesson that they must not be complacent.

The element of complacency has reared its ugly head in the twenty-first century with the West not taking Russia and its leaders seriously, allowing incursions into Ukraine and elsewhere. The shock of another war in Europe has surprised many, and the balance of the NATO powers is being reorganised with new members joining, much to the concern of Putin. Sweden and Finland have become NATO members since Ukraine was invaded by Russia. This change is the opposite of what the Russian leader intended. The modern trend of a build-up of conflict involves using forces that are not wearing the uniforms of the attacking state or country, but are mercenaries. These will probe and attack another country or area to see how far they can get away with it before the West intervenes. The rogue state watches with interest in the background, supplying weapons, ammunition, equipment, and training to the men, and denies direct involvement themselves, militarily and politically. Eventually, the rogue state does bring tanks and personnel forward as part of the incursion, making excuses to protect their citizens from harm. Sham elections in the occupied parts of the country are then carried out. Weak Western leaders are taken advantage of by the leader of the rogue state, and they can easily make strong alliances with others where they have a mutual interest.

Spying, clandestine operations, and hacking digital systems has become the norm in the modern world. The technology may have changed but the principles of gathering intelligence, filtering it, and scrutinising it to find out about others seen as a potential threat have not really altered that much. What is interesting is how rogue states deal with censoring social media from the West, and the impact this has on their population. Social media has a mix of truth, facts, lies, misleading information and everything in between. Deepfakes are now becoming more common, and quite frightening if an innocent person is involved, and his or her identity is hacked or reproduced digitally. Tracking all this on a day-to-day basis is extremely challenging, mainly due to the amount of information out there. It was bad enough when Bletchley Park had hundreds of messages to be decoded each day, but the equivalent for GCHQ now may be in the millions, or more. While it is the case that a handful of intercepted enciphered and decoded messages may be the most significant ones of interest, identifying real threats to a nation or country, finding those few messages is not easy; like finding a needle in a large haystack. AI will be relied upon more in the future to help organisations such as GCHQ and the National Security Agency (NSA) find those threats.

Data destruction and concealing material from an enemy

Within both war and peacetime, there will be opportunities to discover data, documents, and information that can be advantageous to a nation or state, and expose weaknesses in another. Shredding of documents is commonplace, but as so much data and information is now digitally stored, a whole industry has evolved in managing that data. Methods of destroying it have had to become very sophisticated, especially since pressing 'delete' on your computer does not actually delete the file or data. In the Second World War, as the Russians and other allies were invading

Germany, coming closer to Berlin and the centre of the Third Reich, the Nazis were destroying large volumes of documents to conceal evidence of torture and murder, financial information on theft from the Jewish people, and lists of concentration camps, often just burning the items en masse. But there were so many documents to destroy, some were overlooked. Japanese diplomats destroyed many diplomatic papers and documents in the final days before Pearl Harbor, covering their tracks on the messages sent and reports obtained.

Code and cipher books were considered as important as gold dust in wartime, and they must never be allowed to fall into the enemy's hands. Some did, however. The change of codes and code books frequently was some degree of defence to theft, but complacency was also a problem with personnel becoming sloppy in their operational protocols. Basically, not everyone followed the rules. In any security system, one can issue information to selected groups of people on a 'need to know' basis. Churchill adopted this approach on certain matters, including Enigma and the existence of a codebreaking machine to crack it. The Russians were actively excluded from knowledge about the Bombe as were so many senior politicians and others. But leaks can compromise such a policy or strategy. A leak within Bletchley Park could have been damaging to Britain's security and its allies.

Churchill instructed that all the codebreaking machines and drawings be destroyed at the end of the war. His fear was that the Russians might acquire that technology and use it against the West. Not all the codebreaking machines were dismantled initially. Several Bombes remained at GCHQ Eastcote, and they acquired the last two Colossus machines nicknamed 'Red' and 'Blue'.[7] The other eight machines were destroyed. Some of the dismantled parts were recycled to build other equipment in Manchester and elsewhere in the age of new computers post-war. In some ways it is a bit like inventing the wheel, using it, then destroying all evidence, so your rivals and competitors cannot benefit from its use. It is a fruitless exercise, and one that does more damage to the nation that has invented the item than its enemies. Destroying the codebreaking machines, or most of them, did little to prevent the Russians and others acquiring Western technology and make advances themselves to save valuable time. This was true with regard to the acquisition of state secrets in the design and construction of the atomic bomb.

Fast forward into the 1960s to the '80s and many of the design secrets of Concorde, the supersonic airliner developed by Britain and France, were also compromised and fed through to the Russians. The theft of intellectual property was bad enough economically, but such technology could also be adapted for military use, presenting a greater potential threat to a nation that had done all the arduous and costly development work. Stealth technology was allegedly stolen by the Russians after it was developed by the Lockheed Corporation's Skunk Works in the USA. The most one can hope for is for the original designers and their organisations to buy some time, with the technology gaining one an advantage over an enemy or competitor for at least a short while. Sooner or later the design drawings and supporting calculations will be leaked to other countries, and not all of them friendly. During the Second World War and post-war, there was a whole network of spies and agents passing military secrets to enemy states. But as Russia was an ally to Britain, US, and the West for a good part of the Second World War, could the passing of confidential information to them from Bletchley Park at that time be regarded as spying? Surely, they should be sharing key intelligence and information with their known allies?

Here the dilemma lies. Any country, its security services, and political leaders must be given the choice of what information and intelligence to share, and when to share it, if at all. Otherwise, there could be exposure to potential attack, or clandestine operations after the war has ended and the alliances dissolved, or at the least restructured. Some of that intelligence may have to be effectively 'managed', as to who should see it, the level of personnel cleared for security, and so on. There could be political repercussions if certain information got out, and that could result in a change of government, high-level criminal court cases, imprisonment, and worse, in some situations. There might arise economic instability from sharing some data with other nations, or even political revolution. So, there needs to be some degree of control and choice in the matter. None of these arguments will, of course, prevent rogue nations from acquiring secrets from other nations using a wide range of clandestine methods. Secrets that have been passed across to other states have not always been labelled as such. At Bletchley Park, John Cairncross was able to collect papers that had been just left on the floor of the hut, so sloppy and casual was the management of technical data. He accessed 'Tunny' decrypts with ease and passed them to the Russians. Of course, originally, no one would suspect a codebreaker in a Bletchley Park hut as a spy working for Russia. That made his job so much easier. He was given immunity from prosecution when he confessed in the 1960s to his spying activities. Cairncross was labelled as one of the 'Cambridge Five' group of educated spies working for Russia and the Eastern Bloc. He did not consider that he had been disloyal to Britain in his activities and the passing over of state secrets.

People, by and large, trusted their leaders in the Second World War. Most leaders were respected, such as Churchill, even if the public did not always agree with decisions. It is the case, however, that overall, the integrity of leaders at the top would be scrutinised through their speeches and their results in wartime. This included how well they communicated with other allied leaders, and worked as a team. If there was a setback temporarily, how that was overcome.

However, certain facts will always be hidden from the public, such as concealing the actual losses at the Dieppe raid, or when hundreds of American marines and soldiers were attacked by German E-boats practising for D-Day at Slapton Sands in Devon, southern England, in April 1944, with numerous casualties.[8] This event took place only a few weeks prior to D-Day itself. The public and press were not informed of the disaster. Maintaining morale was seen as more important. Many things can be forgiven, even forgotten over time if the overall picture is constructive, positive, and works. The public and the general population will be less inclined to forgive complacency, carelessness, lies, deceitfulness, and cover-ups that innocent people can suffer from as a result of concealment of information. The overall objective in wartime is to win the war, or at least not to be overrun by the enemy. In peacetime, it is much more difficult and challenging to measure success. Is a state economy run by a ruthless dictator successful in the eyes of the people? How much should we value freedom and democracy? The world is currently asking itself those very same questions, and there is no agreement currently between nations as to where the balance should lie. This issue will not go away. Lessons can be learned from actions during wartime, but few learn from the mistakes made in history, or so it would seem.

In spring 2024, a conference was held at Stanford University, California, by the *Five Eyes Alliance* comprising security agencies across the UK, USA, Canada, Australia, and New Zealand. Concerns were raised by the increase in Chinese attempts to steal intellectual property, company secrets, and acquire innovative technologies from the West using clandestine methods. Intellectual property can be worth billions of dollars and some countries and states will try to gain an advantage by stealing secrets if given the opportunity. China, of course, denies such accusations and puts them down to Western propaganda. FIORC, or the *Five Eyes Intelligence and Review Council*, exchanges and shares information between members on areas of mutual concern, discussing potential action to protect the interest of members. It appears that the fight to defend intellectual property is now as high profile as ever before. The impact of stealing company and research secrets can have catastrophic effects economically and geopolitically for a nation. Countering it in practice will be a real challenge for the Western powers. It could even bring us closer to the Third World war.

Effectiveness of codebreaking in wartime

There can be no doubt that Allied codebreaking using a variety of different methods and systems was worthwhile, and had a favourable impact as the Allies tried to reduce the length of the war. This is not to say that everything went according to plan. Long periods of failing to crack Enigma to counter the U-boat threat would prove frustrating and concern Churchill and his military commanders. Professor R.V. Jones, in his book *Most Secret War*, stated that even without cracking Enigma or other Nazi encoding systems, Peenemünde would have still been raided by the Allies to stop Nazi missile development.[9] That was his opinion. But did the gathered intelligence via Bletchley save the Allies time? Probably.

It took the development of centimetric radar at TRE to fundamentally challenge the U-boats in the Atlantic, and reduce their effectiveness, allowing D-Day to proceed with sufficient supplies, resources, and a lowered risk of submarine attack. Codebreaking certainly had its place in decoding intelligence, and saved lives, but it was just one of many systems and tools used in the defeat of the Axis powers. The challenge with codebreaking is that it requires certain highly specialist and talented individuals to be brought together from a variety of different backgrounds to tackle the technical problems encountered. Many of these people are irreplaceable, as are support teams, so they have to be protected from attack by the enemy. This is partly why codebreaking outstations were developed remotely from Bletchley Park in order to spread the risk, even though most actual codebreakers were largely situated there. Learning the codebreaking techniques from other experienced cryptographers took time, even if new systems and methods were developed. If outstations had been destroyed by the Luftwaffe, this would have severely reduced the capacity for processing Enigma messages, and hence less gathered enemy intelligence could be passed on to Allied commanders.

By 1942 Bletchley was deciphering around 39,000 Enigma messages per month, and later this would increase with the help of more outstations to around 84,000.[10] The large volume of deciphered intelligence would help change the war in the Allies' favour, but the reader should not underestimate a wide range of other systems and events that eventually drove victory forward due to perseverance, organisation, training, teamwork, and sheer hard work. What matters less are the claims made by organisations and individuals about who had the greatest influence in defeating the enemy. The reality is that it was a major team effort involving countless countries, states, and organisations around the world. It was touch and go at times when Hitler was developing advanced weaponry, and moving towards intercontinental ballistic missiles and possibly an atomic bomb.

The Nazi plans for further advancement

Following the conclusion of the war and the gathering of information for study, there is evidence that some significant advancements were being planned across a range of weapons and codebreaking technology by the Nazis, but these were stopped in their tracks by the fall of the Third Reich. In codebreaking terms this included further development of the secret writer teleprinter attachments. The Germans even produced prototypes for a fifteen-rotor Enigma, but this was never put into production. We do have to be cautious about this as it may have been a planned development of Lorenz, from the twelve-wheel standard version to a more advanced one with fifteen rotors. No photographs or drawings of this prototype are available for study.

Clearly Hitler and his team of experts planned to develop their missile technology and even to make a bomb from atomic fission. This would have brought the war into a particularly dangerous era, with an unstable dictator in control of nuclear weapons.[11] The efforts of Dr Barnes Wallis and Professor R.V. Jones in England during the war proved that applied physics and engineering could be used to counter the Nazis in respect of tackling problems such as deep underground Nazi factories making missiles and long-range weapons, as well as Luftwaffe radio beam tracking for their bombers. The establishment of places such as TRE, PORES, and others in England gave the Allies an advantage. The same is true of research and development in the United States, including development of the improved naval four-wheel Bombe. Technology shared between nations made the Allies stronger and much more effective in wartime. While the Nazis did encourage the use of Enigma by Italy and some other allies, they very much kept their technology and developments to themselves. There is no evidence that the Lorenz teleprinter attachment encoding machine or the secret writers were shared with the Italians, for example.

If time had been on the side of the Nazis, the Allies could well have been overwhelmed with larger missiles in great quantities, or even nuclear weapons stopping the allied advance into occupied countries and Germany. The rate of enemy missile production was increasing rapidly, and only the combined forces of the British and Americans was able to slow it eventually with both bombing and troop assaults on the ground. The creation of a system of mobile launch pads or semi-mobile facilities was a clever Nazi strategic move, making it harder to wipe them out as compared with fixed installations. The combined expertise of Allied photo reconnaissance pilots and photogrammetry observers scrutinising thousands of aerial photos identified many of the Nazi installations to target. Use of shadows from the sun helped gain intelligence on the missiles and fuel supplies when viewed in 3D through stereoscopic glasses. Bletchley Park was looking out for evidence of where they would be located, including the production of fuel and fabrication of the rockets and launch facilities, to help the commanders plan raids.

The introduction of jet aircraft such as the Messerschmitt Me 262 would have been a game-changer if introduced earlier by the Luftwaffe. It was first flown in July 1942, around two years before D-Day. Operational versions could achieve a maximum speed of 540mph, far faster than anything the Allies had to counter it. However, of more than 1,400 Me 262s produced, only around 300 ever saw combat, many being destroyed on the ground by US bomber raids.[12] The outcome could have been very different with a drive for production of these high-performance aircraft on a large scale in earlier stages of the war.

Following the outcome of the war, both Russia and the US took several German physicists and scientists into their countries to benefit from their research and to help develop weapons of mass destruction. It is a paradox that such efforts were in principle to maintain world peace, by being as strong, or stronger, than one's enemies technologically.

The moral argument for eavesdropping on PoWs in wartime

The work carried out by the British at Nazi detention centres such as Trent Park during wartime produced useful results by secretly recording the inmates' conversations. These were not secret conversations, as such, but if the German prisoners of war had known they were being recorded by the Allies then they may have been more careful. After all, some of the conversations amounted to an admission of being involved directly in the mass murder of Jews and others.

However, if one does not act on the information then why record the conversations in the first place? The Allies desperately wanted an insight into some of the Nazi secrets, particularly information and intelligence on advanced technology such as weapons of mass destruction. Some of this was forthcoming. Much of the transcripts typed from recordings would amount to trivia, and of no military use at all. It was a bit like the decoding of many Enigma messages by the British, with only a small percentage being of real importance, but several may be quite useful if added to the content of other messages. At places such as Trent Park, German officers were allowed access to the BBC news and certain newspapers, so it would have been of interest if they gave their opinion on a news item to a colleague. Information may have come out that could be of use to an Allied commander, but often that was just wishful thinking. However, was it morally correct to eavesdrop on prisoners who were just waiting for the war to end? Many were decent German officers just doing their duty for the Third Reich and Hitler in wartime. Many of them would be horrified at the mass murder of innocent people and wish to disassociate themselves from it. Some even despised Hitler openly, and there would be arguments and disagreements on this very matter between certain officers.

It was surely the role of the security services to use whatever methods possible to glean intelligence from the enemy to help end the war as soon as possible. The methods used effectively indicated there was no right to privacy for prisoners of war. However, even if an officer was recorded admitting he had shot unarmed Jewish people, bringing that person or individual to court and prosecuting him for the war crime was still a challenge, as one needed evidence. The officer accused could say it was a fantasy, that the incident did not occur, but may have wished it did in his mind. Therein lies the problem. Many perpetrators of vicious and violent crimes in wartime will not, unfortunately, be brought to justice. There are too many incidents to gather the evidence conclusively to prosecute many of those who were at fault. So, the organisers of the security services were selective on the information they acted upon, leaving aside many other recorded conversations that would alarm us all.

At Trent Park, RCA 88A pressure microphones were concealed everywhere from light fittings, ceilings, plant pots, even in a billiard table. Hundreds of 12in double-sided acetate/metal discs were used for recording conversations. Most of the recording equipment came from America under Lend-Lease agreements. To make the listening process easier for those within secret rooms in the basement, wearing headphones, the turntables would have variable speed controls to be able to slow down certain passages for transcription.[13] The sophisticated system used was just another tool for the Allies. Many of the transcripts were kept under wraps until the end of the twentieth century, some fifty or so years after they were recorded.

We must not forget that Stalin bugged the British and Americans at some of the high-level wartime conferences, ignoring moral arguments to be open and transparent in politics. Knowing what his opposite numbers were thinking and planning in terms of strategy for post-war Europe was of great value to him. Equipment is now be much more sophisticated than before, and micro-miniaturised, so eavesdropping for security purposes is here to stay.

The overlap of military and civilian personnel and sites

Codebreaking and intelligence gathering and processing during both peacetime and wartime falls into a peculiar category, inasmuch there is a substantial mix and overlap between civilian and military input. This can be demonstrated by looking at the Y-stations, which covered a broad church of management, i.e. Army, Royal Navy, Post Office, Foreign Office, Marconi, etc. Furthermore, Bletchley Park itself was a mix of civilian and military personnel, with many more civilians on balance. Outstations were run by Navy personnel (WRNS), but on sites under the Foreign Office, or commandeered from country estate owners. BTM was, of course, a civilian company, as were the Spirella support team in Letchworth, who made numerous components for the Bombes. Post Office Research Engineering was again civilian, but Government owned and funded at the time. Several of the codebreakers at Bletchley were Army or Navy personnel, and of some form of military background, working alongside civilians such as Gordon Welchman. VIs operating radios voluntarily would be principally civilians, some of whom would later be called up in the services to work on radio intelligence as the war progressed.

The RAF were supported by private factories using civilians to build military planes such as the Spitfire, engines, and armaments. The Royal Navy was also largely supported by contractors made up of civilians, building and repairing ships, engines, and naval equipment. The operation of that equipment once handed over would come under the Navy.

The objective of breaking the enemy's messages and intelligence was to provide the Allied forces with crucial information that could save lives, reduce the length of the war, and help dismantle and destroy the Axis powers. But those largely in control of the processes were often civilians: mathematicians, classicists, linguists, and so on. Commander Travis may have been 'in charge' for a time, but the initiative came largely from the workers at Bletchley, and the outstations, together with the listening stations and support bases such as TRE and PORES. Drayton Parslow, the punched card base, arguably worked more efficiently as a separate Hollerith processing base than when it was at Bletchley Park. It certainly grew in numbers of personnel to meet the needs of the Park.

Knockholt was not a military base, coming under FORDE, and yet it became crucial to the success of the decoding of non-Morse Fish or Tunny enemy intelligence, which arguably helped to shorten the war. What is surprising is how well the overall system worked in practice. There would be changes to systems, processes, the re-siting of bases, and alterations to the quantities of staff and personnel, as the need arose, etc, but the commanders and senior military officers generally received their intelligence to act upon it, in good time, with some exceptions.

Had the request for further resources to Winston Churchill by four enthusiastic Bletchley Park codebreakers been carried out at a military base with all the staff being military officers, arguably those involved could have been severely disciplined, or even court-martialled, for going over the heads of senior ranks. They were not as they were civilians, and any reprimand was minor. Churchill immediately approved the resources. One could then say that there are some advantages at times to adopting a civilian network, with a more flexible approach compared to a military one. However, that rarely works in battle, where discipline, following the rules, and recognising the hierarchy of the chain of command becomes essential.

Analysis of Bombe Machines

The British Bombe codebreaking machines amounted to 211 in number, built in Letchworth during the war by the British Tabulating Machine Company. The official Bombe Registers have been studied at great length over several years, and provided below are some statistics and facts from the information available. The analysis is purely based on detailed study of the registers and the author summarising the quantities or percentages. The process is complex due to the way the information is recorded in the registers. The Bombe Registers are on loan to the National Archives in Kew at the time of writing.

A. The Bombes had both individual numbers and names, but the number generally remained the same, whereas the name could change when machines were moved around the outstations, or from Bletchley Park to an outstation. Because the Bombe number was generally consistent, it is easy to track a particular machine, and if there were changes of names these are listed in the Bombe Register entries against the number.[1]
B. While the numbers of Bombes at the end of the war at Outstation Eastcote amounted to 103 machines, due to various factors up to 119 Bombes that went through the doors there. Stanmore had seventy-six machines at the end of the war, but had up to eighty overall.
C. The three country house outstations near Bletchley would have a total of forty-nine machines, or around 23 per cent of the total, at some stage during the war. These were at Adstock, Gayhurst, and Wavendon. Seventeen Bombes were at Gayhurst at the end of the war, with five at Adstock. Many of the others had been transferred to the outstations as the war progressed and more codebreaking sites were established. By the end of the war, there were between nineteen and twenty-two Bombes at the country house outstations, or around 10 per cent. It can therefore be stated that while there was a peak in the number of machines at the country house outstations in the earlier or mid-part of the war, the quantities declined considerably as several machines were transferred across to Outstation Stanmore, and later, to Outstation Eastcote, as they were developed.[2]
D. 3.8 per cent of the codebreaking Bombes were at Bletchley Park, i.e. eight machines. (Note that Bletchley Park had all the advanced codebreaking machines, such as Robinson and Colossus.)

E. The combination machine known as *Giant* comprised four Bombes linked together, and these were numbered 266, 267, 268, and 271. This was operated at BTM factory in Letchworth for a time before it was eventually dismantled, split back into individual Bombe machines and redeployed to Bletchley Park and Outstation Eastcote. Machines 266, 267 and 271 went to Bletchley, and 268, redesignated as *Chaos*, to Outstation Eastcote. *Giant* was the only machine not to be operated by Wrens, but by male personnel under the direction of Bletchley Park at the factory.

F. While several Bombe machines were moved only once during the war, several others were moved twice, and therefore were operated at up to three different codebreaking outstations. An example of this is Bombe 57, which started off at Outstation Gayhurst on 22 January 1943, moved to Adstock on 19 December 1943, and moved finally to Outstation Stanmore on 14 June 1944, just after D-Day.

G. Outstation Stanmore (OSS) became a type of 'clearing house' for the Bombes being transferred from country house outstations over time. It became an important hub to accept new machines manufactured and delivered from the BTM factory at Letchworth, as well as the transfer of existing Bombe machines from the country estates. Then, when Outstation Eastcote (OSE) became operational in late 1943, some machines from OSS would be moved across there, as well as newer machines. Bletchley Park Bombes remained relatively stable and largely stayed in position, in comparison to other sites. However, two were relocated and used for training. See under J.

H. Unusually, a few of the codebreaking Bombes were moved three times in their lives, an example being Bombe Number 15, which started off at OSW on 24 December 1941, then went to OSS on 8 December, 1942, later to OSE, and finally back to OSS on 2 October 1944.

I. The last new Bombes to be sent to codebreaking outstations were in 1945, eighteen in number. The last would be dispatched to Outstation Stanmore in May 1945.

J. Out of the first ten Bombes produced, four would end up being used purely for instruction or training purposes. That included the first two machines, named *Victory* and *Agnes Dieu*, which both started off at Bletchley Park but ended up at Outstation Eastcote in 1942 and 1944 respectively.

K. While towns and cities were used for Bombe names at codebreaking outstations, there is also evidence that states were also used as names, such as for Canada: e.g. Alberta, Quebec, and Ontario. These were situated adjacent to other Bombes including Vancouver, Winnipeg, and Halifax. Following detailed checking by the author with the official Bombe Registers, it appears all of these were at Outstation Stanmore.

L. Below is a table of the years in which the codebreaking Bombes were produced and became operational. This is based on scrutinising the records in some detail and checking the dates listed against Bombe number and names:

Year	Quantity of Bombes produced	Remarks
1940	2	Bletchley Park (OSP)
1941	14	Including some machines at Bletchley, but mostly for codebreaking outstations
1942	33	OSS established late 1942
1943	50	OSE established late 1943. (By end of the year just under 50 per cent of the final total of Bombes had been produced)
1944	94	The peak year for Bombe production. OSS and OSE dominate the outstations
1945	18	Declining production
Total	**211**	Grand total of British Bombes produced in Second World War

NB: All British Bombes were produced by BTM, in Letchworth, Hertfordshire, with Harold Keen as the chief engineer.[3] Almost all Bombes were operated by WRNS personnel with RAF engineering support for maintenance.[4] The concept of the idea for a Bombe codebreaking machine to emulate the Nazi Enigma was via Alan Turing at Bletchley Park, although engineering design and the detailed production drawings and blueprints were produced at BTM. Post-war, most machines were dismantled, but some were left at OSE for several years before eventually being dismantled and destroyed. No originals remained.[5]

M. It would not be until 29 September 1942 that Outstation Gayhurst (OSG) would receive any Bombes, it being the last of the three country house bases. OSA (Adstock) and OSW (Wavendon) were already well established by then.
N. Two Bombes would be delivered, and became operational at Outstation Eastcote (OSE), on 6 June 1944, D-Day, being Bombe Numbers 286 and 287, named Houston and Astrakhan, respectively. Houston was for the American 6812th Signals operators working in the American Bombe bay.
O. This table lists the Bombes transferred between bases:

Year	Bombes transferred	Remarks
1940	1	
1941	0	No transfers in this year
1942	10	
1943	16	
1944	48	Includes allocating Bombes for US Signals at OSE
1945	11	Figures to mid-1945 at VE day

In total, there were eighty-six transfers of Bombes, although a small handful of these would include reallocation of Bombes for the US Signals team at Outstation Eastcote. The peak of transfer activity came in 1944.

P. Outstation Wavendon received a maximum of sixteen Bombes, Outstation Adstock ten, and Outstation Gayhurst twenty-three. These would be reduced considerably in quantity as the war progressed, and many Bombes were transferred across to other newer outstations such as Stanmore and Eastcote. It can be stated that initially these three outstations had under 25 per cent of the total Bombes, but that by the end of the war Stanmore and Eastcote combined had around 85 per cent of the total. Of course, a proportion of these would have started their lives at the country house outstations, and this should be taken into account. Modifications and improvements were made to many of the Bombes to improve efficiency and reliability.

Q. An enemy V1 missile attack on Stanmore damaged a perimeter wall at the outstation, and an incendiary bomb dropped on Outstation Eastcote during wartime, but remarkably no Bombe machines were damaged during the air raids, and the efficiency of the operations for working on message settings were not apparently disrupted or delayed by enemy action.

R. A small proportion of Bombes were moved to the 'Works' according to the official registers. In the absence of other information, we must assume this was the BTM factory in Letchworth for the repair or modification of machines.

NB The above concentrates on the British Bombes made and used during WW2. The American Bombes were a different design to the British versions, and amounted to 121 four-wheel-Enigma based bombes, built at the NCR factory in Dayton, Ohio. These were relocated to Washington for wartime operation by the US Navy. *Refer to page 73 for more details.*

Questions and Answers

This a range of questions with answers on topics of codebreaking, deception, and intelligence during the Second World War.

Q. *How were the decoding processes during wartime split, if one compares manual methods and machine-based processes?*

A. There would be multiple stages to progress in order to decipher enemy an Enigma message, from initially receiving the intercept via Morse code at one of the Y-stations. Around nine or ten sub-stages were necessary to progress the work. Some would be carried out in different huts, such as with traffic analysis or the crib/clue hunt. Once machines became an option, a key stage would be the data processing using the Bombes, set up on a daily basis to crack the message keys. With more advanced machines as the war progressed, complete sections were established such as the Newmanry and the Testery, with specific roles to take on as part of the decryption process. The use of machines had to be part of an overall team-based approach. Machines alone were not capable of arriving at the end result. Now, in modern times, that would change, and AI may have advanced the codebreaking methods.

Q. *Apart from Alan Turing, which individuals influenced the outcome of the Second World War most as regards cracking enemy ciphers, codes, and intelligence gathering and processing?*

A. There would be many who influenced the outcome of the Second World War, some on a very small scale and some significantly. Names who may be considered here include Gordon Welchman, Donald Michie, Dilwyn Knox, William Tutte, Thomas Flowers, Alastair Denniston, Commander Edward Travis, Hugh Alexander, Max Newman, Frank Tester, and Mavis Lever.

Q. *Arthur Scherbius invented the Enigma machine, but who was working on rotary-based encoding machines before Scherbius?*

A. The Dutch had worked on designing and inventing rotary-based encryption machines some years before Scherbius, and had a degree of success. However, they were slow in obtaining patents for such machines. Scherbius would later acquire the Dutch patents himself, putting him in a strong position commercially.

Q. *Was Arthur Scherbius aware of the impact of his Enigma machine was having in the Third Reich during the war?*

A. As Arthur Scherbius died prematurely before the war commenced, he would not have been aware of the significant impact it made on the Third Reich, the Axis powers, and indeed the Allied codebreaking effort, which was to consume many resources of men, women, and equipment. Scherbius was involved in improving the design and manufacture of Enigma and ensuring the machine was portable. The early versions were not easy to transport as they were heavy, very expensive to make and sell.

Once the German military saw the potential of the Enigma, it was a captive market, and the factory had to scale up production, licensing manufacture to locations where demand could be met. The acquisition of Enigma was not restricted just to the military, as the German railways used it, as did the secret service, the *Abwehr*. It would also find use in neutral Switzerland, and the Nazis became curious as to what messages were sent back and forth in that country. Knowledge is power, and even neutral countries were investigated and monitored by the Third Reich.

Q. *Who decided to have two specialist sections at Bletchley Park, the Newmanry and the Testery, to help decode advanced Nazi encoded messages?*

A. These were evolved over time by Max Newman, for the machine-based Newmanry, and Frank Tester, for the Testery, which concentrated on manual codebreaking after the message settings had been analysed to a degree by advanced machines. Both men were experienced mathematicians and codebreakers. Separate sections and areas at Bletchley Park, they worked independently initially, but later were instructed to liaise with one another to improve efficiency. This appeared to work reasonably well. It is a misconception that one codebreaking machine did everything and decoded the Nazi messages. This was a complex, but effective, team effort of personnel in different sections and departments, and specialist machines, some designed and built by the Post Office Research Engineering Station. The Newmanry, while concentrating on development of machines to assist the codebreaking process, relied on skilled and knowledgeable personnel who understood the challenges.

Q. *Were the Wrens aware of what the decoded messages stated when they were setting up and operating Bombes, and other decoding machines on Nazi messages and intelligence?*

A. The Wrens were never aware of the content of the message even though they were assisting in identifying the message settings from the enemy Enigma encoding machine. This must have been frustrating for them. However, from time to time at some of the outstations such as Eastcote, a talk would be given to the Wrens who worked on the Bombes by someone senior, giving them some limited information on the impact of breaking certain messages. At Eastcote this talk would sometimes be given in the Assembly Block, near Lime Grove.

That was near one of the entrances on the south of the outstation site. This may have improved morale, and given the Wrens a real purpose. Those staff, often female, who worked at Bletchley Park on Typex machines, to display the messages following Bombe analysis at outstations, would also not understand the message appearing in front of them in German, unless they were German speakers. Most were not. However, they would recognise German text when it appeared and that would give them some comfort that the message had been decoded. Translators would carry out the final stage of the decoding process.

Q. *How did the wartime codebreaking systems influence post-war intelligence gathering and decoding, if at all?*

A. A clue in this is the publication of Gordon Welchman's book, *The Hut Six Story*, being stopped from mass circulation after the war ended, by the NSA in America and the British Government. The authorities were very concerned that some of the descriptions of the approach to codebreaking and the techniques used could be applied to the Cold War period, giving rogue nations and enemy states crucial information that may weaken the West in terms of cryptography and intelligence gathering and analysis. Welchman had thought he had not betrayed secrets and was innocent, but he was nearly prosecuted and imprisoned for his writings. The message here is that the approach to gathering, analysing, and decrypting intelligence in modern times has much to thank Second World War processes, which can still be applied in principle today.

Q. *Could Alan Turing's Bombe machines have been adapted to decode the non-Morse messages from Lorenz and similar machines?*

A. This would not have been practical as there were significant differences between the Enigma and the Lorenz machines in how they were designed, constructed, configured, and operated. The Lorenz and secret writer machines used a Vernam-Baudot non-Morse encoding system, which was not the case in the Enigma. Modifications were made of the Bombe codebreaking machine over the war, and even a 'super-Bombe', but this was targeted at versions of Enigma encryption. One only has to consider the highly complex Robinson advanced machine, and the need to synchronise two separate reels of paper punched tape that would then be read by electronic magic-eye sensors, to realise that this was very different in design to the Bombe machine.

Q. *What was the frequency of errors and mistakes in the Nazi operating of Enigma or Lorenz encoding machines, and how did that impact on the Allied codebreakers from a practical viewpoint?*

A. Mistakes and errors were made on both sides during wartime, but initially we should consider the Enigma and how it was used in practice to encode and decode messages for the enemy. One, two, or even three individuals were needed to operate Enigma efficiently. This was because the message had to be typed into the machine, the illuminated encoded letters identified and written down, and then the encoded message sent via Morse code to the recipient. While one person could do this, it was likely there would be usually a minimum of two. There could be errors in recording the encoded letters on the lamp board, errors in typing in the message text and errors in sending the Morse transmission. At the receiving end there could be more errors in recording the message and turning it into plain text. It was bad enough that the Allied codebreakers had to try and break the Enigma cipher keys each day, but add in the errors and this made the task much more challenging. Another aspect was that the German operators sometimes did not always follow the security protocol required. Some encoded messages were sent twice, which gave the Allies an opening to compare the two decrypted messages to help break the code. The Lorenz teleprinter attachment was a very complex machine but did not need several operators, and was fast to encode and then transmit messages. There would be fewer opportunity for errors with Lorenz, as compared to using Enigma.

Q. *What prompted Hitler to decide there was a need for an advanced encoding machine for the German high command if the Enigma was already considered to be unbreakable?*

A. Some German generals had been sceptical that Enigma was completely unbreakable and were concerned about the security of encoded messages. The security of Enigma was improved over time, but it had weaknesses, and some of the operational personnel made errors that compromised its security. This was an opening for the Allied codebreakers to break the keys for the Enigma ciphers. Hitler wanted something special for communication with his elite hierarchy of field marshals and generals; something that was different to Enigma and would not be used by lower-ranking officers or enlisted men. This gave rise to the Lorenz teleprinter attachment machines, or 'Tunny', as the Bletchley Park boffins called them. As they were operated by one person, there was far less possibility of errors. It was much faster to operate than Enigma, and used non-Morse output, which was more of a challenge for the Allies.

Q. *After the war ended, was Tommy Flowers of PORES at Dollis Hill used to develop more advanced machines and computers for Britain?*

A. Unfortunately not. The Official Secrets Act imposed a severe restriction on the work done in wartime around the subject of decryption techniques and machines. While America seemed to develop modern computers without such restrictions, those involved in Britain had their hands tied. This was made worse with decisions taken by Churchill to destroy all the codebreaking machines after the war, although some survived for a time at GCHQ Eastcote. Flowers was put back on the Post Office research work that he was employed to do, and became rather frustrated as a consequence. His role was as head of the switching division, possibly seen by him as a step backwards compared to the excitement of developing the Colossus semi-programmable computer.

He did later approach a bank for funding for the building of a new computer, but was turned down by them. They did not believe a machine as he described could possibly work. Flowers was unable to tell the bank that he had already designed and built an advanced machine due to it being on the secret list. Flowers attended a personal computer course at Hendon College in 1993 to learn how to programme computers as they were becoming more popular for industry and private use. By that time, he would have been allowed to talk to his lecturers or fellow students about his pioneering work for the Post Office Research Engineering Station in wartime. That barrier would be lifted and a certain number of activities and records were eventually declassified by the Government. Arguably, Flowers' greatest post-war achievement would be to assist the development of the National Savings computer, or ERNIE, which generated random numbers for the Premium Bond prizes.

Q. *How did checking the frequency of letters in message settings and messages assist the codebreakers at Bletchley Park?*

A. The operation of studying the frequency of letters in the enemy messages would prove to be invaluable as the war progressed. One could apply various mathematical ratios and statistical analysis to identify patterns and deviations from those patterns in letters and cipher text. Jack Good at Bletchley was proficient in this process, as were others. It was a more sophisticated and reliable method than just trial and error, and based upon proven mathematical and statistical concepts. The idea was to home in to what certain groups of text might be, how they may be configured, and the statistical probabilities of the letters being the correct ones. In modern times, computers aided with artificial intelligence can quickly process many millions of bits of data to eliminate what is of little or no interest, leaving just the specific data that the reader wishes to study in detail. Even without computers in wartime, the codebreakers were trying out different approaches and methods to make the decryption process more efficient and much quicker to achieve a satisfactory output, as compared to not introducing frequency and statistical analysis. Today, we may apply various algorithms to problem solving, and some of those may be highly structured and complex, but developed with AI to save time.

Q. *Was ENIAC a computer and was it more advanced than perhaps Colossus?*

A. ENIAC (Electronic Numerical Integrator and Computer) was devised initially around 1943 by the Americans for the purpose of calculating trajectories of military shells and missiles. A number of women were recruited to operate switches and set it up. After the war, it would be developed further. Colossus was seen as semi-programmable but arguably ENIAC was not quite there, although developed versions did make it more programmable over time. There would be 17,468 vacuum tubes, or valves within this machine, a quantity that significantly surpassed Tommy Flowers' Colossus, the Mark 2 having some 2,400 valves in comparison. ENIAC was completed in February 1946, but

Colossus had beaten it by a year or two in terms of development. Computer experts will argue the various technical points about comparisons between the machines, but ENIAC would be a very useful tool and, in fact, helped produce the technical calculations for the hydrogen atomic bomb.

Q. *How effective were the Y-stations in feeding back intercepted intelligence to Bletchley Park for analysis and decoding?*

A. The Y-stations and their organisation were critical to the whole process of traffic analysis and decoding intercepted information. The Y-stations were reorganised and expanded considerably throughout the process of the war, training became more formal, and tests and examinations had to be passed for a recruit to be accepted within the listening service. Standards were raised and it took around eighteen months for a trained signals listener to be useful and productive at his or her listening station post, which relied as much on gathering valuable experience 'in the field' as did learning the rudiments of Morse code, and the speed of sending and receiving transmissions. Given that variable atmospherics greatly affected the transmissions, there would be a skill in locating and retuning the frequency of a fading signal on the receiver, and doing it promptly to pick up the remains of the message. The use of teleprinters was expanded and assisted with speedy transmission of coded messages to Bletchley Park and elsewhere. Thousands of personnel were involved in the Y-station service across many different locations across Britain and abroad. The direction-finding, or D/F, activities by selected stations would pinpoint and locate transmissions intercepted from the enemy and from Allied agents, and become a crucial tool in defeating the Axis powers over time. The combination of RAF, Army, GPO, and ATS personnel would make an important difference to the outcome of the war. Sharing intelligence with our allies, particularly the Americans, Canadians, Australians, and other Commonwealth countries, would enhance the system and provide a robust service to support the commanders preparing to move into the occupied countries and into Germany.

Abbreviations

ACSWSA	Admiralty Civilian Shore Wireless Service
AFHQ	Armed Forces Head Quarters
AFSA	Armed Forces Security Agency
AI	Artificial Intelligence
APO	Army Post Office
ASDIC	Anti-submarine detection investigation committee (Sonar)
ATS	Auxiliary Territorial Service
BP	Bletchley Park
BTM	British Tabulating Machine Company
CESD	Communications Electronic Security Group
CESG	Communications Electronic Security Department
COMINT	Communications Intelligence
CPC	Communist Party of China
CSDIC	Combined Services Detail Interrogation Centre
CSO	Composite Signals Organisation
D/F	Direction finding
EDSAC	Electronic Delay Storage Automatic Calculator
ELINT	Electronic Intelligence
ENIAC	Electronic Numerical Integrator And Computer
ETOUSA	European Theater of Operations United States Army
FECB	Far East Combined Bureau
FID	Field Intelligence Division
FIORC	Five Eyes Intelligence and Review Committee
FORDE	Foreign Office Research and Development Establishment
FRUEF	Fleet Radio Unit Eastern Fleet
FUSAG	First US Army Group
GC&CS	Government Code and Cipher School
GCHQ	Government Communications Head Quarters

GPO	General Post Office
HSK	High-Speed Keen
HUMINT	Human Intelligence
ISK	Intelligence Services Knox
JDU	Joint Discrimination Unit
JISD	Japanese Intelligence Signals Digest
JSRU	Joint Speech Research Unit
JSSU	Joint Service Signal Unit
JTLS	Joint Technical Language Service
LCSA	London Communication Security Agency
LEO	Lyons Electrical Office
LSIC	London Signals Intelligence Centre
MCIC	Maritime Cryptologic Integration Center
MI 1(b)	War Office/British Army intelligence in Whitehall, London
MILDEC	Military Deception
NASD	Naval Air Signals Intelligence Digest
NATO	North Atlantic Treaty Organisation
NCM	National Cryptologic Museum
NCML	National Computing Machine Laboratory
NCSC	National Cyber Security Centre
NSA	National Security Agency (USA)
OKW	Oberkommando der Wehrmacht. High Command of German Armed Forces
OKW-Chi	OKW-Chiffrierabteilung. Decryption department of the German high command.
OP-20-G	Office for Chief Naval Operations (US Navy)
OSA	Outstation Adstock
OSE	Outstation Eastcote
OSG	Outstation Gayhurst
OSP	Outstation (Bletchley) Park
OSS	Outstation Stanmore
OSS	Office of Strategic Services (USA)
OSW	Outstation Wavendon
PCM	Pulse Code Modulation
PLUTO	Pipeline Under the Ocean
PORE	Post Office Research Establishment

ABBREVIATIONS

PORES	Post Office Research Engineering Station
RNELH	Ruislip Northwood Eastcote Local History Society
RSRE	Royal Signals & Radar Establishment
SCAG	Special Cryptologic Advisory Unit
SCDU	Services Communication Development Unit
SCU	Special Communications Unit
SIGINT	Signals Intelligence
SIGSALY	Signal voice encoding/decoding US-built machine
SIS	Signals Intelligence Service
SLU	Special Liaison Unit
SOE	Special Operations Executive
RAF	Royal Air Force
RN	Royal Navy
SHAEF	Supreme Headquarters Allied Expeditionary Force
SIGINT	Signals Intelligence
TA	Traffic Analysis
TICOM	Target Intelligence Committee
TNMOC	The National Museum of Computing
TRE	Telecommunications Research Establishment
VI	Voluntary Interceptor
WAAF	Women's Auxiliary Air Force
WATU	Western Approaches Tactical Unit
WAVES	Women Accepted for Volunteer Emergency Service
WEC	Wireless Experimental Centre
WRNS	Women's Royal Naval Service, abbreviated as Wrens
Y-Station	Wireless intercepting station

Terms and Names

Abwehr German Secret Service.

Adstock (OSA) A codebreaking outstation during the war near Bletchley Park.

Aspidistra A joint Anglo-American transmission system used to fool the Germans during the war, principally developed by RCA in America and installed in Crowborough, England.

Banburismus A system devised by Alan Turing, mathematician, and codebreaker at Bletchley Park, to improve efficiency of codebreaking when attacking enemy messages to establish Enigma wheel settings.

Baudot International teleprinter code invented by Emile Baudot. A version of special binary digital code applied to punched paper tape using the alphabet, and some additional characters and commands.

Bodyguard The code name for the Allied deception operation in 1944 comprising projects Fortitude North and Fortitude South.

Bureau B A name given to conceal the identity of Bletchley Park and used by BTM in Letchworth.

Cadix The code name for the intelligence centre used by the Poles in southern France at Uzès, under the control of Vichy France before German occupation of the area.

Cambridge Five A group of five British individuals educated at Cambridge University in England, in positions of trust, such as within MI5, who passed secrets to the Soviet Union, and acted as spies either during the Second World War, post-war, or both. Anthony Blunt, Guy Burgess, John Cairncross, Donald Maclean, and Kim Philby formed the Cambridge five.

Cantab The name given to the project for the design and construction of codebreaking Bombe machines at BTM in Letchworth.

Cipher A term often synonymous with code. It is a process for encoding or decoding a message or similar. One may speak of cipher 'keys', and this is a type of cipher that can be deciphered with knowledge of the 'key' settings. Enigma was one encoding/decoding machine that relied on the settings of a 'key', and the Allies were tasked with cracking as many keys as possible to read enemy messages.

Cobra A separate and specialist piece of codebreaking equipment that would be attached to Bombe machines with a long thick cable to improve the performance.

Code Synonymous with the term cipher or cypher, a code is a set of rules applied, usually in secret, to enable communication with others who can access those rules. It can be based upon a system of letters of the alphabet, numbers, hieroglyphics or images applied in a particular sequence, or via a specific set of rules. The object is to maintain secrecy and to have control over who can access the message or data being encoded. One encodes messages or data, and then another decodes them, using the relevant rules.

Code book A book or document that contains the rules applicable to a particular cipher or code, to enable consistency of approach by those who wish to encode messages or data. Distribution of such code books must be controlled to maintain secrecy and confidentiality. There would be various versions used by the enemy.

Colossus The world's first semi-programmable computer designed and built by the engineering part of the Post Office (PORES) for Bletchley Park. It was designed utilising 1,500 valves, and used to attack the German Lorenz and advanced teleprinter-based encoding machines used by the German high command. A Mark 2 version was produced near the start of D-Day in 1944, which was several times faster than the original.

Cottages Buildings at Bletchley Park that housed codebreaker teams for a period of time.

Crib Clue.

Cryptography Writing of hidden messages, also known as encrypting.

Cryptanalysis A method of codebreaking using a mathematical or statistical approach.

Cryptology A codebreaking method that uses a more linguistic approach.

De-Chi Part of the Colossus decode element of advanced teleprinted non-Morse messages, which was stripped away using the Colossus and Robinson codebreaking machines. This is discussed in some detail in *Codebreaker*, Captain Jerry Roberts' book on Lorenz.

Divisions The Navy term for 'parade' used by Wrens.

Dolphin The name given to the Enigma cipher used by U-boats to attack Allied shipping in the Atlantic.

Eastcote (OSE) A codebreaking outstation in north-west London.

Enigma A rotary-based encoding machine designed by Arthur Scherbius, and used by the Nazis and other enemy countries during the war. Enigma literally means riddle or puzzle. Different versions were made; some with three wheel rotors, others with four.

Fish Communication links across Europe used by Hitler and his generals for German high command communication. Around nineteen links were established. The routes would have names of Fish to identify them, such as 'Gurnard' or 'Bream'. Fish was a Bletchley Park code name for this traffic. Fish link messages were often 10,000 characters long, and needed special equipment and processes to analyse and decode.

Some examples given below:

Squid – To Army Group South
Octopus – To Army Group A and 7th Army. (later replaced by Stickleback)
Trout – To German authorities in Memel
Bream – To Rome
Herring – North Africa
Gurnard – Berlin to Zagreb
Dolphin – U-Boats Atlantic (Heimisch)
Jellyfish – Berlin to Paris

Fortitude The operation for deception of the Nazis, split into two parts, Fortitude North, and Fortitude South.

Fortitude North The code name for the operation by the Allies to deceive the enemy, with activities and radio transmissions in Scotland, to tie up Nazi forces in Norway in 1944. Part of Operation Bodyguard in deception activities.

Fortitude South The code name for the operation by the Allies to deceive the enemy about where the main force in England would attack occupied France in 1944, and relevant to preparations for D-Day.

Freebornery A name given to the tabulating section under Freddie Freeborn from BTM, processing message data deciphered by codebreakers at Bletchley Park, for a database using Hollerith punched card machines.

Garble check An encoder's check to ensure the encrypted coded message could be decrypted by the receiver. Used by the Japanese and the Americans in reports.

Gayhurst (OSG) A codebreaking outstation during the war near Bletchley Park.

Geheimschreiber A Nazi secret writer advanced encoding machine based upon the Siemens T-52.

Ghost army An American specialist division that acted using deception techniques and operations to support main forces and commando units during the war.

Giant A combined codebreaking machine built at Letchworth during the war, comprising several Bombes linked together.

Green Hornet The nickname for the SIGSALY voice-encoding and decoding system designed by the Americans during the war.

Hagelin An American cipher machine.

Heath Robinson See Robinson.

Hellschreiber A German teleprinter-based encoding machine.

HMS Pembroke See Pembroke.

Hydra A cipher key used by U-boats for Enigma communication.

Jellyfish The Berlin to Paris high command Nazi communication link, being one of several 'Fish' communication links used by the enemy in the war.

Job's up Indication of a verbal statement by WRNS personnel in a Bombe machine room that the message settings had been calculated correctly and could be transferred to Bletchley Park for final processing via Typex machine.

Key Cipher letters and or numbers relating to an encoding machine.

Kriegsmarine German Navy

Lorenz A German teleprinter-based attachment used by the Nazis to encode German high command messages. These would be in various models such as SZ40, SZ42a, SZ42b. Relatively few were made compared to the mass-produced Nazi Enigma machines.

Luftwaffe German Air force.

Magic The Americans referred to wartime Japanese intelligence decoded via codebreaking staff and machines as Magic.

Mansion House The large house by the lake at Bletchley Park, which dominated the site for codebreakers and support staff. (NB: Not to be confused with the Mansion House in central London).

Medusa A cipher key used by OKW to command U-boats in the Mediterranean with Enigma.

Menu A set of instructions using letters and graphical connected lines provided by Bletchley Park codebreakers to set up the Bombe codebreaking machines to tackle Enigma message settings.

Message key The cipher key to expose a particular encrypted message or series of messages with the same message key.

Message settings The configuration of an encoding/decoding machine or system to enable encoded messages to be sent elsewhere.

Mill Hill An area in north London where a WRNS training school was located.

Morse code Communication system of dots and dashes transmitted electrically via an electro- mechanical key, sent either via wires or transmitted via radio telegraphy. Often encrypted during wartime.

Newmanry A specialist codebreaking section at Bletchley Park involved with advanced codebreaking machines.

Non-Morse A type of system for communication of messages and data that was used extensively during the last war by the Nazis for high-speed, teleprinter-based communication. It was based on the Baudot code of dots and crosses to communicate the alphabet, plus certain punctuation marks. This was used to communicate messages from the German high command using teleprinter attachments, machines such as Lorenz and more advanced German secret writers.

One-time pad A method or tool used in encoding messages for encryption using random letters or numbers, which makes them virtually impossible to duplicate by the enemy. One-time pads are often used by modern organisations to send a code to a client or customer by text or telephone to be then inserted on a computer screen. A code that is re-sent to the customer will use completely different numbers or alphanumeric codes to aid security.

Overlord The code name for the operation for D-Day invasion in June 1944.

Paddock The secret underground facility at Dollis Hill, London, for alternative Cabinet rooms for the Prime Minister. Located in Brook Road, Dollis Hill. (Used for only a limited period by Churchill.)

Pembroke The first part of the naval term for administration and associated bases, which were Special Duties X bases, and often established as codebreaking outstations. Pembroke V was the most used term for codebreaking stations from an administrative viewpoint, but Pembroke III was previously used at some locations, if only for accounting purposes. Official Royal Navy onshore bases were termed HMS *Pembroke*, and were run as though they were Navy ships.

The Pound A name sometimes used at Knockholt listening station in Kent for the base that occupied Ivy Farm, i.e. Knockholt Pound.

Purple A Japanese encoding machine, broadly speaking being an equivalent of Enigma but with different design features. Known also as the Type B Cipher machine.

PV Royal Navy/WRNS abbreviation for Pembroke V, a codebreaking base. This superseded the Station X designation.

Reflector Part of an Enigma encoding machine to re-route the electrical signal in the machine and effectively increase the security of encoded letters.

Robinson A codebreaking machine used at Bletchley Park to decipher message settings of the advanced German encoding machines. Also sometimes referred to as Heath Robinson, although not designed by that inventor.

Rodding A system to assist the decoding of enemy messages at Bletchley Park.

Room 40 British Naval intelligence HQ based in London and evolved from the First World War onwards.

Rotors Wheel rotors used in the Enigma series of machines and similar rotary-based encryption machines. These were installed using a code book with instructions, and the sequence could vary. Rotors were increased to give more permutations of message settings and improve security. A series of rotors would be selected from a box and placed in a particular specific sequence in the Enigma machine, based upon a code book with instructions. The rotors would be identified with Roman numerals such as I, II, III, IV, V. The quantity of rotors would increase over time for some machines, increasing the permutations of message settings by a considerable degree.

Sagefisch The German name for wireless teleprinter-encoded transmissions, which would be termed 'Fish' by the British.

Secret writer An advanced type of Nazi encoding machine based upon the Siemens T-52 model and called *Geheimschreiber*.

Settings (Enigma) The configuration of the Enigma machine prior to either sending or receiving an encoded message. The settings must match exactly on both the sending and receiving machines in order to be able to read and decode the message.

Siemens relay An electrical component originally made by the Siemens factory in Germany and copied by British engineers to use in codebreaking machines as they were more efficient.

Shark Bletchley Park's name for the German Triton Navy cipher used to transmit U-boat positions, movements, and associated intelligence over the airwaves using Morse code and enciphered via Enigma.

SIGABA An American encoding machine.

SIXTA Hut Six Traffic Analysis at Bletchley Park.

Special Duties X Another term for a top-secret base with intelligence processing and codebreaking. Many WRNS (Wrens) were allocated to such bases and specialist duties, although their administrative name for the onshore locations was Pembroke V, or HMS Pembroke V.

Stanmore (OSS) A codebreaking outstation during the war in north-west London.

Station X Another name for Bletchley Park. Headquarters of GC&CS in Buckinghamshire.

Steckerboard The plugboard on certain Enigma machines with connecting cables to increase the permutations and security.

Sturgeon The code name for the German T52 secret writer encoding machines and group of machines.

Teleprinter An electro-mechanical machine for communication of text from one site to another. Used at Bletchley Park, Y-stations and several codebreaking outstations during the war, and elsewhere.

Testery A specialist section at Bletchley Park during the war with a team of codebreakers and mathematicians working closely with the Newmanry on decoding advanced enemy messages.

Tetragram A word consisting of four letters. Repeated four-letter or four-character strings of data that were used to assist codebreaking during wartime.

Torch Operation Torch was the amphibious landing on a large scale in North Africa in November 1942.

Traffic analysis The process by which analysts and codebreakers at Bletchley Park would scrutinise enemy messages to help identify the source, priority, direction, and other information that may be invaluable to the Allies. A map or block diagram could sometimes be created from analysis by log readers of intercepted enemy messages.

Triton A cipher used to send messages between U-boat HQ and operational Atlantic U-boats. Bletchley Park called Triton 'Shark'.

Tunny The British nickname for the Lorenz SZ40 advanced teleprinter attachment used by the Nazis for encoding messages for the German high command. Also, an advanced British designed and built machine situated within the Bletchley Park section termed the Newmanry to emulate the Lorenz teleprinter attachment. Tunny messages were the Fish communications across Europe and the Mediterranean sent via advanced Nazi encryption machines.

U-boat *Kriegsmarine* submarine that attacked Allied shipping in the North Atlantic and elsewhere.

Ultra The high-level intelligence encoded by the enemy during the last war, and largely or substantially decoded by personnel at Bletchley Park with the support and assistance of others.

Venona A post-war project to expose and examine foreign intelligence intrusion into the secrets of Western powers, which had used a number of different methods of espionage, including use of foreign agents to infiltrate Western security services. Initial clues of espionage by the Russians were exposed as far away as Canberra, Australia, and the project lasted several years. GCHQ Eastcote was part of the Venona project, among others. The investigation was funded for many years before winding down in the 1980s.

Voluntary Interceptors Sometimes abbreviated as VIs, these were radio amateurs recruited by the Foreign Office for listening for intelligence on the radio, including for Morse code intercepts. They were recruited via membership of the Radio Society of Great Britain. The original idea of using amateurs can be accredited to Lord Sandhurst.

Watchkeepers A term used by Bletchley Park senior staff when referring to support personnel to operate and manage the Bombe codebreaking machines, such as Wrens. Alternatively, background support in the Bletchley huts.

Wavendon (OSW) A codebreaking outstation during the war near Bletchley Park.

Wheel rotors Another way of describing Bombe machine wheels, which are needed to set up the codebreaking machine and to emulate the Enigma encoding machine. See Rotors.

Woburn A country estate with grounds that was a billet for WRNS personnel who needed easy access to Bletchley Park.

Women Accepted for Volunteer Emergency Services (WAVES) American female volunteer personnel, also used to construct the US Navy version of the British codebreaking Bombe machine.

Wren Name associated with British WRNS female naval personnel. Wrens operated most of the codebreaking machines at Bletchley Park and the outstations during the war.

Wrennery Buildings near or attached to an operational base and usually being adjacent to an onshore naval base with accommodation for WRNS personnel or Wrens. Woburn Abbey was one such 'wrennery' during the war, although it was not a naval base, but a country estate.

Y-station A listening station to intercept enemy messages by radio and Morse code. These were part of a large network of listening stations based in the UK but also located abroad in Allied countries and parts of the British Empire. They were managed by different sections and organisations including the Army, Navy, GPO, Marconi, and the Foreign Office (MI5 and MI6).

Acknowledgements

The Association of Wrens

BBC WW2 People's War – online source

BBC and BBC News – online sources

Bentley Priory Museum, Stanmore

Bletchley Park – Dr David Kenyon Research Historian

Bletchley Park – Guy Revell, Museum Archivist

Bletchley Park Heritage Trust

British Telecom (BT) archives

Channel Islands Military Museum, St Ouen, Jersey, C.I.

The Churchill Rooms, London

GCHQ Archives and Museum, Cheltenham

Headstone Manor and Museum, LB Harrow

Heritage Foundation Letchworth Garden City

London Borough of Harrow

London Borough of Hillingdon

LB Hillingdon, Uxbridge Reference Library

Historic England

Historic England website and photo reconnaissance

Imperial War Museum, London

Institute of Engineering Technology (IET)

Letchworth – Garden City Collection, www.gardencitycollection.com

Letchworth Tourist Information Office

National Archives at Kew

National Cryptologic Museum, Maryland, USA

National Museum of Computing, Bletchley Park, Block H, Bletchley Park, Milton Keynes, MK3 6EB

Pembroke Park (Estate) and Public Footpath – LB Hillingdon

Radio Society of Great Britain (RSGB)

Royal Navy

Ruislip Northwood Eastcote Local History Society

South-East History Board, KSH (Sussex History Forum)

Science Museum, London

United States Navy

WinstonChurchill.org

WRNS *Wren History 1939–1945* online source

Particular thanks to Craig at The Museum of GCHQ for assistance in licensing various photographs.

Bibliography

Books, articles, and publications

Agar, John, *Turing and the Universal Machine* (London: Icon Books Ltd, 2001)

Agar, John, *The Government Machine – A Revolutionary History of the Computer* (Cambridge/London: MIT Press, 2003)

Aldrich Richard James, *GCHQ* (London: Harper Press, 2010)

Avarez, D., *Allied & Axis Signals & Intelligence in WW2* (London: Routledge, 1999)

Batey, Mavis, *Dilly – The Man Who Broke Enigmas* (London: Biteback Publishing, 2017)

Black, Jeremy, *A History of the Second World War in 100 Maps* (London: British Library, 2020)

Brown, Louis, *A Radar History of World War II* (Bristol: IoP Publishing Ltd, 1999)

Budiansky, Stephen, *Battle of Wits – The Complete Story of Codebreaking in World War II* (New York: The Free Press, 2000)

Buttar, Prit, *Between Giants – The Battle for the Baltics in World War II* (Oxford: Osprey Publishing, 2013)

Campbell-Kelly, Martin, *ICL – A Business and Technical History* (Oxford: Oxford University Press/Clarendon Press, 1990)

Cawthorne, Nigel, *Alan Turing – The Enigma Man* (London: Arcturus Publishing Ltd, 2016)

Coghlan, Peter & Dr Thomas Cheetham, *Knockout Punch* (ULTRA Bletchley Park Magazine Issue 18, 2022)

Copeland, B. Jack plus others, *Colossus – The Secrets of Bletchley Park's Codebreaking Computers* (New York USA: Oxford University Press, 2010)

Corera, Gordon, *Intercept The Secret History of Computers and Spies* (London: Weidenfeld and Nicolson/Orion 2016)

Cox, Colleen A., *A Quiet and Secluded Spot – Ruislip, Northwood, and Eastcote* (London: Ruislip, Northwood, and Eastcote Local History Society, 1991)

Critical Analysis of German Operational Intelligence Part II – Unclassified. War Department – Taken From *German Operational Intelligence* (Washington DC, 1946), Author unknown.

Dunlop, Tessa, *The Bletchley Girls* (London: Hodder & Stoughton Ltd, 2015)

Erskine, Ralph & Smith, Michael, *The Bletchley Park Codebreakers* (London: Biteback Publishing, 2011)

Ferris, John, *Behind the Enigma – The Authorised History of GCHQ Britain's Secret Cyber-Intelligence Agency* (London: Bloomsbury Publishing, 2020)

Fry, Helen, *The M Room – Secret Listeners Who Bugged the Nazis* (Createspace Independent Publishing Platform, November 2012)

Fuensantaamon, Ramon, Jose, Francisco Javier Lopez-Brea Espian, Frode Weierud, *Spanish Enigma: A History of the Enigma in Spain* (Taylor & Francis Group LLC, 2010)

Gannon, Paul, *Colossus – Bletchley Park's Greatest Secret* (London: Atlantic Books, 2006)

Gladwin, Lee A., Article: *Alan Turing, Enigma, and the Breaking of German Ciphers in World War II* (Archives.gov., Fall 1997)

Good, I.J., Michie, D., Timms, G., *Breaking Teleprinter Ciphers at Bletchley Park – General Report on Tunny with emphasis on Statistical Methods* (1945) IEEE Press/Wiley [Part: March 1946]

Greenberg, Joel, *Alastair Denniston* (Barnsley: Frontline Books, 2017)

Greenberg, Joel, *Gordon Welchman* (London: Frontline Books, 2016)

Haigh, Alice Elena, *'To Strive, To Seek, To Find' – The Origins and Establishment of the British Post Office Engineering Station at Dollis Hill, 1908–1938* (The University of Leeds School of Philosophy, Religion and History of Science. March 2021) PhD Submission.

Harper, Stephen, *Capturing Enigma* (Stroud: The History Press, reprinted 2016)

Hinsley & Stripp, *Codebreakers – The Inside Story of Bletchley Park* (University of Oxford: Oxford University Press, 2001)

Jenkins, Roy, *Churchill* (London: Pan Books, 2001)

Jennings, Christian, *The Third Reich is Listening – Inside German Codebreaking 1939–45* (Oxford: Osprey Publishing, 2018)

Jones, R.V., *Most Secret War* (London: Hamish Hamilton, 1978)

Kaekamp, Andres, *A History of the Baltic States* (London: Red Globe Press, 2018)

Kenyon, David, *Bletchley Park and D-Day* (New Haven and London: Yale University Press: 2019)

Kerrigan, Michael, *ENIGMA – How Breaking the Code Helped Win World War II* (London: Amber Books, 2018)

Kippenham, Rudolf, *Codebreaking – A History and Exploration* (New York: 1999)

Koorm, Ronald, *Backing Bletchley – The Codebreaking Outstations from Eastcote to GCHQ* (Stroud, Amberley Publishing, 2020)

Koorm Ronald. *WW2 Codebreaking – People and Places – A Wartime Glossary* (Barnsley/ S. Yorkshire – Pen & Sword 2024)

Koorm Ronald. *WW2 Codebreaking – Events and Organisations – A Wartime Glossary* (Barnsley / S. Yorkshire – Pen & Sword 2025)

Lamb, Christian, *Beyond The Sea – a Wren at War* (London: Mardle Books, 2021)

Levine, Joshua, *Operation Fortitude* (London: Harper Collins Publishers, 2012)

Lopez, Aubin, Bernard, Guillerat, *World War II INFOGRAPHICS* (London: Thames & Hudson, 2019)

Lucas, Russell, *German Secret Service*, Glossary chapter (2016)

Macintyre, Ben, *Double Cross* (London: Bloomsbury Publishing, 2012)
Matthews, Peter, *SIGINT* (Stroud: The History Press, 2018)
McKay, Sinclair, *The Secret Life of Bletchley Park* (London: Aurum Press Ltd, 2011)
McKay, Sinclair, *The Secret Listeners* (London: Aurum Press Ltd, 2013)
McKay, Sinclair, *The Lost World of Bletchley Park* (London: Aurum Press Ltd, 2013)
McKay, Sinclair, *The Spies of Winter* (London: Aurum Press Ltd, 2016)
McKay, Sinclair, *100 People you Never Knew Were at Bletchley Park* (London: Safe Haven Books Ltd, 2021)
McKay, Sinclair, *Secret Britain* (London: Headline Publishing Group, 2021)
Messenger, Charles, *The D-Day Atlas* (London: Thames & Hudson, 2014)
Miller, Russell, *Codename Tricycle* (London: Pimlico, 2005)
Montefiore, Hugh Sebag, *ENIGMA – The Battle for the Code* (London: Weidenfeld and Nicolson/Orion 2011)
Morris, Moses & John Wade, *Spycamera – The Minox Story* (West Sussex, Hove Collectors Books 1998)
Page, Gwendoline, *We Kept the Secret* (Norfolk. Geo. R. Reeve Ltd, 2008)
Patch, John. Commander, US Navy (Retired), *Fortuitous Endeavour-Intelligence and Deception in Operation Torch* – (Naval War College Review Volume 61 Number 4 Autumn Article 9, 2008)
Paterson, Michael, *Voices of the Codebreakers* (Barnsley: Greenhill Books, 2018)
Pearson, Joss, *Bletchley Park's Secret Room* (Stroud, Amberley Publishing, 2015)
Philpott, Colin, *Secret Wartime Britain* (Yorkshire: Pen and Sword Books Ltd, 2018)
Ramsay, Winston G. *The War in the Channel Islands – Then and Now* (Poland: After the Battle Magazine Publications, 1981/2012.
Rich, Ben R. & Leo Janos, *Skunk Works* (New York: Back Bay Books Little Brown and Company, 1994)
RNELHS, *The Home Front Ruislip, Northwood and Eastcote in Wartime* (London: Ruislip, Northwood and Eastcote Local History Society, 2007)
Roberts, Captain Jerry, *Lorenz* (Stroud: The History Press, 2018)
Sherman, David, *The First Americans – The 1941 US Codebreaking Mission to Bletchley Park* (National Security Agency – Center for Cryptologic History, Special series Volume 2, 2016)
Singh, Simon, *The Code Book* (London: Fourth Estate Limited 2000)
Smith, Michael, *Station X – The Codebreakers of Bletchley Park* (London: Pan Books, 2004)
Smith, Michael, *Bletchley Park – The Code-Breakers of Station X* (Oxford: Shire Publications, 2014)
Smith, Michael, *The Debs of Bletchley Park* (London: Aurum Press Ltd, 2015)
Storey, Neil R., *WRNS The Women's Royal Naval Service* (Oxford: Shire Books/ Osprey Publishing, 2017)
Summers, Julie, *Our Uninvited Guests* (London: Simon & Schuster, 2018)
Taylor, Neil, *Estonia – A Modern History* (London: Hurst & Company, 2018)
The National Archives, *Operational Selection Policy OSP28 – Government Communication Headquarters & its Predecessors* (National Archives Revised January 2006)

Tidy, Josh, *Letchworth Garden City in Old Photographs* (Letchworth: Heritage Foundation Letchworth Garden City, 2016)

Tidy, Josh, *Letchworth Garden City Through Time* (Stroud, Amberley Publishing Ltd, 2015)

Turing, Dermot, *XY & Z – The Real Story of How Enigma was Broken* (Stroud: The History Press, 2018)

Turing, Dermot, *PROF – Alan Turing Decoded* (Stroud: The History Press, 2016)

Vogal, Steve, *Betrayal in Berlin* (London: John Murray 2018)

Welchman, Gordon, *The Hut Six Story* (Kidderminster, M&M Baldwin, 2018)

Weller, A., *Secret Eastcote* (London: Friends of Eastcote House Gardens Community Archive Publication, Date Unknown)

Articles/Papers

Abrutat Dr David – GCHQ Historian, RSGB 2022 Convention: *Stoking Bletchley – The Story of the Y Services 1939–1945*

After the Battle, Issue 37 (Historical society)

Atlas – Company historical information ICL and ICT

Avery, Andrew J., *All The King's Men – British Codebreaking Operations 1938–43*. Thesis, East Tennessee University (2015)

Benson, Robert Louis, *SIGINT and the Holocaust*, Approved for release by the NSA on 22 March 2010 FOIA Case #60309 (2010)

Boon, Rachel, PhD student University of Manchester. 2020 Thesis: *Research is the Door to Tomorrow – The Post Office Engineering Station Dollis Hill 1933–1958* (University of Manchester. Centre for History of Science, Technology and Medicine.

COBRA, Paper by David Whitehead CEng MIEE (1994)

Ford, Steve, *RAF Eastcote High Road, Eastcote – Archaeological Desk-Based Assessment* for George Wimpey (West London) Ltd, (March 2007)

Fox, Barry, *Secrets and Spies*, Hi Fi News, March 2024 AV Tech Media Ltd, (Queenborough.)

Edited by J. Gilbert & J.P. Finnegan, *US Army Signals Intelligence in World War II – A Documentary History* (Center of Military History United States Army, Washington D.C. 1993)

Graces Guide to British Industrial History, Graces Guide, 2012 (Graces Guide Registered Charity) Information on BTM Co.

Hanyok, Robert J., *Eavesdropping on Hell – Historical Guide to Western Communications Intelligence and the Holocaust 1939–1945*, Series IV Volume 9 (Center for Cryptologic History, National Security Agency 2005, Second Edition. United States Cryptologic History/ADET)

Dr Judkins, Phil, *Enigma: On Cruise Missiles, Rockets and Superguns – First Time Around* (Chairman, Defence Electronic History Society: Paper presented 15 October 2013)

Large, Christine (Director at Bletchley Park), 'Some Human factors in codebreaking', From a paper published in 2002 given at RTO HFM Symposium

Local Paper article (2014), on unveiling of the commemorative plaque at Pembroke Park for Outstation Eastcote and GCHQ.

Mowry, David P., *Cryptologic Aspects of German Intelligence Activities in South America in WW2*, Series IV, WW2, Vol. 2 (National Security Agency, Center for Cryptologic History, 2011)

Newton, Katherine, History of Government/gov.uk, *Aspidistra: The wartime breakthrough you've never heard of* (Blog August 2019).

Oleson, Peter. *Guide to Study of Intelligence – From Axis Surprises to Allied Victories – The Impact of Intelligence in World War II* (Journal of US Intelligence Studies, Vol. 22, No. 3. Winter 2016–17, Virginia 2017)

The Independent, article on Dorothy O'Grady (date unknown)

The National Archives, *Operational Selection Policy OSP28-Government Communications Headquarters and Its Predecessors* (Revised January 2006)

Putney, T. Diane, *Ultra and the Army Air Forces in World War II (Interview with Associate Justice of the Supreme Court, Lewis F. Powell)* Office of Air Force History, United States Air Force, Washington DC, 1987

The Rutherford Journal, The Turing Bombe (Online)

Sale, Anthony, *The American 6813th Technical History 1945*, reformatted, 2003

Signal City, Geoffrey Dykes/RN Communications Branch Museum/Library

Swartz, John, *Voluntary Interceptors tribute at the RSGB Radio Centre* – Adapted from RSGB Magazine RadCom, September 2018

TICOM Archive, *FISH and the Jellyfish Convoy*, Case Studies, Secret Intelligence in Nazi Germany

Toms, Susan (RN&E LHS), *The History Behind the Road Names for Pembroke Park, Eastcote*

Toms, Susan (RN&E LHS), Papers and articles from The Ruislip, Northwood, Eastcote Local History Society, *Codebreakers at Eastcote*

Toms, Susan (RN&E LHS), *Enigma and the Eastcote Connection – 2005*, The Ruislip, Northwood, Eastcote Local History Society

Wilcox, Jennifer, *Solving The Enigma, History of the Cryptanalytic Bombe*, reprinted 2015, Center for Cryptologic History, National Security Agency (NSA)

Other Sources of Information/Websites

www.airmuseum.com/archives

www.bcs.org

www.BletchleyPark.org.uk (Traffic analysis)

www.Bombe.org.uk (Bombe types)

www.Britishtelephones.com (UK telephone history)

https://chris-intel-corner.blogspot.com/search?q=italian+cryptography (Italian cryptography)

www.codesandciphers.org.uk (The British Bombe, 6812th Signal Security Detachment (Prov) APO 413 US Army/pdf scan via Tony Sale)
www.codesandciphers.org.uk/anoraks/menus.htm
www.commsmuseum.co.uk
www.Cryptomuseum (Netherlands)
www.dni.gov
www.electronicsdesk.com (Adcock antenna)
www.Firstworldwar.com
www.gchq.gov.uk
www.goldbeach.org.uk
Hertsmemories.org.uk (BTM webpage)
www.hifinews.co.uk
www.HistoryNet
www.history.navy.mil, Naval History and Heritage Command
www.nationalmuseum.af.mil, National Museum of the United States Air Force
Online Podcast E80 by Bletchley Park, October 2019, on Outstation Eastcote.
Online Podcast E145 Torch to Tunis – Bletchley Park
Online Podcast E128 by Bletchley Park, 'Whitehall 7947'
www.maproom.net
www.Pastscape, Drayton Parslow
www.portsdown-tunnels.org.uk
www.Prabook.com
www.theintercept.com
www.radioblvd.com, Radio Boulevard, Western Historic Radio Museum
Rusilip.co.uk, Ruislip Online, online source, including extracts from DTI staff articles relevant to Eastcote, post-war.
www.rbth.com, Russia Beyond
www.shaunlewis-theauthor.com, 'The use of secret inks for espionage'
www.sussexhistoryforum.co.uk
www.steelsoldiers.com (Military Vehicles Supersite) (Forum Web Entry, 14 November 2014, Corpus Christi, Texas)
www.theintercept.com
www.theyservice
www.ticomarchive.com/iv-case-studies/geheimschreiber-t-52
(FISH and the Jellyfish Convoy – 2018)
www.troodosmountain.org
eu.Usatoday.com – Brian Eason (Article on Tom Kimmel and Admiral Kimmel)
War History online
The Wartime memories project
www.wartime memoriesproject.com
RSGB 2022 Convention: Stoking Bletchley – The story of the Y Services 1939–1945
www.youtube.com/watch?v=ia9kw_WOM0A
Central Bureau and Australia's Codebreaking Operations in the Second World War, 9 April

Miscellaneous Sources

Atlas – company historical information ICL and ICT.

BBC, television documentaries on the rise of the Third Reich.

BCS, The Chartered Institute for IT.

Bill Thompson USN (Ret).

Commanders of World War Two, Key Publishing Ltd.

Correspondence with Bletchley Park in May 2024 regarding publishing extracts of an account of Foreign Office civilian Doris Jenny Stockdale, neé Gummerson, Decoder and Teleprinter Operator at Knockholt, 1942–45, and also on the Bletchley Roll of Honour.

Correspondence and discussions with ex-Wren Eileen Lawrence (née Hughes), who worked at two codebreaking outstations during the war, and who became an MI5 officer after the war. Eileen is also on the Bletchley Roll of Honour.

Discussions, letters, and communication with certain ex-Wrens (WRNS) who worked on codebreaking machines and equipment during the war and who contacted the author's publisher following reading his book, *Backing Bletchley*, published in 2020.

Damien Horn: Jersey, C.I., curator of the Channel Islands Military Museum at St Ouen, Jersey, to allow reproduction of certain photographs of wartime military equipment to be used within the Glossary from a private collection.

Discussions with Betty Hollingberry, ex-Wren, based at Eastcote during wartime as Betty Vowles. (At time of writing, Betty was 101 years young).

Discussions with a Bletchley Park voluntary guide at Northwood Hills Library in 2018.

Discussions with a member of the National Museum of Computing at both Northwood Hills Library and at Ruislip Manor Libraries in 2018.

Discussion with a number of ex-British Telecom engineers who trained at Bletchley Park after the war.

Discussions with Mr T. Voore, ex BBC test engineer, on radio equipment and electronic equipment used in wartime.

Discussion with a person at Bentley Priory museum who had knowledge of several of the satellite outstations.

Emails and correspondence with members of the Association of Wrens over the last few years.

Researching wartime WRNS officer records online.

Research and investigation of various relevant maps, charts, diagrams, statistics relevant to the subject matter.

Discussions with members of the IET on aspects of Polish history regarding codebreaking machines.

Examination of local maps of the Eastcote and surrounding areas sourced at Uxbridge Reference library and elsewhere.

Exhibition at the Science Museum in 2019 on GCHQ and codebreaking.

Extracts from Microsoft Powerpoint Presentation (R. Koorm FRICS) on Codebreaking Outstations – Eastcote to GCHQ (copyright 2018).

BIBLIOGRAPHY

Extracts from Microsoft Powerpoint Presentation (R. Koorm FRICS) on Support Services to Intelligence Operations during WW2 (copyright 2019).

Extracts from Microsoft Powerpoint Presentation (R. Koorm FRICS) on D-Day and Codebreaking during WW2 (copyright 2019 and 2024).

Extracts from Microsoft Powerpoint Presentation (R. Koorm FRICS) on Fake News or Deceiving the Enemy During WW2 (copyright 2020).

Investigation and study of the two volumes of the Bombe Registers on loan to the National Archives at Kew. (HW25/19 and HW25/20).

Maps, photographs, and information via the Collections Officer at The Garden City Collection, Letchworth, following detailed discussions with the Collections Officer.

Maproom.net – My thanks to this online organisation for their help and assistance in providing certain specific maps. Also, in their excellent communication and prompt response to the author's queries on maps of London.

My thanks to the GCHQ Museum Archivist in email correspondence and in licensing of selected photographs from GCHQ.

The National Cryptologic Museum in Maryland, USA, and my particular thanks to Robert J. Simpson, Museum Archivist and Librarian, who was of considerable assistance in my research on Second World War American cryptologic equipment, systems, and photographs.

Personal War diary entries of Corporal Edward Thomas William Pearce, Royal Engineers 238th Field Company, 1943 and 1944.

Radio Society of Great Britain (RSGB). Emails exchanged, 2021/2022.

PBS America, documentaries about wartime subject matter including D-Day, Nazi weapons of mass destruction, codebreaking, Navy campaigns, BEF and Dunkirk, Stalin, etc.

Smithsonian Channel, various documentaries on the Second World War.

The Valve Museum and articles by Tony Sale on Colossus.

Various TICOM reports: TICOM Secret Intelligence in Nazi Germany – Fish and the Jellyfish Convoy.

Personal war diaries of a Royal Engineer (E.W. Pearce).

NB a proportion of the above presentations were prepared by the author for museums, history societies, and similar. Some were given in person and some online. The presentations are the copyright of the author. Photographs within the presentations are credited to the source or sources where appropriate.

Some of the National Archives reference documents (reference codes) researched are listed as follows, but are not a complete list, only a snapshot of some that have relevance to the subject. Note that the endnotes also contain references in places to specific National Archive documents:

HW 8/98, HW 25/19, HW 25/20 [Vols 1 and 2 Bombe Registers], HW 25/22, HW 14/4, HW 14/9, HW 14/20, HW 14/22, HW 14/23, HW 14/24, HW 25/20, HW 14/57, HW 14/48, HW 14/43, HW 14/48, HW 14/51, HW 14/60, HW 14/56 (cover story for Stanmore and WRNS staff recruitment), HW 14/62, HW 14/58, HW 64/63, HW 64/65, HW 14/119, HW 14/123, HW 14/126, HW 14/128, HW

14/164, HW 25/5, HW 25/5 (1) HW 25/5 (2), HW 25/22, HW 34/17, HW 34/21, HW 40/87, HW 40/88, HW 40/89, HW 47/1, HW 64/25, HW 50/6, HW 50/79, HW 51/40, HW 15 (GC&CS Venona Project Records) HW 64/63, HW 64/25, HW 64/45, HW 64/68, HW 64/76, HO 192/420, HW 120.

FO 371/43399, FO 366/1332

FO 366/2221 (Financial arrangements GC&CS Eastcote)

WO 208/5092 (Polish outstations), HW 4, HW 2/69, HW 25/20, HW 25/22, HW 25/36, HW 41/401, HW 50/72, HW 55/1, HW 64/28, HW 192/420, HO 391/12, HW 8/97, WO 208/5109

AVIA 7/146, AVIA 7/966

KV 2/40, KV 2/63, KV 2/65, KV 2/66, KV 2/101, KV 2/4195, KV 2/4191, KV 2/4212, KV 2/4204

Museums of interest in the United Kingdom

Imperial War Museum, Lambeth, London, www.iwm.org.uk

Bletchley Park, Bucks, bletchleypark.org.uk

TNMOC, The National Museum of Computing, Bletchley Park, Bucks, www.tnmoc.org

Battle of Britain Bunker Museum, Uxbridge, Middlesex, www.battleofbritainbunker.co.uk

Bentley Priory Museum, Stanmore, Middlesex, www.bentleypriorymuseum.org.uk

Royal Signals Museum, Blandford Camp, Dorset, www.royalsignalsmuseum.co.uk

The D-Day Story, Portsmouth, Hampshire, www.theddaystory.com

The National Army Museum, Royal Hospital Road, Chelsea, London, SW3 4HT, nam.ac.uk

Museums of interest in the USA

The National Cryptologic Museum, Maryland, USA.

Note on selected images and photographs

Those monochrome images provided by GCHQ and the Museum of GCHQ under licence are by kind permission of Director GCHQ © Crown Copyright.

We have tried to acknowledge all those contributors who provided photographs, diagrams, charts, maps, tables, or statistics within this Glossary and the series of Glossary volumes. Several of the diagrams provided are the author's sole copyright, and are annotated as such. Permission to use these diagrams or images must initially be obtained via the publishers to seek the author's approval.

Photos and diagrams selected amplify the information in the book.

Author's Note

The author sought consents and permissions from relevant organisations, persons, and parties to include relevant text and/or images and diagrams. Persons and organisations have been credited where appropriate for such content. If anyone has been missed out, the author apologises for the omission as there was no intention to exclude them.

Some of the persons and individuals that the author had been in contact with have since passed away. Where possible, the author has, in some cases, spoken to, or emailed family members of those deceased, to clarify certain points, or to obtain approval for certain text entries and descriptions. Responses to date have been both constructive and positive. It is extremely important that persons who played a part in codebreaking or intelligence or in a support role, are recognised for their contribution in wartime, and beyond, and their legacy continues for particularly younger readers to study and to learn from.

Omission of a person or organisation does not mean that person was insignificant, or not worthy of this volume, more that space was limited.

The author's intention in writing the three-volume Glossary on codebreaking and intelligence was to give a balanced view to the reader of what really happened in the build-up to the Second World War, the war itself, and some aspects post-war. It is my intention to take the reader on a journey of knowledge, to understand better the inter-relationships between people, places, events, organisations, systems, equipment, and deception techniques used. I hope you have gained something constructive from studying the detailed entries across the volumes. Those individuals who participated in wartime should not be forgotten, whichever side of the conflict they were on.

Finally, Betty Hollingbery (née Vowles), a WRNS codebreaker at Outstation Eastcote during the second world war, and who had the second volume of this series of books formally dedicated to her by the author, achieved 102 years young in April 2025. She was invited to attend the VE day celebration parade the following month. Our very best wishes to Betty!

Other books in the same series

WW2 Codebreaking – People and Places – A Wartime Glossary, Ronald Koorm
ISBN 9781399053495 Publisher: Pen & Sword
WW2 Codebreaking – Events and Organisations – A Wartime Glossary, Ronald Koorm
ISBN 9781399053440 Publisher: Pen & Sword

Endnotes

Introduction

1. Two films or movies have been made about Operation Mincemeat. Both are worth viewing, and appear to follow the facts reasonably closely. The first film in 1956 was *The Man Who Never Was. Operation Mincemeat* was released in 2022 and starred Colin Firth.

Systems

1. The Ava factory in Poland made replica Enigmas secretly for Polish codebreakers and mathematicians.
2. In 1932, Marian Rejewski, a Polish mathematician, cracked Enigma for the first time in Warsaw.
3. Photographs exist of women making and assembling components to fit within the Bombe machines at Spirella and Letchworth. One famous photograph is called 'Wizard with Wires' in the Heritage Garden City Collection at Letchworth, and can be viewed online.
4. 203 out of 211 Bombe codebreaking machines went to codebreaking outstations, or around 96 per cent of them.
5. Projections in early June 1942 were around forty-five machines required with twenty actual machines available at the time. (Memo to Commander Travis from HD Fletcher Hut 6 Bletchley Park on 4 June 1942.)
6. The Official Bombe Registers are on loan to the National Archives in Kew, and are comprised of two volumes, roughly A5 in size. Entries are handwritten.
7. Extract courtesy of the National Archives.
8. Source: Bletchley Park Roll of Honour. Officer Canale was at Bletchley Park from December 1941 to October 1942.
9. Source Wikipedia on the Manhattan project text.
10. Betty Hollingberry, nee Vowles, who worked at Eastcote, remembered this at the age of 101 in 2024!
11. TNMOC is on the same site as Bletchley Park in Buckinghamshire but as a separate charitable trust.
12. Think of this as the background to a manual 'Google'-type database with hundreds of thousands, even many millions of records, which could be sorted

and filtered down. It was in an age well before computers were used. Hollerith were electro-mechanical machines, but not computers as such.

13. Two million punched cards per week was about average and they all had to be stored.
14. Kenyon, David, *Bletchley Park and D-Day* (Chapter The Intelligence Factory)
15. Prior to 1942 entry to the WRNS was purely voluntary, and attracted women from the middle and upper classes. After conscription, the balance was changed to a broader input of women from varied backgrounds. Initially, the Wrens were generally those from an upper-class background.
16. ATS military personnel and other women would work at Bletchley Park, including many civilians too.
17. Just over 2 per cent of WRNS personnel would work on Special X duties on codebreaking during the war.
18. Welchman was a senior codebreaker who worked closely with Alan Turing and who invented the 'diagonal board' circuit to make the Bombe machine even more efficient.
19. Some radio receivers would require inserting a coilset into the receiver to listen to a range of specific frequencies, and a set of these had to be available to change between them. It was a clumsy system but apparently worked well once you got the hang of it.
20. The RSS had both male and female personnel at Y-stations across the UK. Some reports indicate as many as 25 per cent women at Y-stations.
21. Many wireless stations or Y-stations were used for direction-finding operations to pinpoint transmission sources.
22. South-East History Board, extract from account online via Doris (Jenny) Stockdale (Nee Gummerson).
23. Refer to the interview of Eileen Lawrence, nee Hughes, in the appendix at the end of the first volume of this series, *People and Places*.
24. Evaluation tests were carried out to verify the suitability of Wrens for Special X duties on the codebreaking machines to replace men in the early years. Most Wrens were able to deal with the technical aspects with some guidance and training, but not all. There would have been a certain amount of initial prejudice by male management against using women for this sensitive work.
25. There is a wall plaque on the wall of the house in Hendon that was used by agent Garbo and his handler to commemorate the historical significance of the espionage work carried out against the Nazis in wartime.
26. The public footpath still exists at Eastcote but now separates two parts of a residential housing development. The original footpath is supposed to have origins in the sixteenth century.
27. Wilcox, Jennifer, *Solving The Enigma, History of the Cryptanalytic Bombe*, National Security Agency.
28. Ibid.
29. Although now privately owned by the Fort Southwick Company Limited, the public can attend ticketed, guided tours of the tunnels, of the UGHQ site.

30. The American Bombes would be transported to Washington and operated from there. There would be some coordination with Bletchley Park, too.
31. ERNIE was developed largely by a Post Office Engineering team including Thomas Flowers, Harry Fensom to a concept of Sidney Broadhurst at PORES, in north-west London. There have been five iterations of ERNIE to date.
32. Extract statistics from Table within a Thesis on Post Office Research Engineering Station and originally sourced from BT Archives. (Research is 'The door to tomorrow – The Post Office Engineering Station – Dollis Hill 1933–1958', Rachel Boon, University of Manchester.)
33. Gordon Welchman, codebreaker at Bletchley Park, was highly critical of Flowers and his use of valves and resources.
34. Various attempts have been made by the author to communicate with Stowe School on this matter to obtain some feedback, but no response has been received at the time of writing.
35. The commemorative plaque at Eastcote by the old codebreaking site records 110 Bombe machines, but study of the official Bombe Registers, there were 103 machines at the end of the war.
36. The Battle of Britain Bunker at Uxbridge is a museum and open for guided tours of the underground control room, although steep steps must be negotiated, and unfortunately it is not suitable for wheelchairs or those with mobility issues. People who have gone down those stairs in wartime include Winston Churchill, King George VI, and famous RAF officers such as Air Vice Marshal Trafford Leigh-Mallory, who was in charge of No. 11 Group early in the war.
37. A blue plaque exists on the front wall to the site where St Paul's school existed commemorating the event. The school was demolished in 1968.
38. Colossus Mk2 was operational from 1 June 1944, a few days prior to D-Day.

Equipment

1. BCS, 'The Enigma of the Polish Bomba', article, July 2019.
2. Extensive use of tweezers by the Wrens enabled adjustment and alignment of the rotor wheel wire brushes to prevent short circuits.
3. Some Bombes did have more than one reference number, explaining why this exceeded 211, which was the number built.
4. The photograph referred to is from the National Cryptologic Museum database.
5. Rochester was marked as Bombe 313 in the Official Bombe Registers. This does not mean there were 313 Bombes, as there were some gaps, anomalies, and some machines may have been renamed.
6. Visually there was often a fourth wheel to one side of the main three drum rotors.
7. From the report by Post Office Engineer David Whitehead, the Cobra machine was originally built in Dursley by Mawdsley, and then tested and modified considerably by the Post Office Engineering branch at Dollis Hill.

8. Four-wheel Bombes were built by the NCR company in Dayton, Ohio, using WAVES personnel for assembly.
9. David Whitehead, paper on Cobra, dated 6 November 1993, report of involvement with the Cobra equipment. Reprint from an article in the BT Retired Staff section of BT Labs Sports and Social Club.
10. Colossus measured approximately 5m long × 3m deep × 2.5m high.
11. 631 CCMs were produced.
12. For around nine months Bletchley Park would be frustrated trying to crack four-wheeled Enigmas.
13. Giant comprised individual Bombe numbers 265, 266, 267, 268 when later split up back to separate machines. Some went to OSE and others to Bletchley Park.
14. Bakelite was an early type of plastic often seen in a brown and black finish. Some contained asbestos material. It was used extensively for telephones, radios, receivers, and housings for loudspeakers.
15. Risk of hearing loss is a combination of the sound pressure level of the noise and the exposure duration, which is the basis of modern risk assessments and regulations in the workplace. Ironically, in the UK there is no legislation or legal limit on exposure to loud noise for members of the public who are not at work.
16. ICT evolved later into ICL and was then acquired by Fujitsu of Japan.
17. Breaking teleprinter Ciphers at Bletchley Park – General Report on Tunny with Emphasis on Statistical Methods (1945). Appendix B: Activities at Knockholt. The Interception of German Teleprinter Communications by Foreign Office Station Knockholt. (via H.C. Kenworthy).
18. Technical information courtesy of the United States Census Bureau online website.
19. By 1959 it is reported that the IBM advanced sorters could process 2,000 punched cards per minute, a big increase over wartime figures.
20. Source Ruislip Online, Eastcote MOD, PD.
21. Korting would go on to make tape recorders and audio equipment in the 1950s.
22. Source: Shaun Lewis, 'The use of Secret inks in espionage'.
23. Manufacturers of Horn loudspeakers included Voigt and Lowther, which later merged.
24. A synthetic flexible rubber surround allows the speaker cone to move substantially air and work more efficiently.
25. The origin of the name 'Madame X' is unclear.
26. Most of these companies had been established for many years prior to the start of the Second World War. Few survive today, although some of the brand names have been acquired by other firms for use under licence. Zeiss makes many high-precision lenses and optical items, some of which can be attached to other camera brands.
27. Auction houses sometimes sell vintage wartime camera models, both still photographic and cine cameras. Also, camera fairs often include vintage models such as Leicas, Rolleiflexes, Super Ikontas, and lenses from Zeiss and Leica. Anything of a rarity will fetch high prices but collectors are always on the lookout for that pristine model of a wartime camera with a famous brand name.

Some modern digital cameras can even accept older vintage camera lenses to be used in a manual mode setting, and many adaptors are available for several models to enable a good fit to the camera body. One final word of warning, there are copies and fakes out there too, just as there are in the art world.

28. Some AR88s were dumped down a well after the war, a terrible waste of resources.
29. AR88s were used extensively in Y-stations too, as the main radio receiver.
30. National Archives AVIA 7/146, AVIA 7/966.
31. See also mention of rhombic aerials at Knockholt Pound Y-station, where some were 105ft high and there were around twelve sets on a large open site with buildings constructed on many acres of farmland acquired by the Government.
32. The Churchill Rooms in Westminster, London, has a small room that was used by Churchill for communications using the SIGSALY voice-encoding system. An information board adjacent to the room provides some background about SIGSALY.
33. Fujitsu was directly involved in a serious scandal in the development and operation of the Horizon accounting software system used by the Post Office and errors in the system resulted in false accusations against sub-postmasters, several who went to prison for theft. In January 2024, a TV dramatisation of the events created uproar in Parliament, with the outcome the clearing of the names of all those prosecuted via a special Act of Parliament, effectively bypassing the judicial system. A public enquiry was still ongoing at the time of writing in 2024, and Fujitsu as a company may possibly have to recompense those who were falsely accused of wrongdoing. In January 2024, TNMOC was approached for comment in a BBC Panorama programme on the Horizon scandal and the use of computers, which were allegedly operated remotely by Fujitsu personnel.
34. See item above for detail on Horizon.
35. American military personnel accessed the Selfridges building through a side door and went down to the basement, the general public having no clue to what was installed there. Without the SIGSALY equipment, transatlantic conversations between Churchill and Roosevelt could have been compromised as regards national security.
36. Source: Russia Beyond, www.rtbh.com/history/330855-soviet-codes-cryptographers-wwii
37. The Railway Executive Committee operated from Down Street station to plan for any eventuality in wartime for running the rail network. It was situated underground in a disused tube station near to what became Green Park station.
38. It was rather unusual for the Tunny to be in the Testery, as the machine section was the Newmanry, and in a separate area. However, the Tunny was used as the final stage for processing the message prior its translation into English.
39. Many of the Typex operators at Bletchley were female, as can be evidenced in various photographs taken during the war.
40. Two Typex machines were abandoned at Dunkirk in 1940, to be picked up by the Germans. The Germans looked at the machines, but spent limited time evaluating them.

41. The New Zealand military used Typex until the 1970s.
42. National Archives FO371/43399.
43. Some other engineers across the world had considered the use of valves as digital switches before the start of the war, although this was a radical approach at the time.

Deception

1. The non-aggression pact with Germany and Russia was dated 23 August 1939, only a few days before the German invasion of Poland. This would effectively convince the Russians that they would be safe from attack by the Nazis, but this was far from the truth as Germany invaded Russia a couple of years later.
2. Source: World War II Infographics.
3. Ibid.
4. Photos exist of the King and Queen visiting TRE during the war, but the author is unsure what the caption accompanying the photo would have reported, given the need for extreme secrecy and security. It would be something like, 'HM The King accompanied by HM the Queen visited a factory and met staff who are doing their bit in helping to defeat Nazi Germany', or something similar, without giving away either the location or the purpose of the site.
5. I had come face to face with George Blake, the famous Russian spy, on the night he escaped from Wormwood Scrubs prison, when his getaway car drove into the rear of my brother's A35 van when I was seated in the back. I was 15 years old at the time, and did not know anything about spying, or Blake stealing secrets from MI5. Surprisingly, he did not hang around to exchange car insurance details, and sped off down the road, almost at the speed of light. The BBC had a newsflash when we arrived home, stating that Blake had escaped. He was never captured. President Putin gave Blake a glowing eulogy when he passed away, referring to him in his speech as 'Colonel Blake'.
6. Some special bombs were developed by Dr Barnes Wallis to target underground Nazi missile factories and were used successfully during the war.
7. Source conveyed to the author by T. Voore in a publication principally about the Cold War, and still to be verified at time of writing.
8. In March 2024, President Putin won another election to remain Russian president for another six years, until at least 2030, which would be the longest term served by a Russian leader.

Commentary

1. For more information on the history of PORES in north-west London, the reader may wish to study the detailed thesis by Rachel Boon on the Post Office PORES site, which tracks the development from the 1930s. 'Research is the Door to Tomorrow – The Post Office Engineering Station Dollis Hill 1933–1958'.

2. Design and research on use of hearing aids was carried out at PORES in north London, but there was no manufacture of hearing aids at the site. That was left to specialist firms, which would later supply the NHS. One of the author's friends recalls as a child being fitted with a large hearing aid of an early type, but it was not very robust when he was climbing trees!
3. Only a relatively small percentage of Wrens worked on codebreaking Special X duties, around 2.2 per cent. The remainder carried out a broad range of military and administrative tasks. The Wrens do not exist in the modern Royal Navy, having been disbanded in the 1980s, but there still exists an Association of Wrens for those who had joined previously in the WRNS capacity.
4. Stealth technology was largely developed in the late 1970s by designers at Lockheed, via Kelly Johnson and Ben Rich, and the reader is referred to *Skunk Works* by Ben R. Rich and Leo Janos.
5. Although Stalin was impatient for the second front in France to relieve the pressure in the East, he had to acknowledge that D-Day would have to work first time around, and that failure could have been catastrophic. However, his trust in the Western Allies diminished further when he was informed there would be a delay.
6. The loss of *Aguila* is commemorated in at least four places: Scarborough, Tower Hill in London commemorating loss of merchant shipping during the war, Plymouth Navy memorial, and the National Arboretum, which has a sculpted Wren on the site. As the leading Wren, Cecilly Bruce Benjamin, came originally from Pinner, north-west London, the St Edmund the King church there also has a commemorative plaque. A lifeboat in Wales had previously been named after *Aguila.*
7. The final two Colossus machines were sent to Cheltenham and later dismantled in the 1960s. A part-built eleventh Colossus machine was dismantled at PORE in Dollis Hill. Parts may have been recycled for other projects, as materials and components were scarce after the war.
8. Around 800 servicemen lost their lives in the Sefton Sands E-boat attack. These were mainly Americans. It was pure luck for the German E-boat commanders that they came across a practise beach assault operation for D-Day on the south Devon beaches, and the Allies were completely unprepared for the attack.
9. R.V. Jones, *Most Secret War – British Scientific Intelligence 1939–1945.*
10. Source: www.britannica.com
11. As a comparison, in March 2024 President Putin of Russia threatened the West with use of nuclear weapons if it went into Ukraine.
12. It was July 1944 before the Me 262 went into combat and attacked a Mosquito.
13. *Hi Fi News*, March 2024, 'Barry Fox Secrets and spies'. Also *The M Room* by Helen Fry.

Analysis of Bombe Machines

1. The reader should note that a handful of Bombes had more than one number, which makes tracking them more complex but not impossible.

2. Information from a study of the Official Bombe Registers held at the National Archives in Kew, London.
3. The table is on British-made Bombes, while figures elsewhere in the book refer to the American four-wheeled based Bombes built by NCR in the USA.
4. Note that the Giant Bombe or Bombes were unusual as they were not operated by WRNS personnel and were based at the BTM factory in Letchworth. However, when they were split up into individual machines and sent to outstations and Bletchley Park they were operated by Wrens.
5. Some detailed drawings of the Bombes can be seen on the Bletchley Park website and are held by the GCHQ Archives.

Index